PEANUTS® Every Sunday

Books by Charles M. Schulz

Peanuts®
More Peanuts®
Good Grief, More Peanuts®!
Good Ol' Charlie Brown
Snoopy
You're Out of Your Mind, Charlie Brown!
But We Love You, Charlie Brown
Peanuts® Revisited
Go Fly a Kite, Charlie Brown
Peanuts® Every Sunday
It's a Dog's Life, Charlie Brown
You Can't Win, Charlie Brown
Snoopy, Come Home
You Can Do It, Charlie Brown
We're Right Behind You, Charlie Brown
As You Like It, Charlie Brown
Sunday's Fun Day, Charlie Brown
You Need Help, Charlie Brown
Snoopy and The Red Baron
The Unsinkable Charlie Brown
You'll Flip, Charlie Brown
You're Something Else, Charlie Brown

PEANUTS®
Every Sunday

By CHARLES M. SCHULZ

HOLT, RINEHART AND WINSTON
New York / Chicago / San Francisco

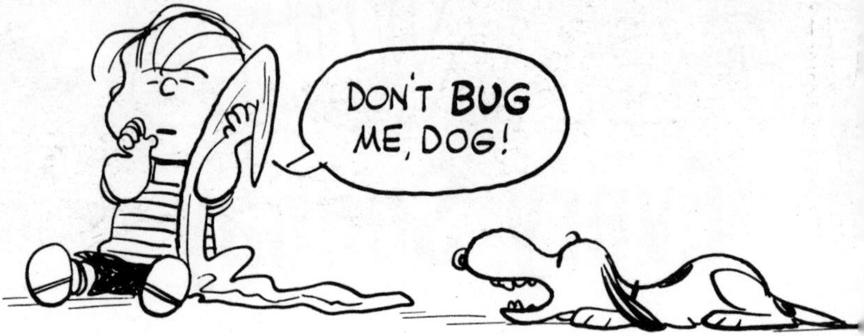
DON'T BUG ME, DOG!

Published simultaneously in Canada by Holt, Rinehart and Winston of Canada, Limited.

Published, April, 1961

Twelfth Printing, June, 1969

Library of Congress Catalog Card Number: 61-7132

SBN: 03–030730–9

Printed in the United States of America

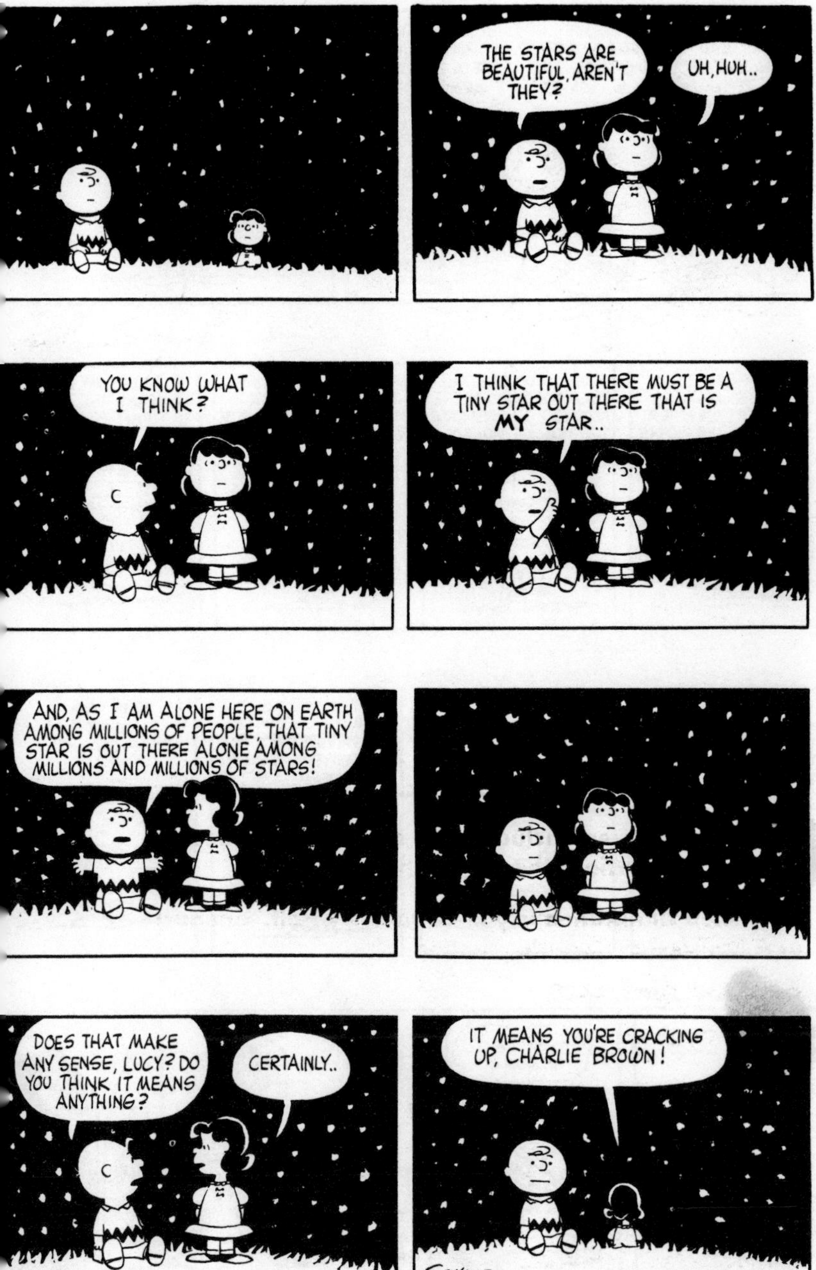
THE STARS ARE BEAUTIFUL, AREN'T THEY?
UH, HUH..
YOU KNOW WHAT I THINK?
I THINK THAT THERE MUST BE A TINY STAR OUT THERE THAT IS MY STAR..
AND, AS I AM ALONE HERE ON EARTH AMONG MILLIONS OF PEOPLE, THAT TINY STAR IS OUT THERE ALONE AMONG MILLIONS AND MILLIONS OF STARS!
DOES THAT MAKE ANY SENSE, LUCY? DO YOU THINK IT MEANS ANYTHING?
CERTAINLY..
IT MEANS YOU'RE CRACKING UP, CHARLIE BROWN!
SCHULZ

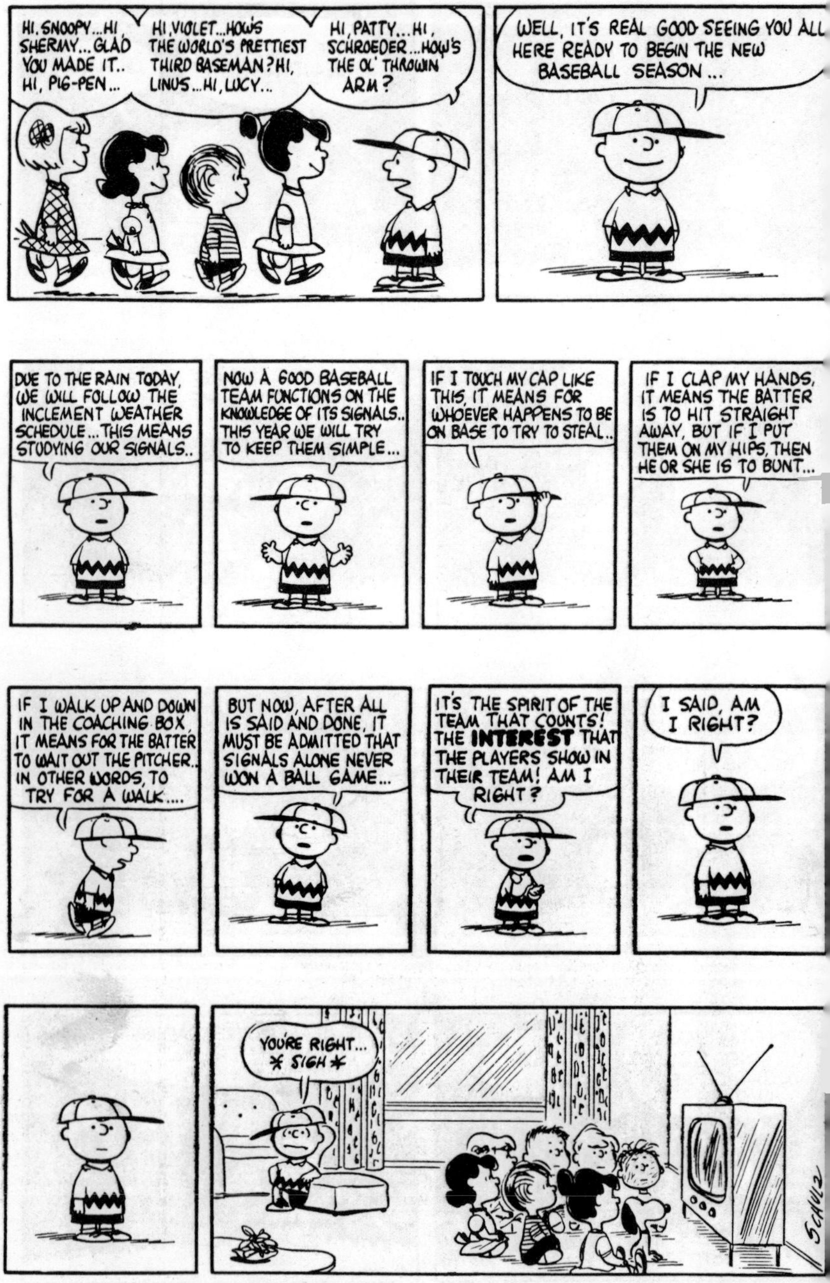
HI, SNOOPY...HI, SHERMY...GLAD YOU MADE IT.. HI, PIG-PEN...
HI, VIOLET...HOW'S THE WORLD'S PRETTIEST THIRD BASEMAN? HI, LINUS...HI, LUCY...
HI, PATTY...HI, SCHROEDER...HOW'S THE OL' THROWIN' ARM?
WELL, IT'S REAL GOOD SEEING YOU ALL HERE READY TO BEGIN THE NEW BASEBALL SEASON...
DUE TO THE RAIN TODAY, WE WILL FOLLOW THE INCLEMENT WEATHER SCHEDULE...THIS MEANS STUDYING OUR SIGNALS..
NOW A GOOD BASEBALL TEAM FUNCTIONS ON THE KNOWLEDGE OF ITS SIGNALS.. THIS YEAR WE WILL TRY TO KEEP THEM SIMPLE...
IF I TOUCH MY CAP LIKE THIS, IT MEANS FOR WHOEVER HAPPENS TO BE ON BASE TO TRY TO STEAL..
IF I CLAP MY HANDS, IT MEANS THE BATTER IS TO HIT STRAIGHT AWAY, BUT IF I PUT THEM ON MY HIPS, THEN HE OR SHE IS TO BUNT...
IF I WALK UP AND DOWN IN THE COACHING BOX, IT MEANS FOR THE BATTER TO WAIT OUT THE PITCHER.. IN OTHER WORDS, TO TRY FOR A WALK....
BUT NOW, AFTER ALL IS SAID AND DONE, IT MUST BE ADMITTED THAT SIGNALS ALONE NEVER WON A BALL GAME...
IT'S THE SPIRIT OF THE TEAM THAT COUNTS! THE INTEREST THAT THE PLAYERS SHOW IN THEIR TEAM! AM I RIGHT?
I SAID, AM I RIGHT?
YOU'RE RIGHT... * SIGH *
SCHULZ

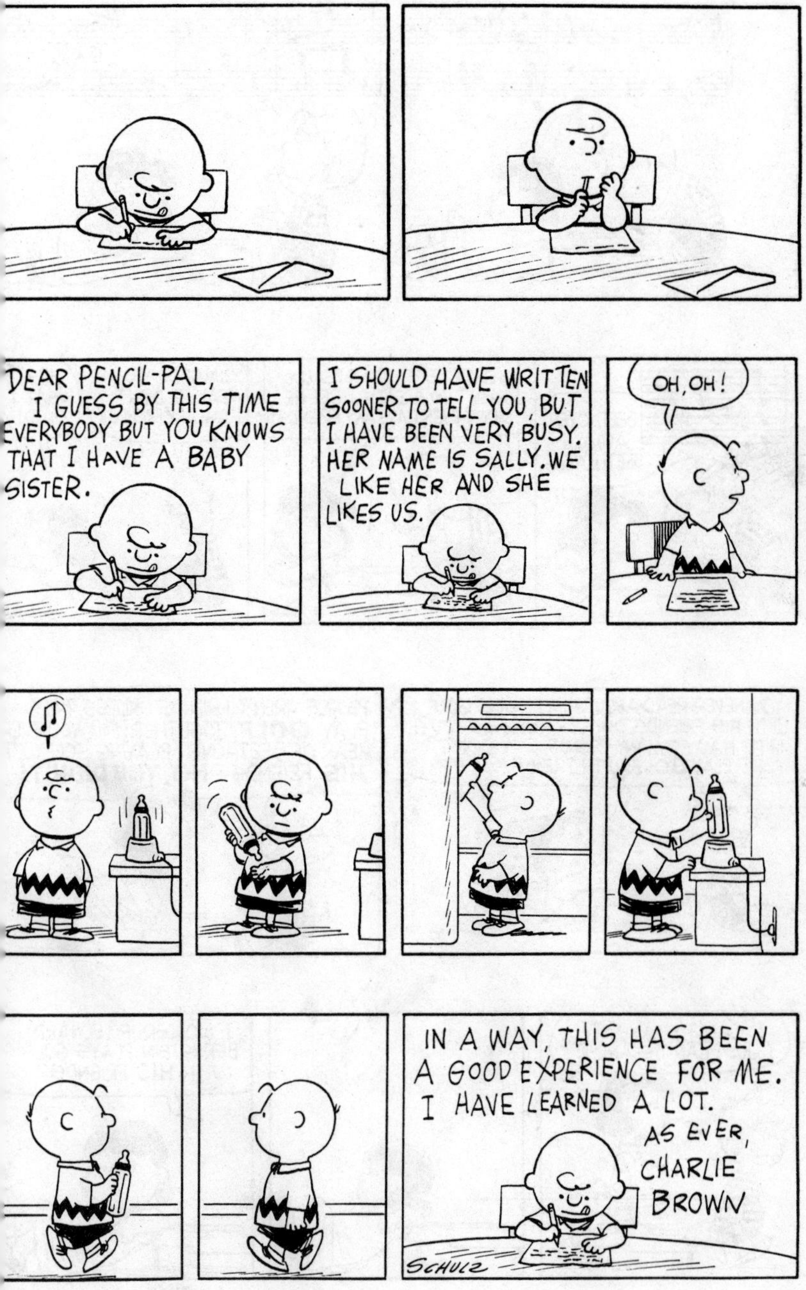
DEAR PENCIL-PAL,
I GUESS BY THIS TIME EVERYBODY BUT YOU KNOWS THAT I HAVE A BABY SISTER.
I SHOULD HAVE WRITTEN SOONER TO TELL YOU, BUT I HAVE BEEN VERY BUSY. HER NAME IS SALLY. WE LIKE HER AND SHE LIKES US.
OH, OH!
IN A WAY, THIS HAS BEEN A GOOD EXPERIENCE FOR ME. I HAVE LEARNED A LOT.
AS EVER,
CHARLIE BROWN
SCHULZ

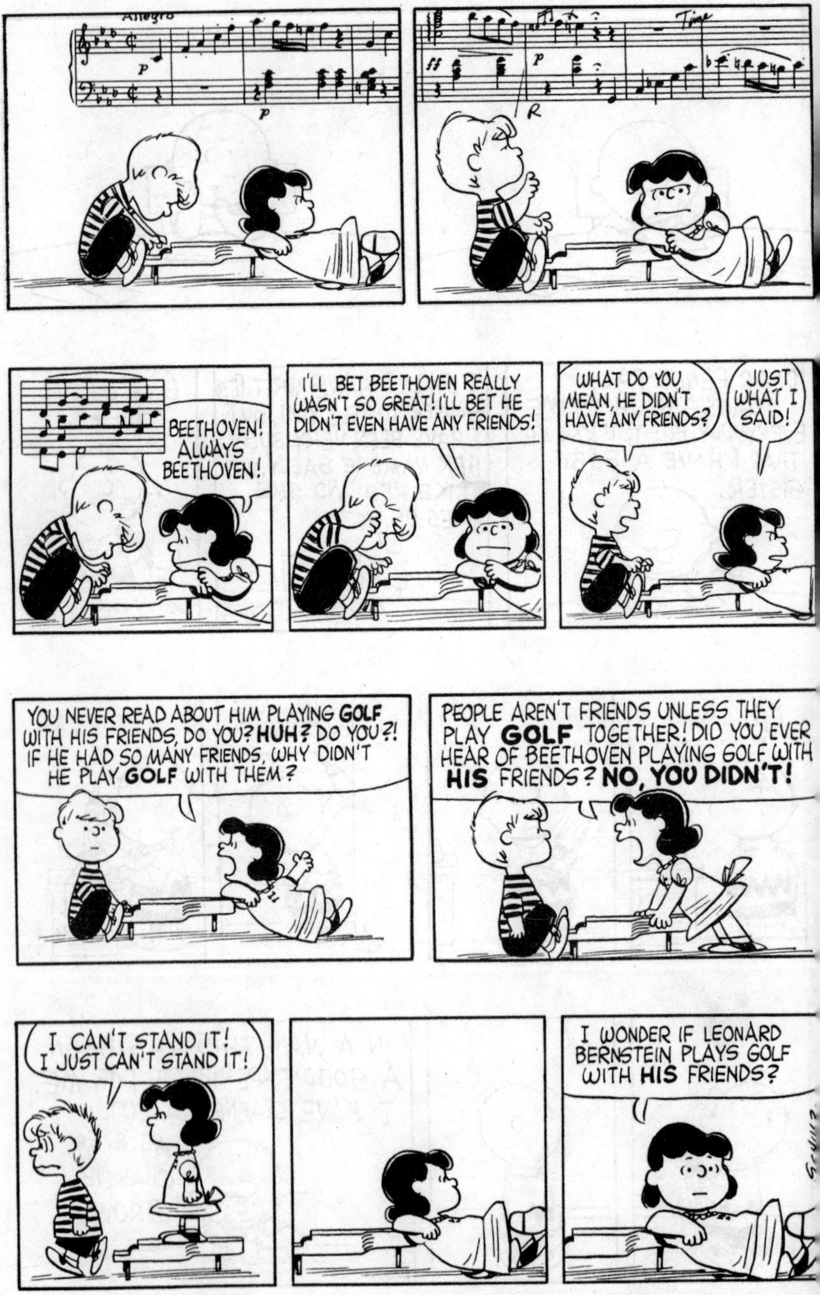
Allegro
BEETHOVEN! ALWAYS BEETHOVEN!
I'LL BET BEETHOVEN REALLY WASN'T SO GREAT! I'LL BET HE DIDN'T EVEN HAVE ANY FRIENDS!
WHAT DO YOU MEAN, HE DIDN'T HAVE ANY FRIENDS?
JUST WHAT I SAID!
YOU NEVER READ ABOUT HIM PLAYING GOLF WITH HIS FRIENDS, DO YOU? HUH? DO YOU?! IF HE HAD SO MANY FRIENDS, WHY DIDN'T HE PLAY GOLF WITH THEM?
PEOPLE AREN'T FRIENDS UNLESS THEY PLAY GOLF TOGETHER! DID YOU EVER HEAR OF BEETHOVEN PLAYING GOLF WITH HIS FRIENDS? NO, YOU DIDN'T!
I CAN'T STAND IT! I JUST CAN'T STAND IT!
I WONDER IF LEONARD BERNSTEIN PLAYS GOLF WITH HIS FRIENDS?

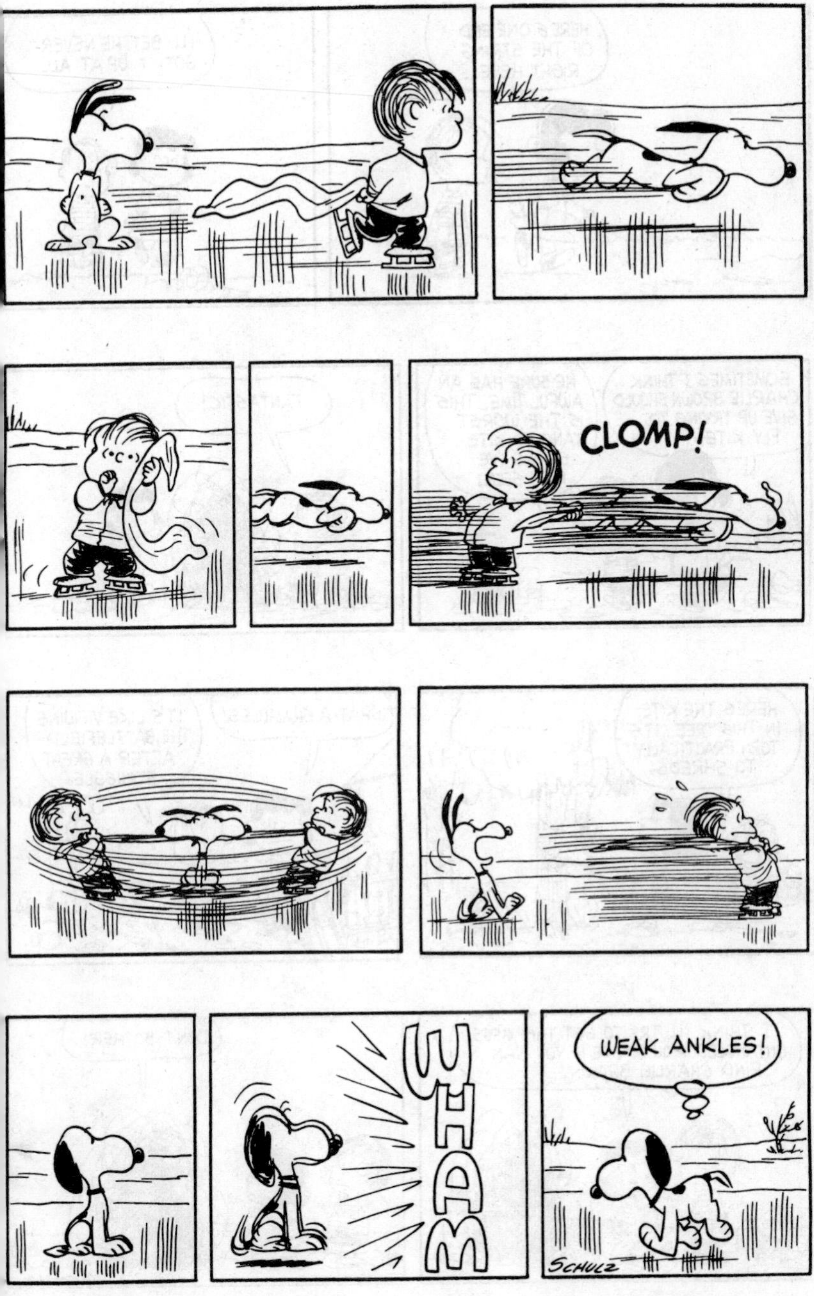
CLOMP!
WHEE
WEAK ANKLES!
SCHULZ

HERE'S ONE END OF THE STRING RIGHT HERE...
I'LL BET HE NEVER GOT IT UP AT ALL...
SOMETIMES I THINK CHARLIE BROWN SHOULD GIVE UP TRYING TO FLY KITES...
HE SURE HAS AN AWFUL TIME...THIS IS THE WORST TANGLED KITE STRING I'VE EVER SEEN!
FANTASTIC!
HERE'S THE KITE IN THIS TREE...IT'S TORN PRACTICALLY TO SHREDS!
WHAT A SHAMBLES!
IT'S LIKE VIEWING THE BATTLEFIELD AFTER A GREAT STRUGGLE
I THINK I'LL TRY TO GET THIS MESS UNTANGLED...YOU GO SEE IF YOU CAN FIND CHARLIE BROWN...
DON'T BOTHER!
SCHULZ

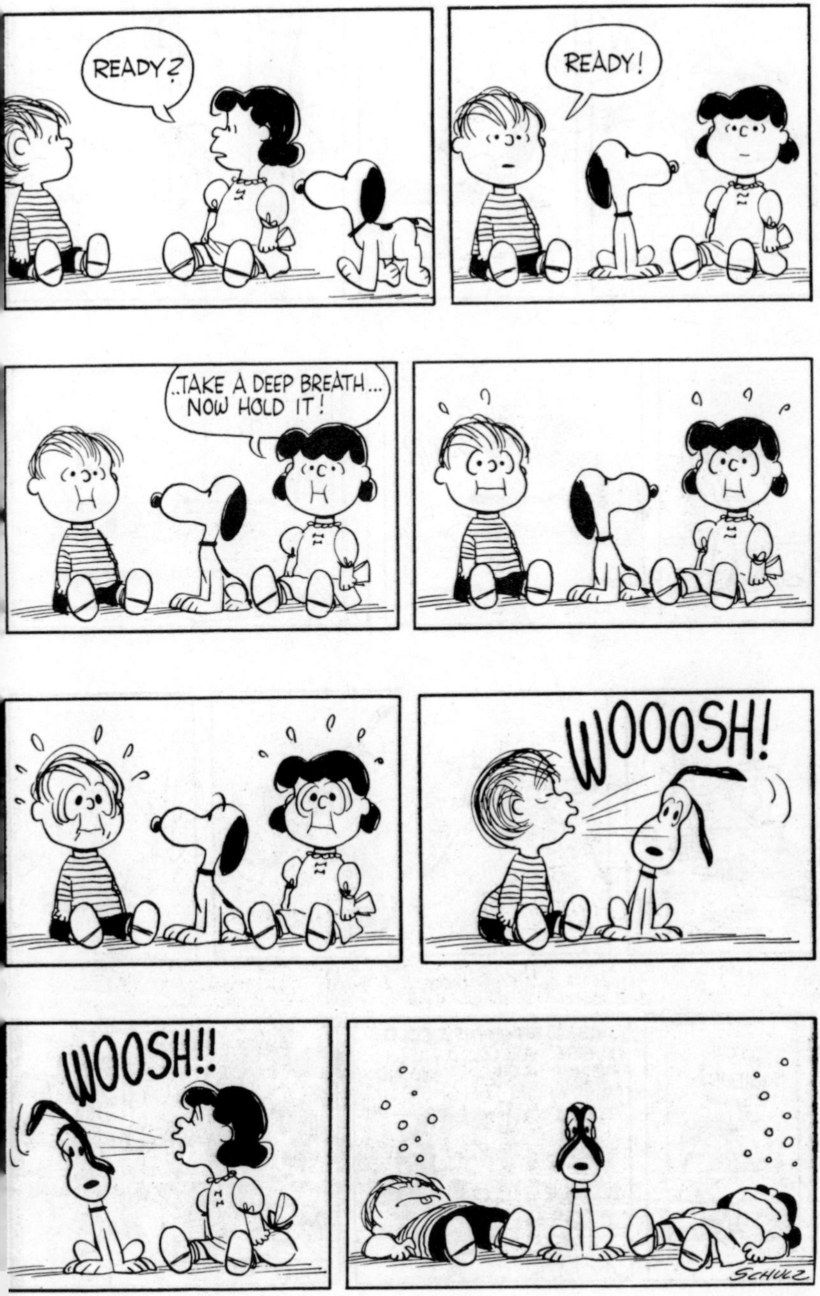
READY?
READY!
..TAKE A DEEP BREATH... NOW HOLD IT!
WOOOSH!
WOOSH!!
SCHULZ

CLOMP

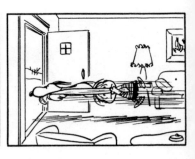

WHEW!

ARE YOU CRAZY? IT'S **COLD** OUTSIDE! YOU COULD CATCH PNEUMONIA ROLLING AROUND OUT THERE IN THE SNOW!

THE STRUGGLE FOR SECURITY KNOWS NO SEASON!

SCHULZ

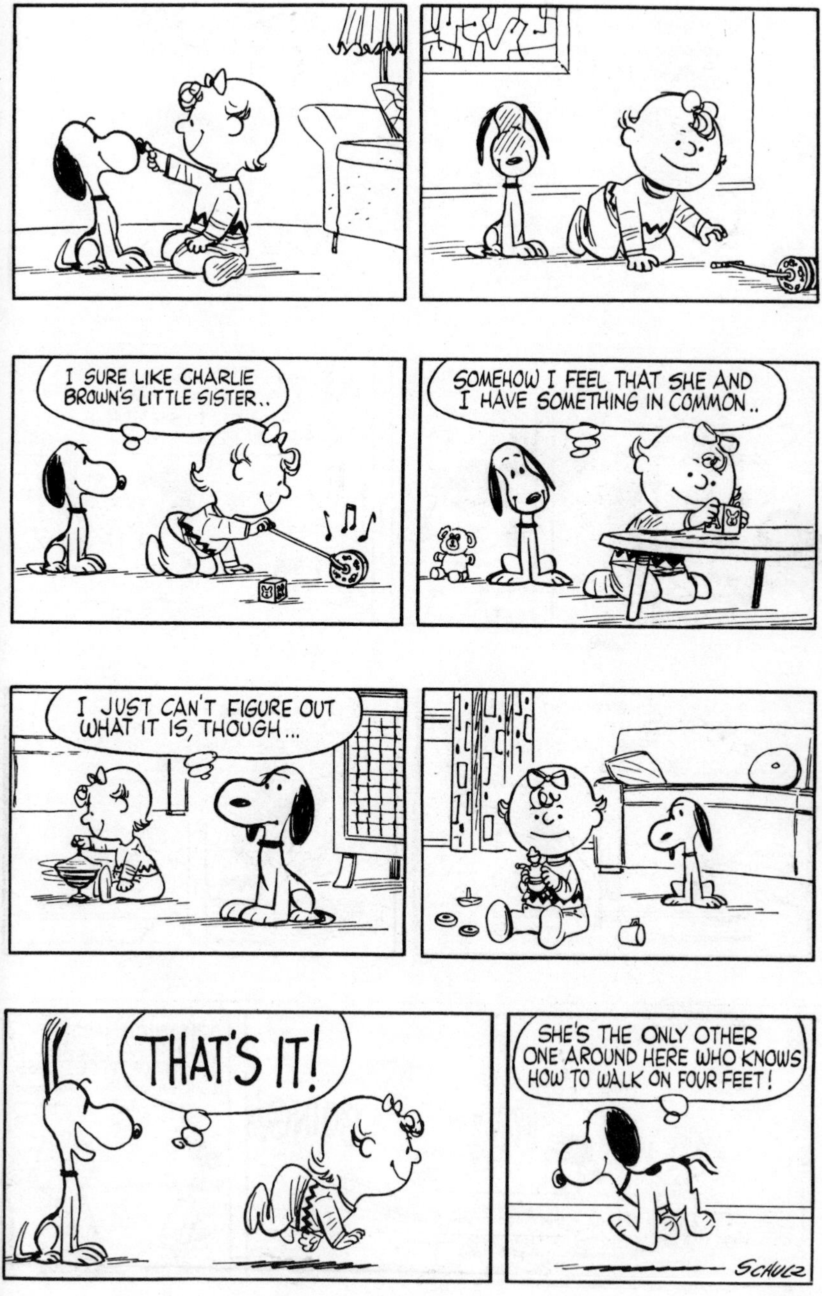
I SURE LIKE CHARLIE BROWN'S LITTLE SISTER..
SOMEHOW I FEEL THAT SHE AND I HAVE SOMETHING IN COMMON..
I JUST CAN'T FIGURE OUT WHAT IT IS, THOUGH...
THAT'S IT!
SHE'S THE ONLY OTHER ONE AROUND HERE WHO KNOWS HOW TO WALK ON FOUR FEET!
SCHULZ

YOU'RE WEAK, YOU'RE WISHY-WASHY, YOU'RE DULL AND YOU'RE BORING!

I DON'T KNOW WHAT ELSE I CAN SAY...

THE WAY I SEE IT, CHARLIE BROWN, YOUR FAULTS SIMPLY OUTWEIGH YOUR VIRTUES!

I WISH THERE WERE SOME WAY TO DEMONSTRATE WHAT I MEAN..

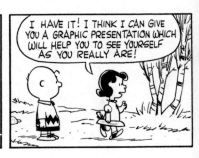

I HAVE IT! I THINK I CAN GIVE YOU A GRAPHIC PRESENTATION WHICH WILL HELP YOU TO SEE YOURSELF AS YOU REALLY ARE!

THIS BOARD WILL REPRESENT AN EVENLY BALANCED PERSONALITY...NOW, ON ONE SIDE I'LL PLACE THIS PEBBLE WHICH REPRESENTS ALL OF YOUR VIRTUES...

ON THE OTHER SIDE I'LL PLACE THIS BOULDER WHICH REPRESENTS YOUR COUNTLESS FAULTS...NOW, WATCH WHAT HAPPENS...

WUMP!

BOING!

DON'T YOU THINK YOU'RE LUCKY TO HAVE ME AROUND TO POINT UP THESE THINGS IN SUCH A GRAPHIC MANNER?

SCHULZ

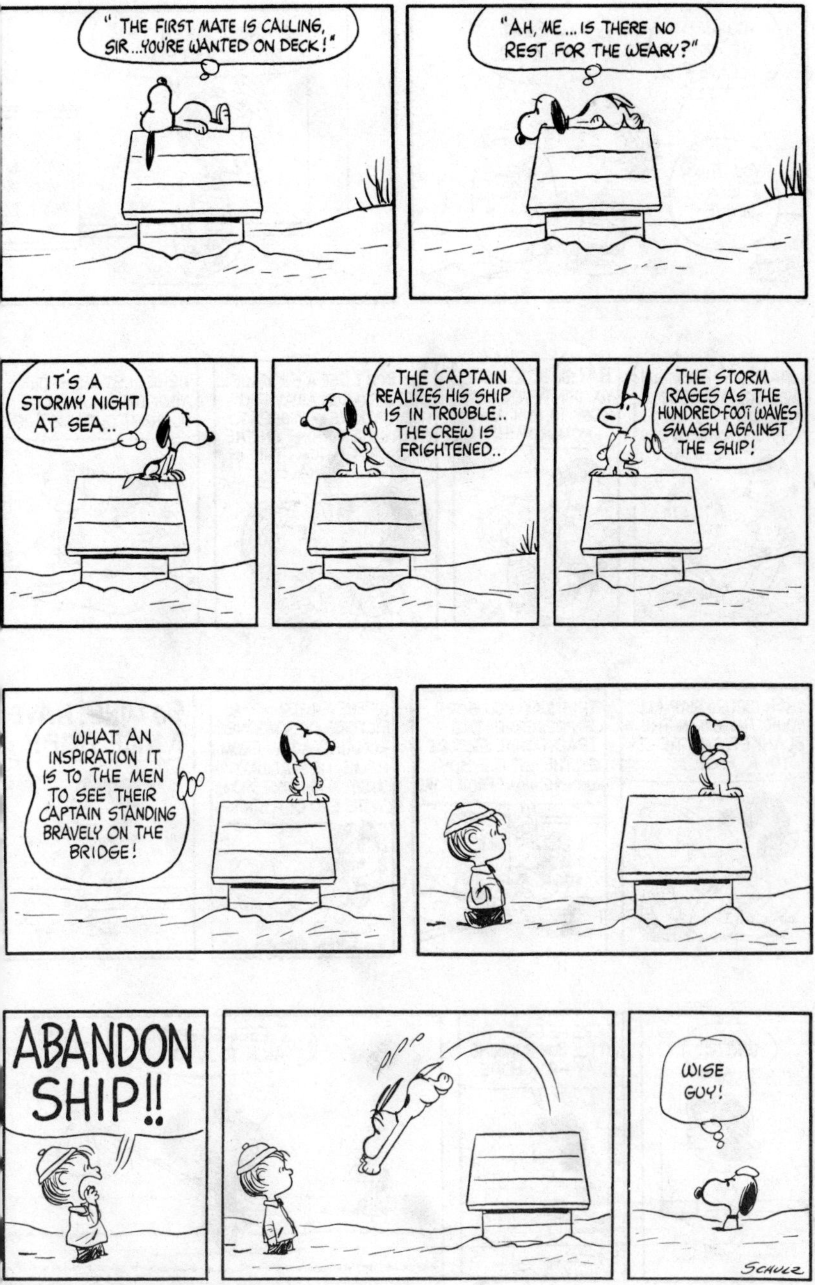

" THE FIRST MATE IS CALLING, SIR...YOU'RE WANTED ON DECK!"
"AH, ME ... IS THERE NO REST FOR THE WEARY?"
IT'S A STORMY NIGHT AT SEA..
THE CAPTAIN REALIZES HIS SHIP IS IN TROUBLE.. THE CREW IS FRIGHTENED..
THE STORM RAGES AS THE HUNDRED-FOOT WAVES SMASH AGAINST THE SHIP!
WHAT AN INSPIRATION IT IS TO THE MEN TO SEE THEIR CAPTAIN STANDING BRAVELY ON THE BRIDGE!
ABANDON SHIP!!
WISE GUY!
SCHULZ

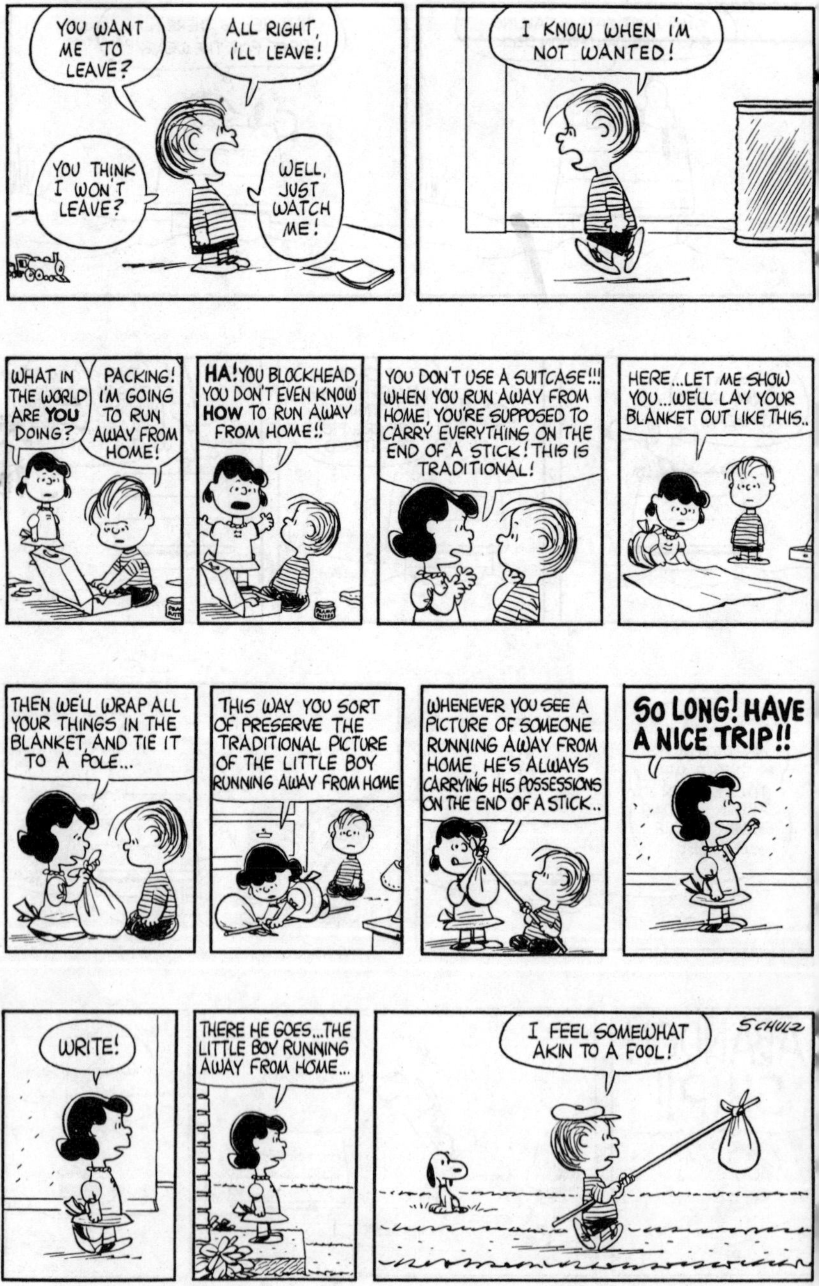
YOU WANT ME TO LEAVE?
ALL RIGHT, I'LL LEAVE!
YOU THINK I WON'T LEAVE?
WELL, JUST WATCH ME!
I KNOW WHEN I'M NOT WANTED!
WHAT IN THE WORLD ARE **YOU** DOING?
PACKING! I'M GOING TO RUN AWAY FROM HOME!
HA! YOU BLOCKHEAD, YOU DON'T EVEN KNOW **HOW** TO RUN AWAY FROM HOME!!
YOU DON'T USE A SUITCASE!!! WHEN YOU RUN AWAY FROM HOME, YOU'RE SUPPOSED TO CARRY EVERYTHING ON THE END OF A STICK! THIS IS TRADITIONAL!
HERE...LET ME SHOW YOU...WE'LL LAY YOUR BLANKET OUT LIKE THIS..
THEN WE'LL WRAP ALL YOUR THINGS IN THE BLANKET, AND TIE IT TO A POLE...
THIS WAY YOU SORT OF PRESERVE THE TRADITIONAL PICTURE OF THE LITTLE BOY RUNNING AWAY FROM HOME
WHENEVER YOU SEE A PICTURE OF SOMEONE RUNNING AWAY FROM HOME, HE'S ALWAYS CARRYING HIS POSSESSIONS ON THE END OF A STICK..
SO LONG! HAVE A NICE TRIP!!
WRITE!
THERE HE GOES...THE LITTLE BOY RUNNING AWAY FROM HOME...
SCHULZ
I FEEL SOMEWHAT AKIN TO A FOOL!

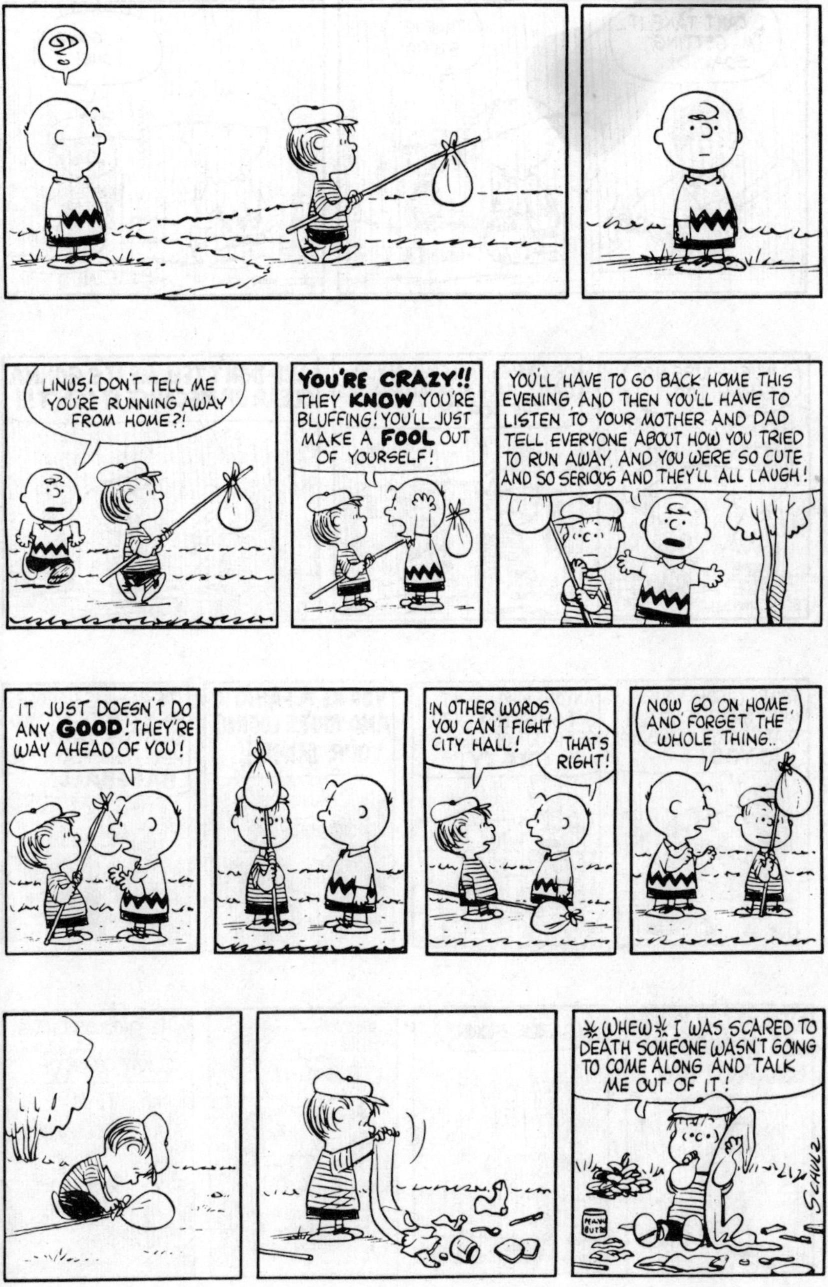
LINUS! DON'T TELL ME YOU'RE RUNNING AWAY FROM HOME?!
YOU'RE CRAZY!! THEY KNOW YOU'RE BLUFFING! YOU'LL JUST MAKE A FOOL OUT OF YOURSELF!
YOU'LL HAVE TO GO BACK HOME THIS EVENING, AND THEN YOU'LL HAVE TO LISTEN TO YOUR MOTHER AND DAD TELL EVERYONE ABOUT HOW YOU TRIED TO RUN AWAY, AND YOU WERE SO CUTE AND SO SERIOUS AND THEY'LL ALL LAUGH!
IT JUST DOESN'T DO ANY GOOD! THEY'RE WAY AHEAD OF YOU!
IN OTHER WORDS, YOU CAN'T FIGHT CITY HALL!
THAT'S RIGHT!
NOW, GO ON HOME, AND FORGET THE WHOLE THING..
WHEW! I WAS SCARED TO DEATH SOMEONE WASN'T GOING TO COME ALONG AND TALK ME OUT OF IT!
SCHULZ

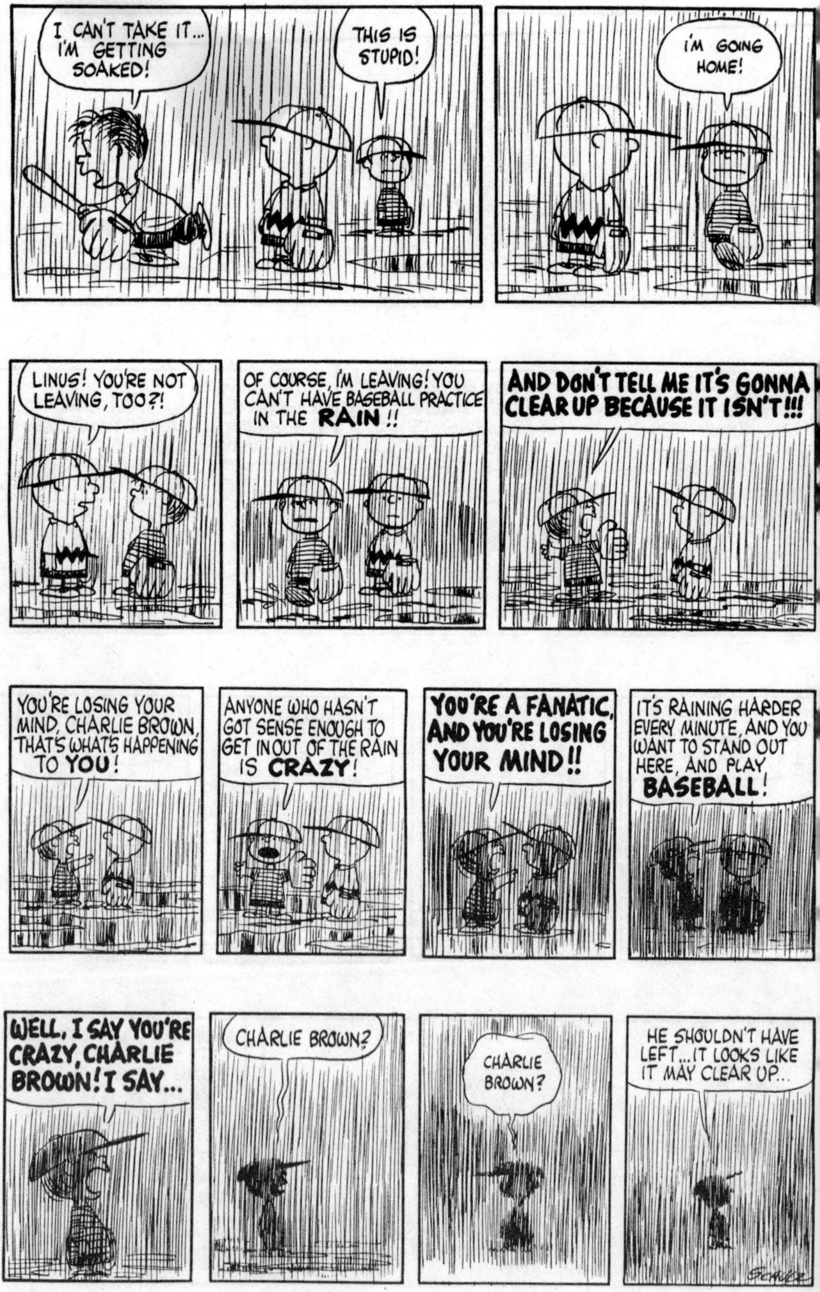
I CAN'T TAKE IT... I'M GETTING SOAKED!
THIS IS STUPID!
I'M GOING HOME!
LINUS! YOU'RE NOT LEAVING, TOO?!
OF COURSE, I'M LEAVING! YOU CAN'T HAVE BASEBALL PRACTICE IN THE RAIN!!
AND DON'T TELL ME IT'S GONNA CLEAR UP BECAUSE IT ISN'T!!!
YOU'RE LOSING YOUR MIND, CHARLIE BROWN, THAT'S WHAT'S HAPPENING TO YOU!
ANYONE WHO HASN'T GOT SENSE ENOUGH TO GET IN OUT OF THE RAIN IS CRAZY!
YOU'RE A FANATIC, AND YOU'RE LOSING YOUR MIND!!
IT'S RAINING HARDER EVERY MINUTE, AND YOU WANT TO STAND OUT HERE, AND PLAY BASEBALL!
WELL, I SAY YOU'RE CRAZY, CHARLIE BROWN! I SAY...
CHARLIE BROWN?
CHARLIE BROWN?
HE SHOULDN'T HAVE LEFT...IT LOOKS LIKE IT MAY CLEAR UP...

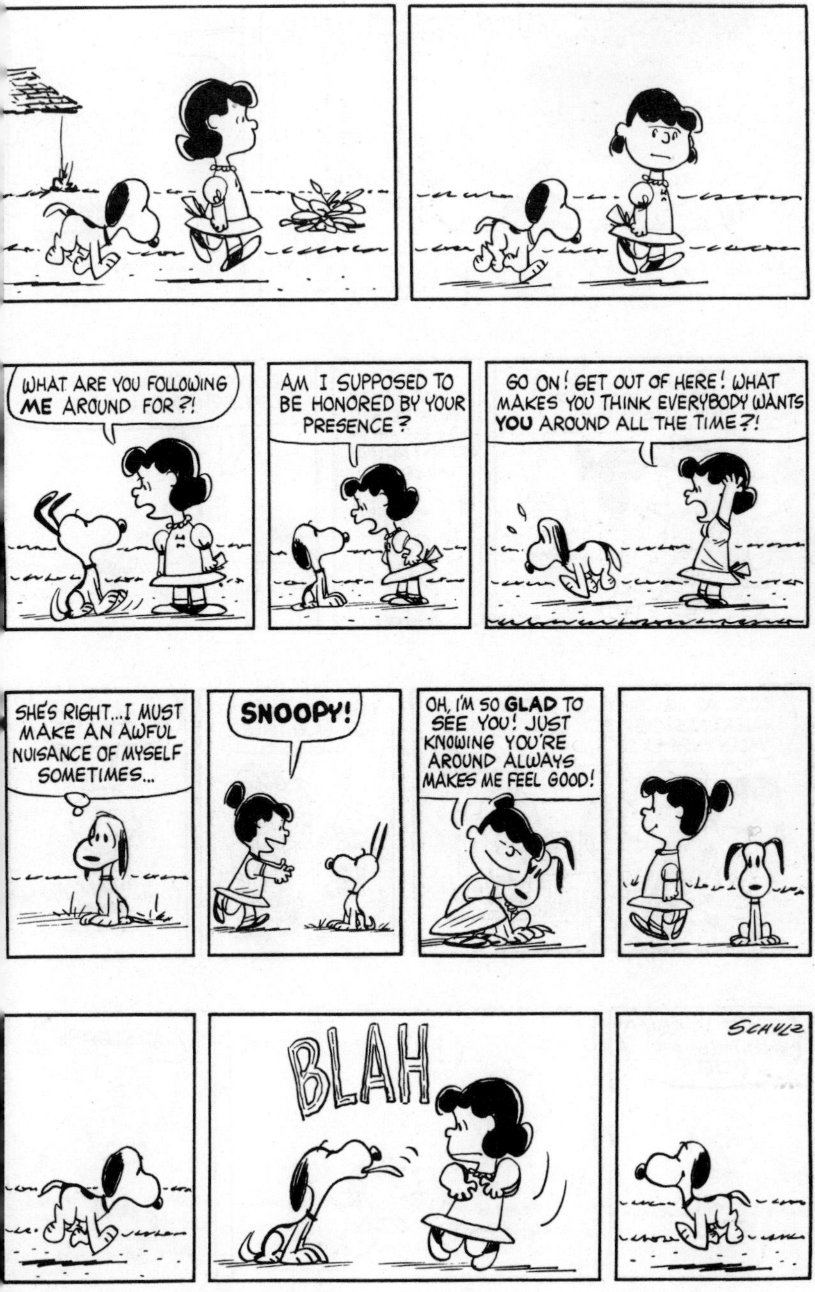
WHAT ARE YOU FOLLOWING ME AROUND FOR ?!
AM I SUPPOSED TO BE HONORED BY YOUR PRESENCE ?
GO ON! GET OUT OF HERE! WHAT MAKES YOU THINK EVERYBODY WANTS YOU AROUND ALL THE TIME ?!
SHE'S RIGHT...I MUST MAKE AN AWFUL NUISANCE OF MYSELF SOMETIMES...
SNOOPY!
OH, I'M SO GLAD TO SEE YOU! JUST KNOWING YOU'RE AROUND ALWAYS MAKES ME FEEL GOOD!
BLAH
SCHULZ

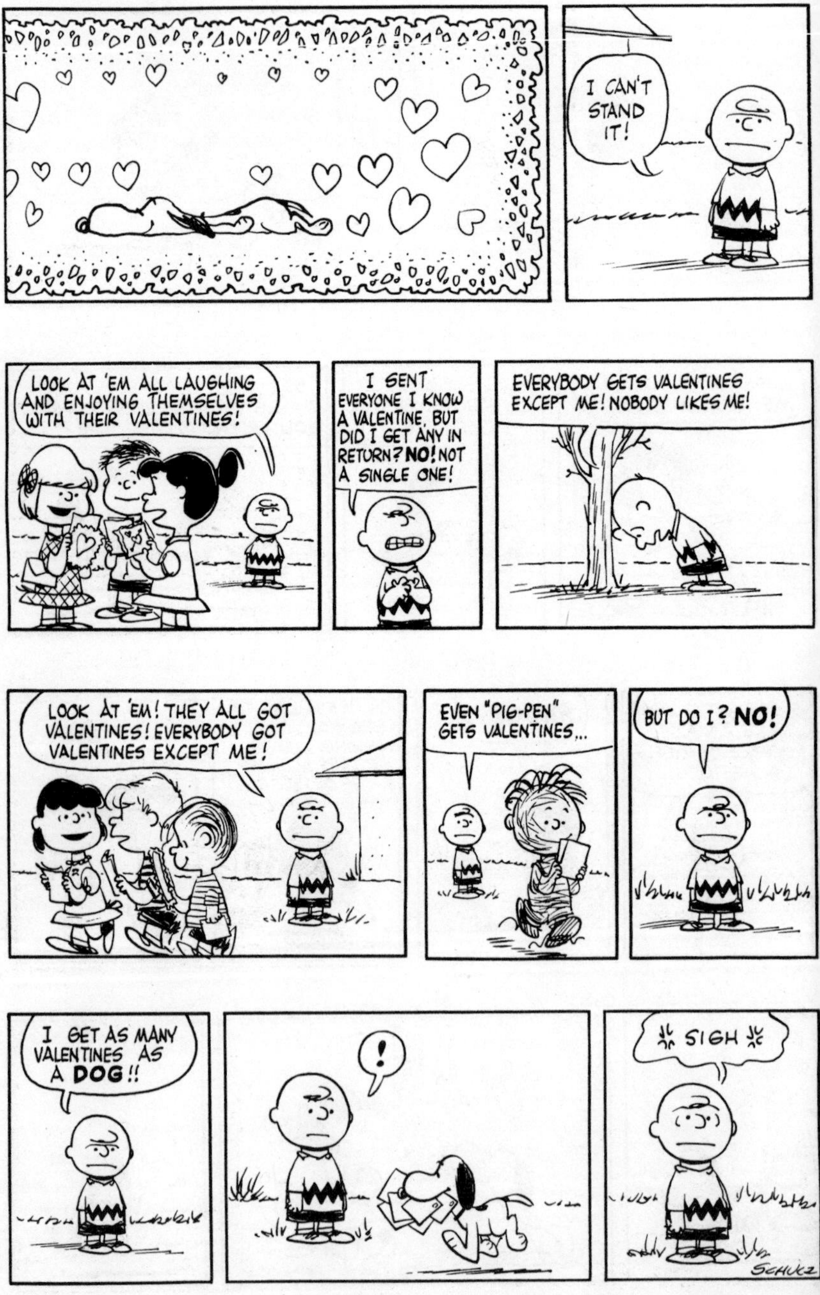

I CAN'T STAND IT!
LOOK AT 'EM ALL LAUGHING AND ENJOYING THEMSELVES WITH THEIR VALENTINES!
I SENT EVERYONE I KNOW A VALENTINE, BUT DID I GET ANY IN RETURN? NO! NOT A SINGLE ONE!
EVERYBODY GETS VALENTINES EXCEPT ME! NOBODY LIKES ME!
LOOK AT 'EM! THEY ALL GOT VALENTINES! EVERYBODY GOT VALENTINES EXCEPT ME!
EVEN "PIG-PEN" GETS VALENTINES...
BUT DO I? NO!
I GET AS MANY VALENTINES AS A DOG!!
!
SIGH
SCHULZ

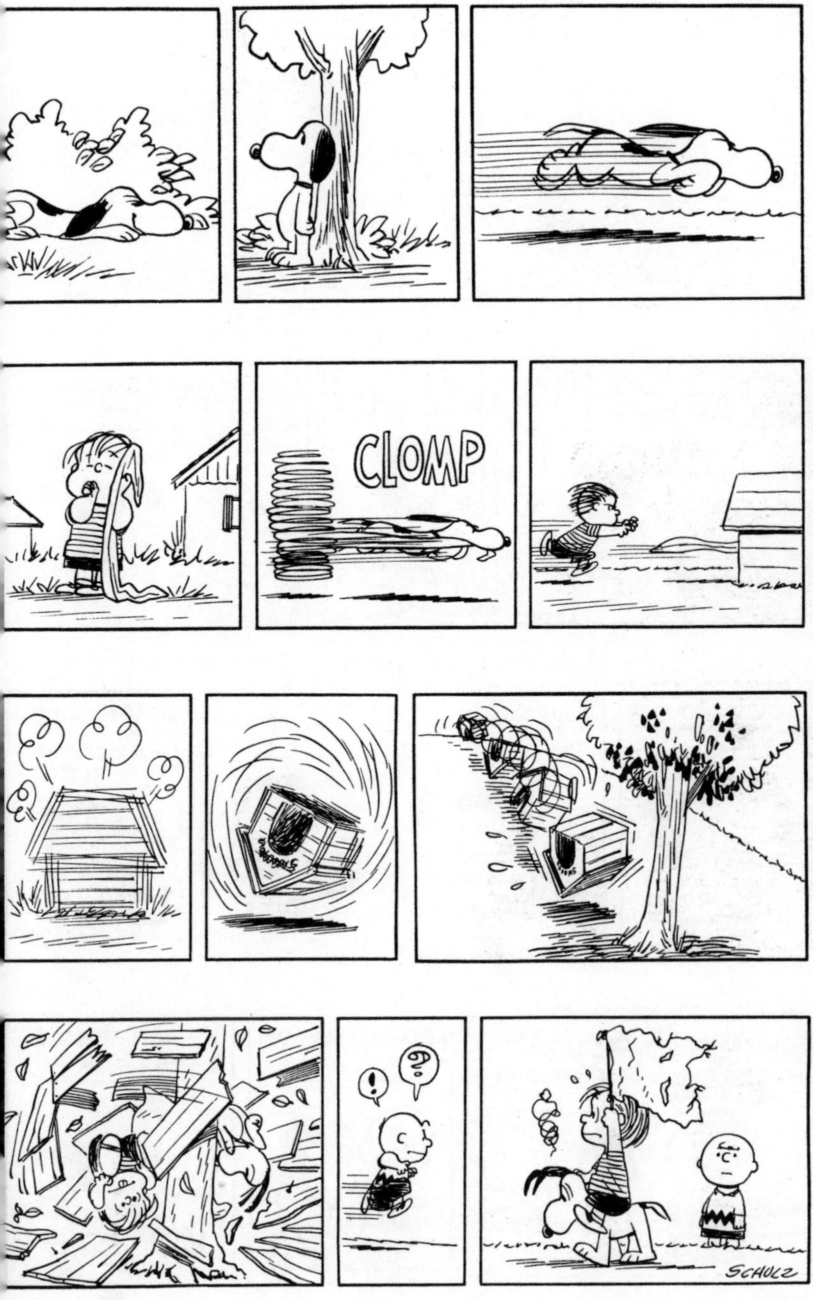
CLOMP
!
?
SCHULZ

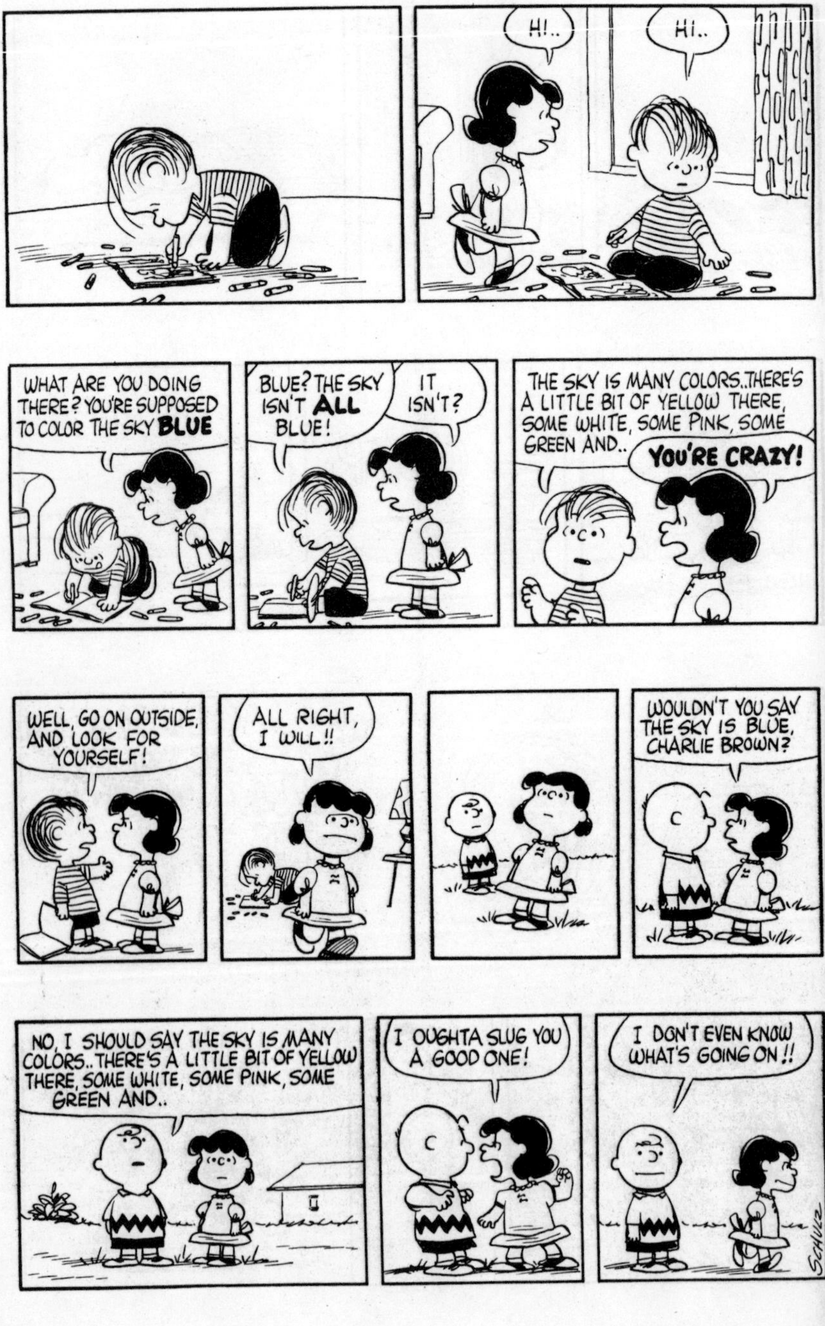
HI..
HI..
WHAT ARE YOU DOING THERE? YOU'RE SUPPOSED TO COLOR THE SKY BLUE
BLUE? THE SKY ISN'T ALL BLUE!
IT ISN'T?
THE SKY IS MANY COLORS..THERE'S A LITTLE BIT OF YELLOW THERE, SOME WHITE, SOME PINK, SOME GREEN AND..
YOU'RE CRAZY!
WELL, GO ON OUTSIDE, AND LOOK FOR YOURSELF!
ALL RIGHT, I WILL!!
WOULDN'T YOU SAY THE SKY IS BLUE, CHARLIE BROWN?
NO, I SHOULD SAY THE SKY IS MANY COLORS..THERE'S A LITTLE BIT OF YELLOW THERE, SOME WHITE, SOME PINK, SOME GREEN AND..
I OUGHTA SLUG YOU A GOOD ONE!
I DON'T EVEN KNOW WHAT'S GOING ON!!
SCHULZ

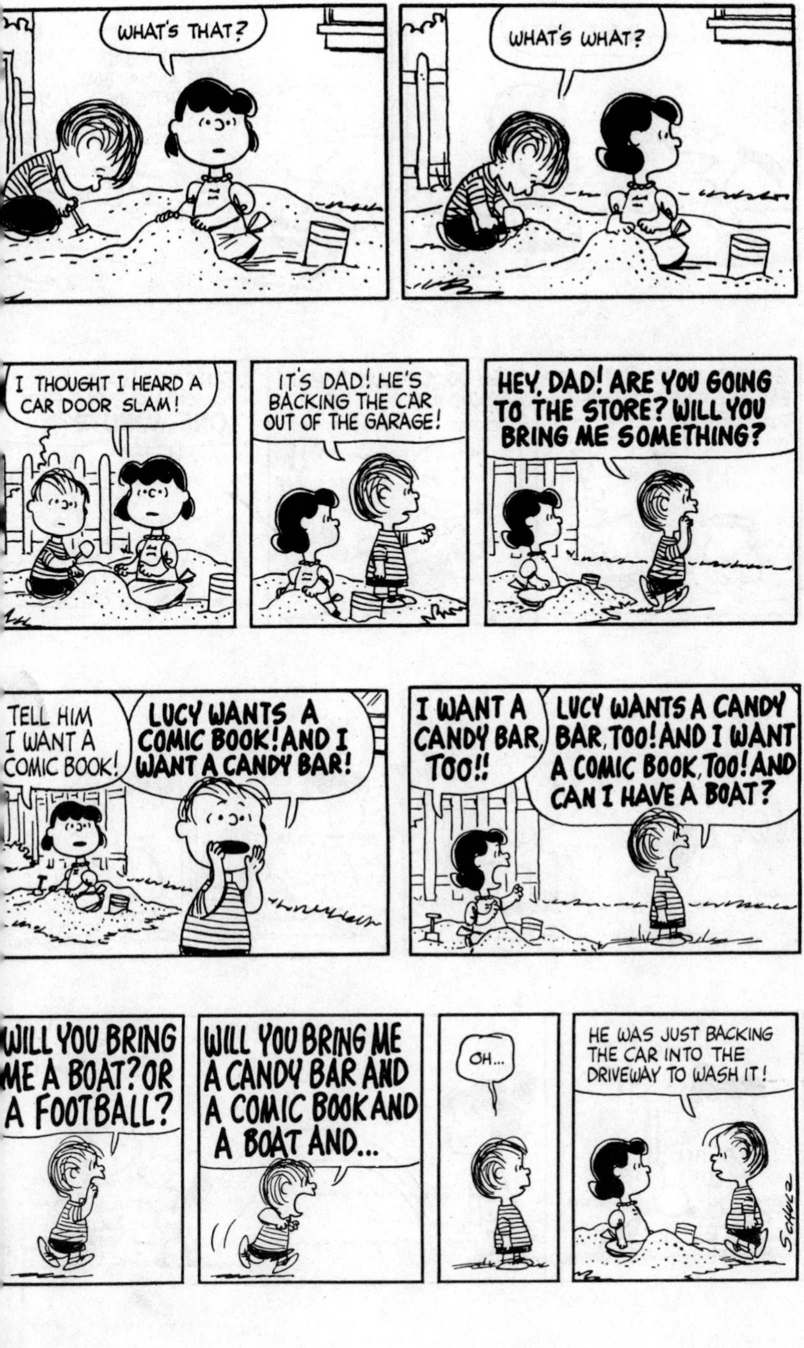
WHAT'S THAT?
WHAT'S WHAT?
I THOUGHT I HEARD A CAR DOOR SLAM!
IT'S DAD! HE'S BACKING THE CAR OUT OF THE GARAGE!
HEY, DAD! ARE YOU GOING TO THE STORE? WILL YOU BRING ME SOMETHING?
TELL HIM I WANT A COMIC BOOK!
LUCY WANTS A COMIC BOOK! AND I WANT A CANDY BAR!
I WANT A CANDY BAR, TOO!!
LUCY WANTS A CANDY BAR, TOO! AND I WANT A COMIC BOOK, TOO! AND CAN I HAVE A BOAT?
WILL YOU BRING ME A BOAT? OR A FOOTBALL?
WILL YOU BRING ME A CANDY BAR AND A COMIC BOOK AND A BOAT AND...
OH...
HE WAS JUST BACKING THE CAR INTO THE DRIVEWAY TO WASH IT!
SCHULZ

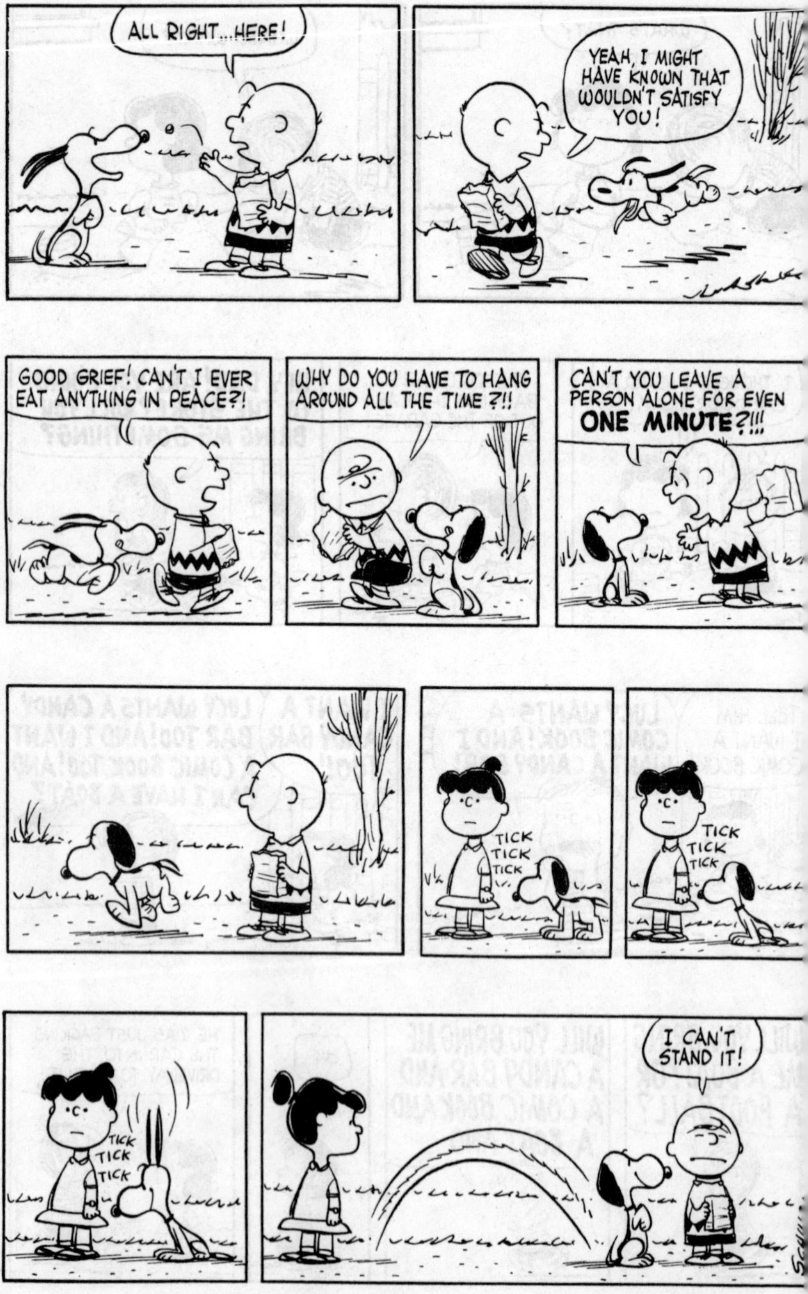

ALL RIGHT...HERE!
YEAH, I MIGHT HAVE KNOWN THAT WOULDN'T SATISFY YOU!
GOOD GRIEF! CAN'T I EVER EAT ANYTHING IN PEACE?!
WHY DO YOU HAVE TO HANG AROUND ALL THE TIME?!!
CAN'T YOU LEAVE A PERSON ALONE FOR EVEN ONE MINUTE?!!!
TICK TICK TICK
TICK TICK TICK
TICK TICK TICK
I CAN'T STAND IT!

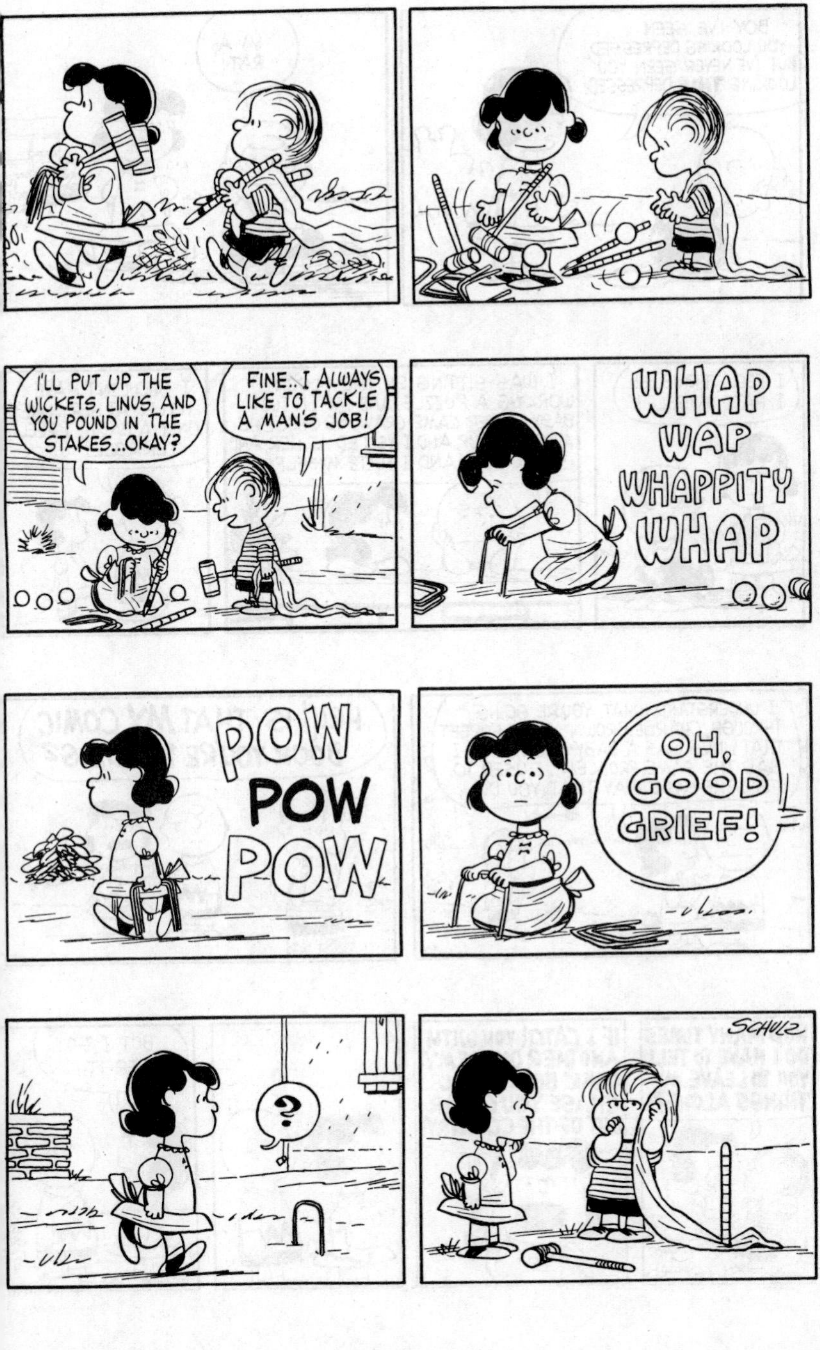
I'LL PUT UP THE WICKETS, LINUS, AND YOU POUND IN THE STAKES...OKAY?
FINE..I ALWAYS LIKE TO TACKLE A MAN'S JOB!
WHAP WAP WHAPPITY WHAP
POW POW POW
OH, GOOD GRIEF!
?
SCHULZ

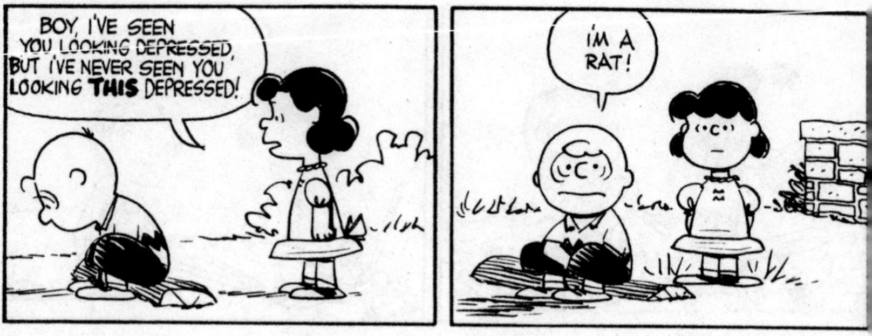
BOY, I'VE SEEN YOU LOOKING DEPRESSED, BUT I'VE NEVER SEEN YOU LOOKING THIS DEPRESSED!
I'M A RAT!

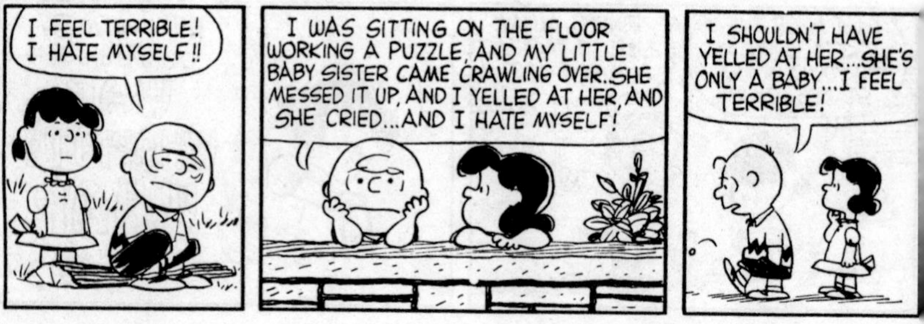
I FEEL TERRIBLE! I HATE MYSELF!!
I WAS SITTING ON THE FLOOR WORKING A PUZZLE, AND MY LITTLE BABY SISTER CAME CRAWLING OVER. SHE MESSED IT UP, AND I YELLED AT HER, AND SHE CRIED...AND I HATE MYSELF!
I SHOULDN'T HAVE YELLED AT HER...SHE'S ONLY A BABY...I FEEL TERRIBLE!

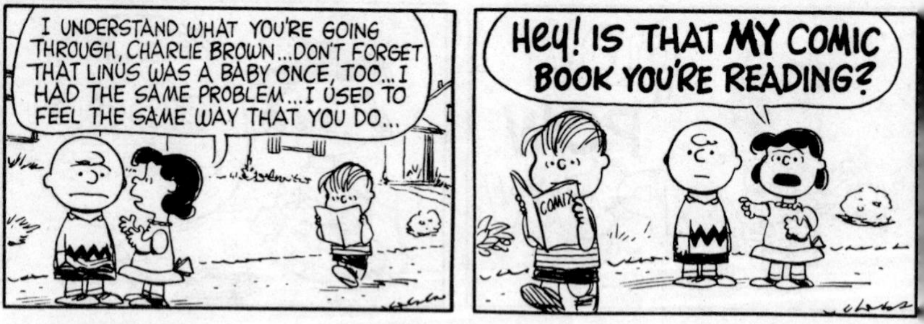
I UNDERSTAND WHAT YOU'RE GOING THROUGH, CHARLIE BROWN...DON'T FORGET THAT LINUS WAS A BABY ONCE, TOO...I HAD THE SAME PROBLEM...I USED TO FEEL THE SAME WAY THAT YOU DO...
HEY! IS THAT MY COMIC BOOK YOU'RE READING?
COMIX

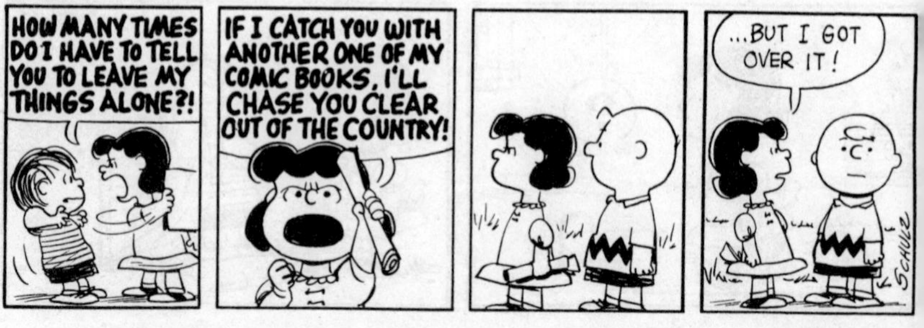
HOW MANY TIMES DO I HAVE TO TELL YOU TO LEAVE MY THINGS ALONE?!
IF I CATCH YOU WITH ANOTHER ONE OF MY COMIC BOOKS, I'LL CHASE YOU CLEAR OUT OF THE COUNTRY!
...BUT I GOT OVER IT!
SCHULZ

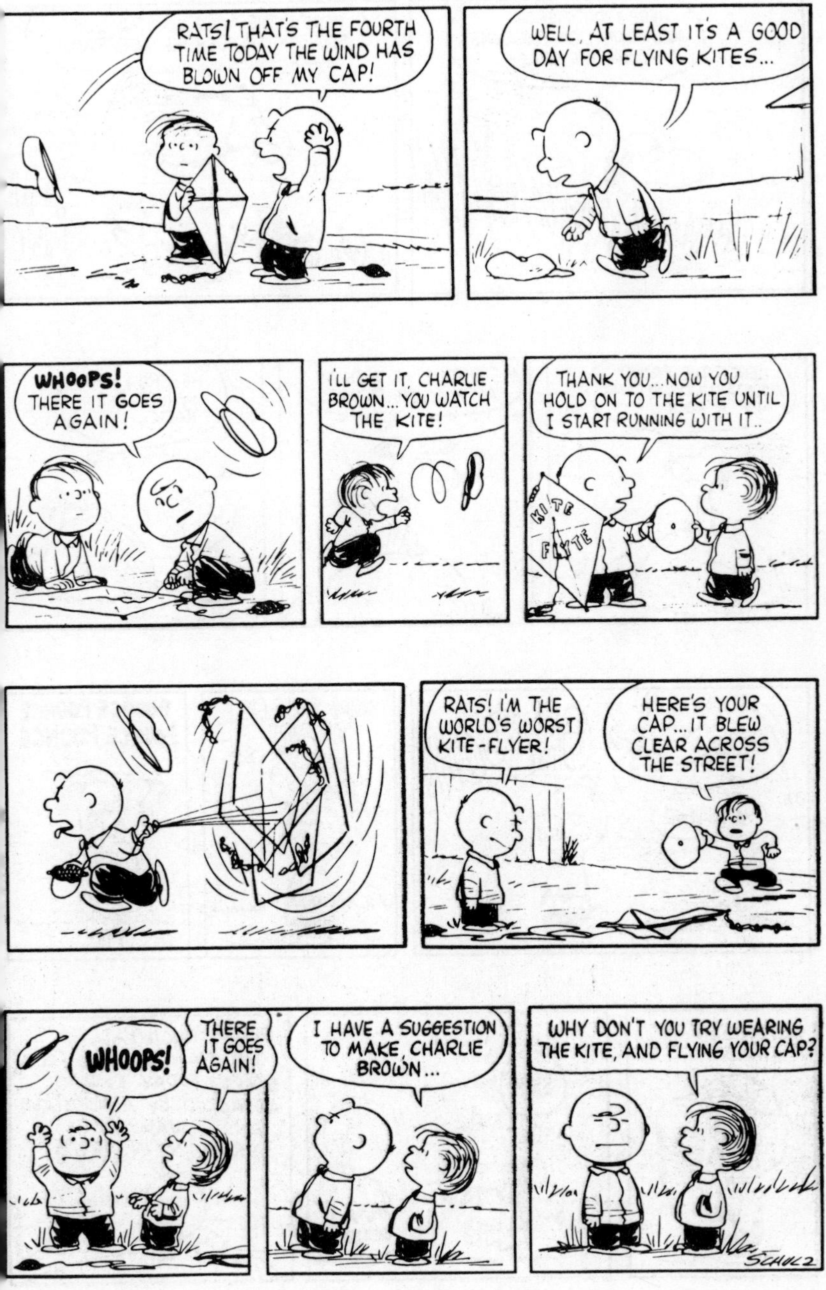
RATS! THAT'S THE FOURTH TIME TODAY THE WIND HAS BLOWN OFF MY CAP!
WELL, AT LEAST IT'S A GOOD DAY FOR FLYING KITES...
WHOOPS! THERE IT GOES AGAIN!
I'LL GET IT, CHARLIE BROWN... YOU WATCH THE KITE!
THANK YOU... NOW YOU HOLD ON TO THE KITE UNTIL I START RUNNING WITH IT..
KITE FLYTE
RATS! I'M THE WORLD'S WORST KITE-FLYER!
HERE'S YOUR CAP... IT BLEW CLEAR ACROSS THE STREET!
WHOOPS!
THERE IT GOES AGAIN!
I HAVE A SUGGESTION TO MAKE, CHARLIE BROWN...
WHY DON'T YOU TRY WEARING THE KITE, AND FLYING YOUR CAP?
SCHULZ

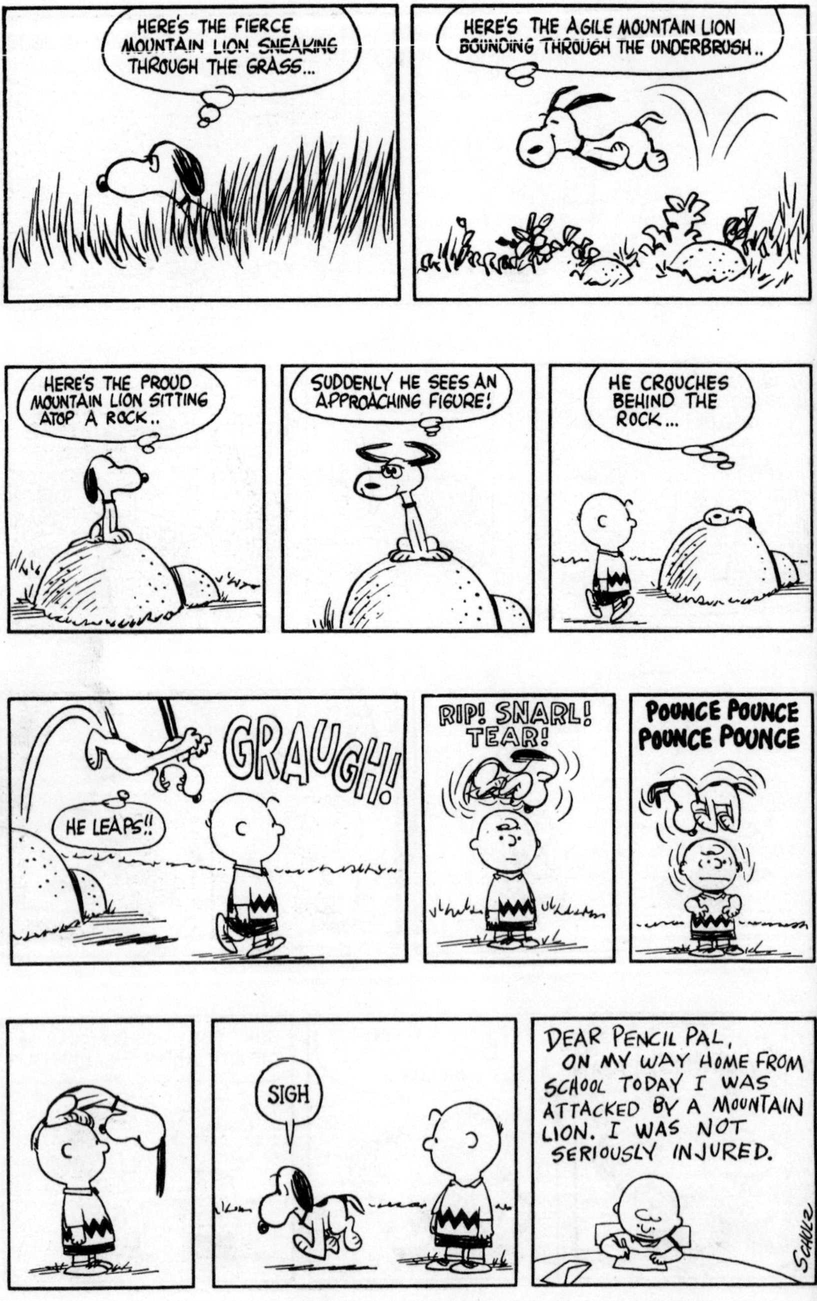
HERE'S THE FIERCE MOUNTAIN LION SNEAKING THROUGH THE GRASS...
HERE'S THE AGILE MOUNTAIN LION BOUNDING THROUGH THE UNDERBRUSH..
HERE'S THE PROUD MOUNTAIN LION SITTING ATOP A ROCK..
SUDDENLY HE SEES AN APPROACHING FIGURE!
HE CROUCHES BEHIND THE ROCK...
HE LEAPS!!
GRAUGH!
RIP! SNARL! TEAR!
POUNCE POUNCE POUNCE POUNCE
SIGH
DEAR PENCIL PAL, ON MY WAY HOME FROM SCHOOL TODAY I WAS ATTACKED BY A MOUNTAIN LION. I WAS NOT SERIOUSLY INJURED.
SCHULZ

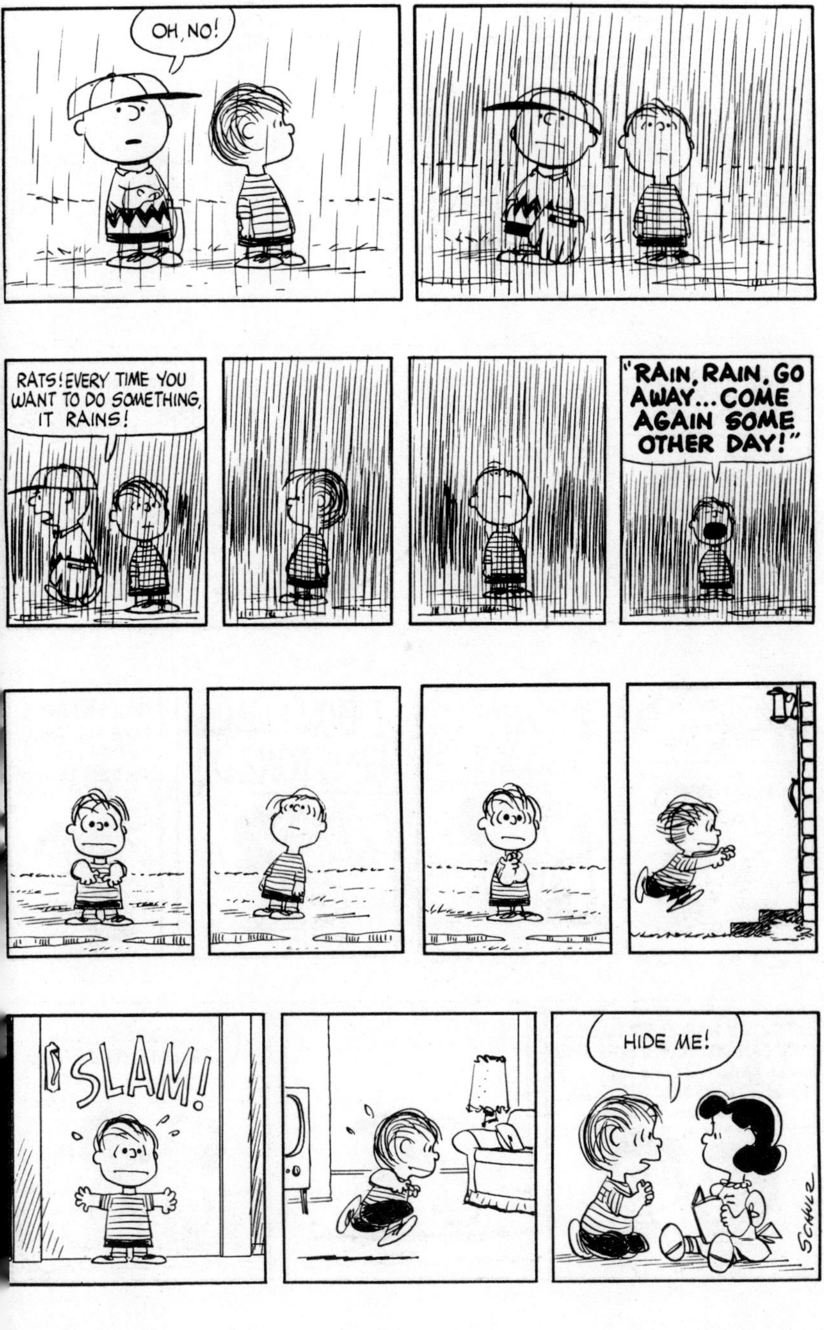
OH, NO!
RATS! EVERY TIME YOU WANT TO DO SOMETHING, IT RAINS!
"RAIN, RAIN, GO AWAY... COME AGAIN SOME OTHER DAY!"
SLAM!
HIDE ME!
SCHULZ

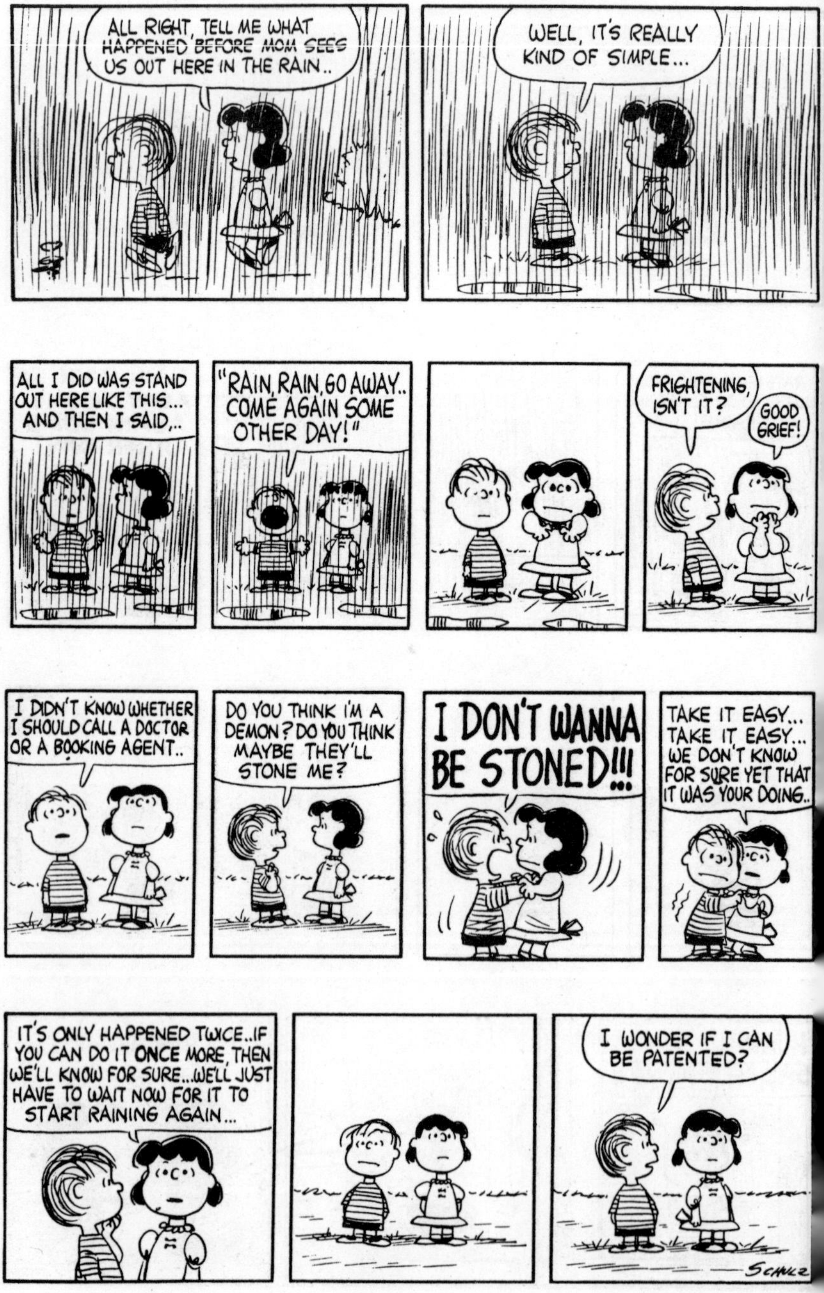
ALL RIGHT, TELL ME WHAT HAPPENED BEFORE MOM SEES US OUT HERE IN THE RAIN..
WELL, IT'S REALLY KIND OF SIMPLE...
ALL I DID WAS STAND OUT HERE LIKE THIS... AND THEN I SAID,...
"RAIN, RAIN, GO AWAY.. COME AGAIN SOME OTHER DAY!"
FRIGHTENING, ISN'T IT?
GOOD GRIEF!
I DIDN'T KNOW WHETHER I SHOULD CALL A DOCTOR OR A BOOKING AGENT..
DO YOU THINK I'M A DEMON? DO YOU THINK MAYBE THEY'LL STONE ME?
I DON'T WANNA BE STONED!!!
TAKE IT EASY... TAKE IT EASY... WE DON'T KNOW FOR SURE YET THAT IT WAS YOUR DOING..
IT'S ONLY HAPPENED TWICE..IF YOU CAN DO IT ONCE MORE, THEN WE'LL KNOW FOR SURE...WE'LL JUST HAVE TO WAIT NOW FOR IT TO START RAINING AGAIN...
I WONDER IF I CAN BE PATENTED?
SCHULZ

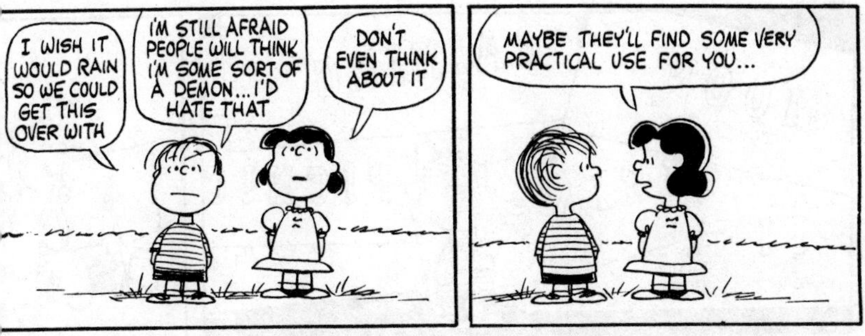
I WISH IT WOULD RAIN SO WE COULD GET THIS OVER WITH
I'M STILL AFRAID PEOPLE WILL THINK I'M SOME SORT OF A DEMON... I'D HATE THAT
DON'T EVEN THINK ABOUT IT
MAYBE THEY'LL FIND SOME VERY PRACTICAL USE FOR YOU...

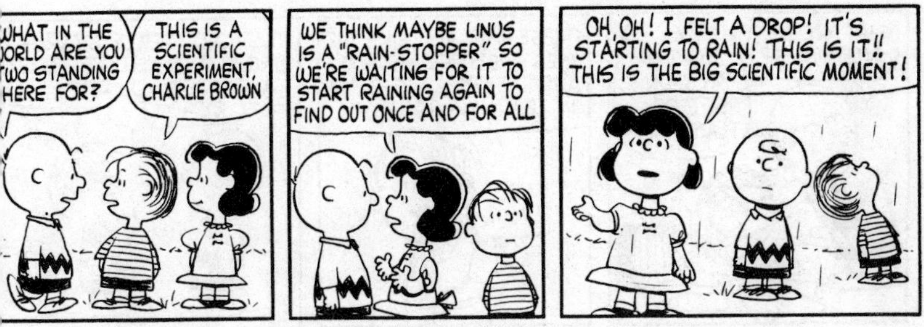
WHAT IN THE ORLD ARE YOU TWO STANDING HERE FOR?
THIS IS A SCIENTIFIC EXPERIMENT, CHARLIE BROWN
WE THINK MAYBE LINUS IS A "RAIN-STOPPER" SO WE'RE WAITING FOR IT TO START RAINING AGAIN TO FIND OUT ONCE AND FOR ALL
OH, OH! I FELT A DROP! IT'S STARTING TO RAIN! THIS IS IT!! THIS IS THE BIG SCIENTIFIC MOMENT!

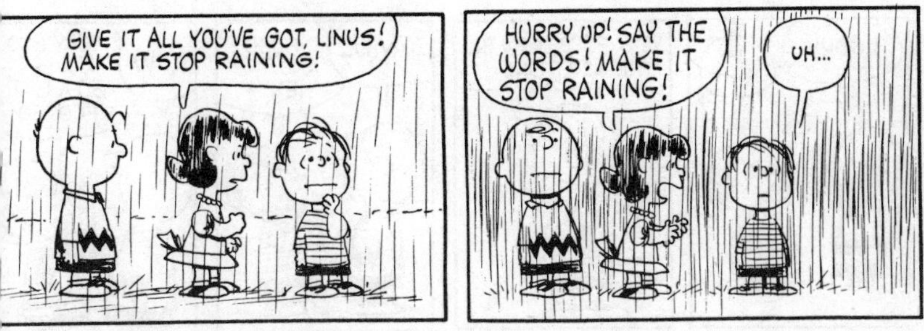
GIVE IT ALL YOU'VE GOT, LINUS! MAKE IT STOP RAINING!
HURRY UP! SAY THE WORDS! MAKE IT STOP RAINING!
UH...

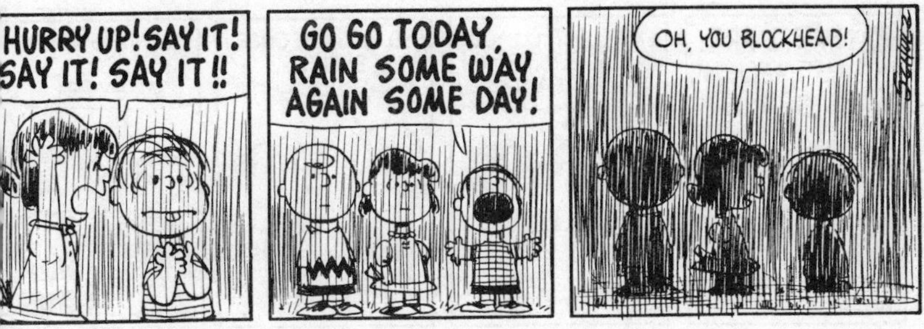
HURRY UP! SAY IT! SAY IT! SAY IT!!
GO GO TODAY, RAIN SOME WAY, AGAIN SOME DAY!
OH, YOU BLOCKHEAD!
SCHULZ

MOON
RAINING
BRIN
PICNIC
FINI
WUN
TU
WHAT ARE YOU DOING, LINUS?
I'M MAKING MY OWN SET OF FLASHCARDS
THESE ARE JUST LIKE THE ONES THEY USE IN SCHOOL, AND THEY'RE A GREAT AID IN LEARNING TO READ..
LOOOK
I'LL HOLD THEM UP, CHARLIE BROWN, AND WE'LL SEE HOW GOO
A READER YOU ARE... READY?
LOOOK
UH HUH!
VERY GOOD...NOW TRY THE NEXT ONE..
TAYBUL
GOOD.. AND THE NEXT?
KOW
VERY GOOD
NOW LET'S GO A LITTL
FASTER..
PAYPUR, DORE, HOWSE, WELKUM, NIFE, SPUNE!
EXCELLENT! DO YOU WANT TO RUN THROUGH THEM AGAIN?
NO, I THINK ONCE IS ENOUGH...
AWL THYS REEDING IS HARRD ONN MI EYYS!
SCHULZ

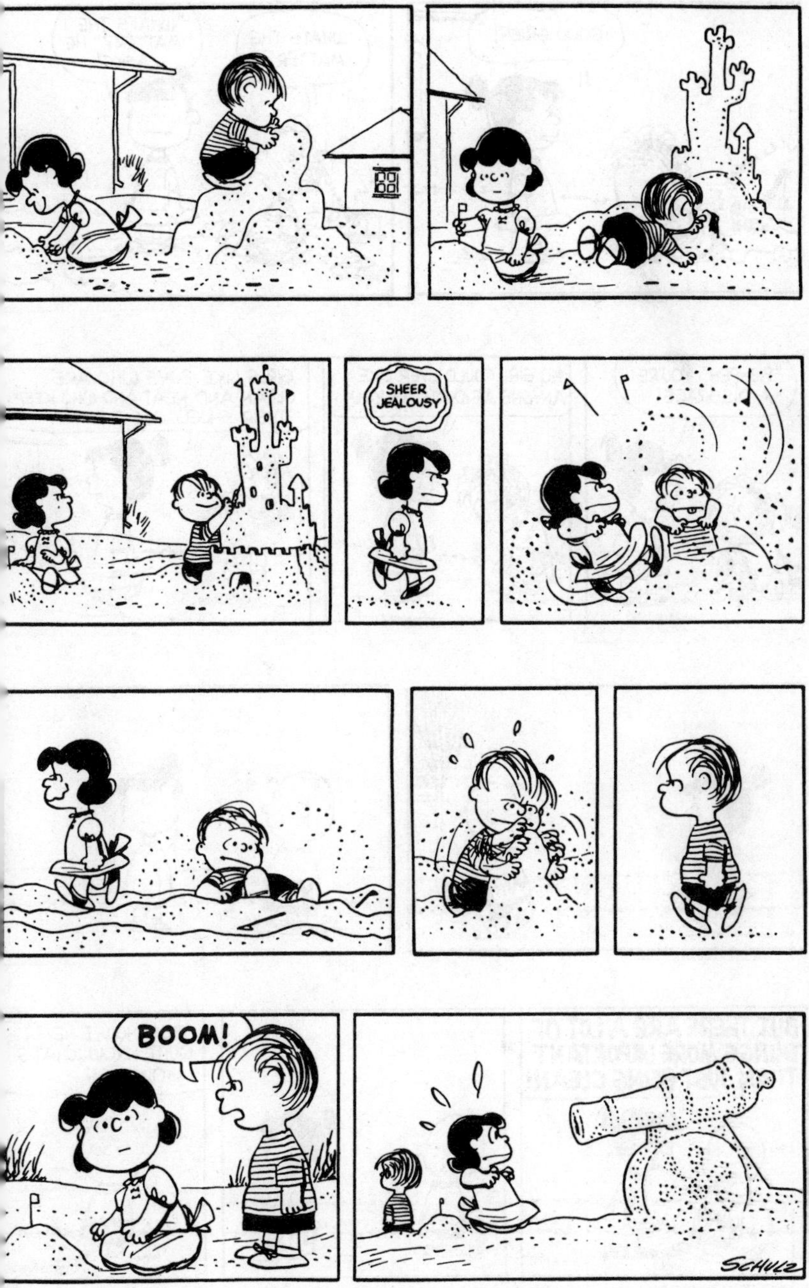
SHEER JEALOUSY
BOOM!
SCHULZ

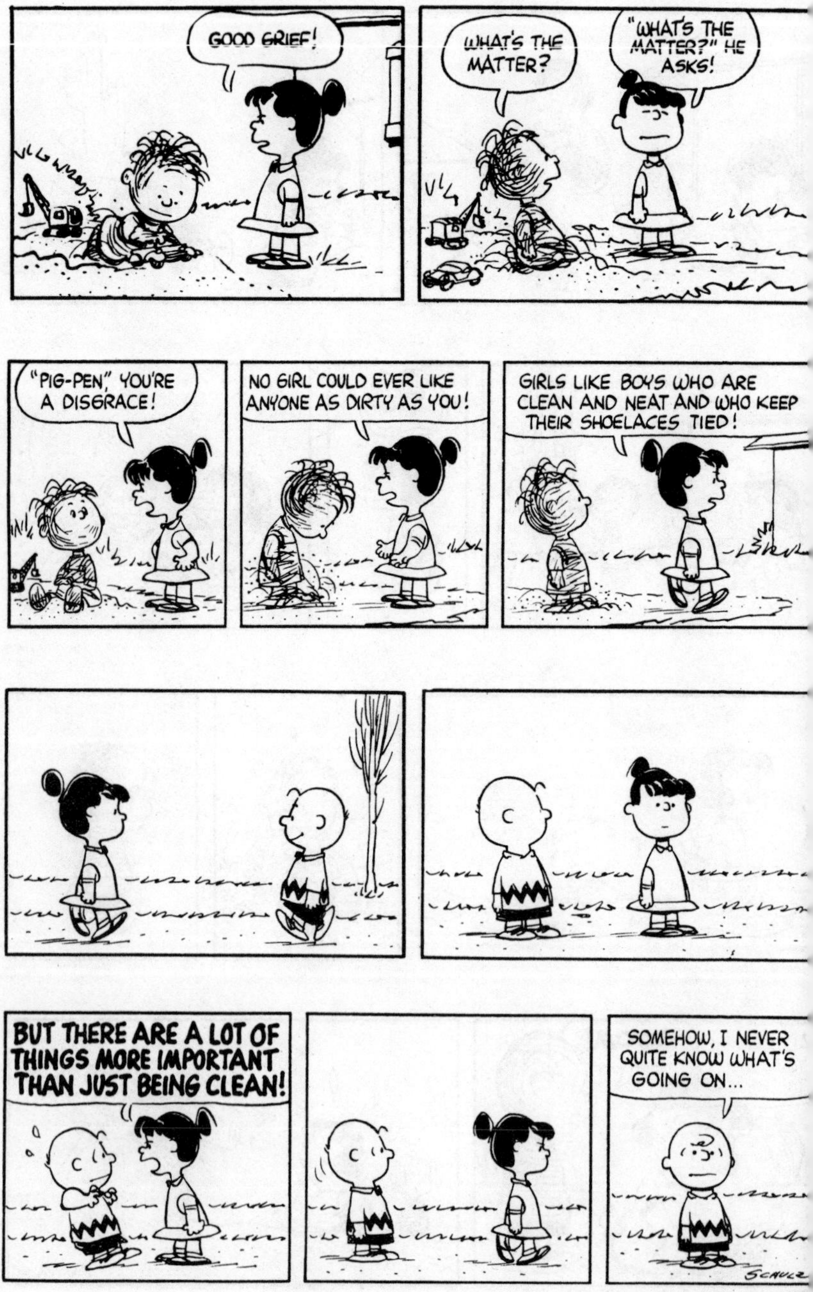
GOOD GRIEF!
WHAT'S THE MATTER?
"WHAT'S THE MATTER?" HE ASKS!
"PIG-PEN," YOU'RE A DISGRACE!
NO GIRL COULD EVER LIKE ANYONE AS DIRTY AS YOU!
GIRLS LIKE BOYS WHO ARE CLEAN AND NEAT AND WHO KEEP THEIR SHOELACES TIED!
BUT THERE ARE A LOT OF THINGS MORE IMPORTANT THAN JUST BEING CLEAN!
SOMEHOW, I NEVER QUITE KNOW WHAT'S GOING ON...
SCHULZ

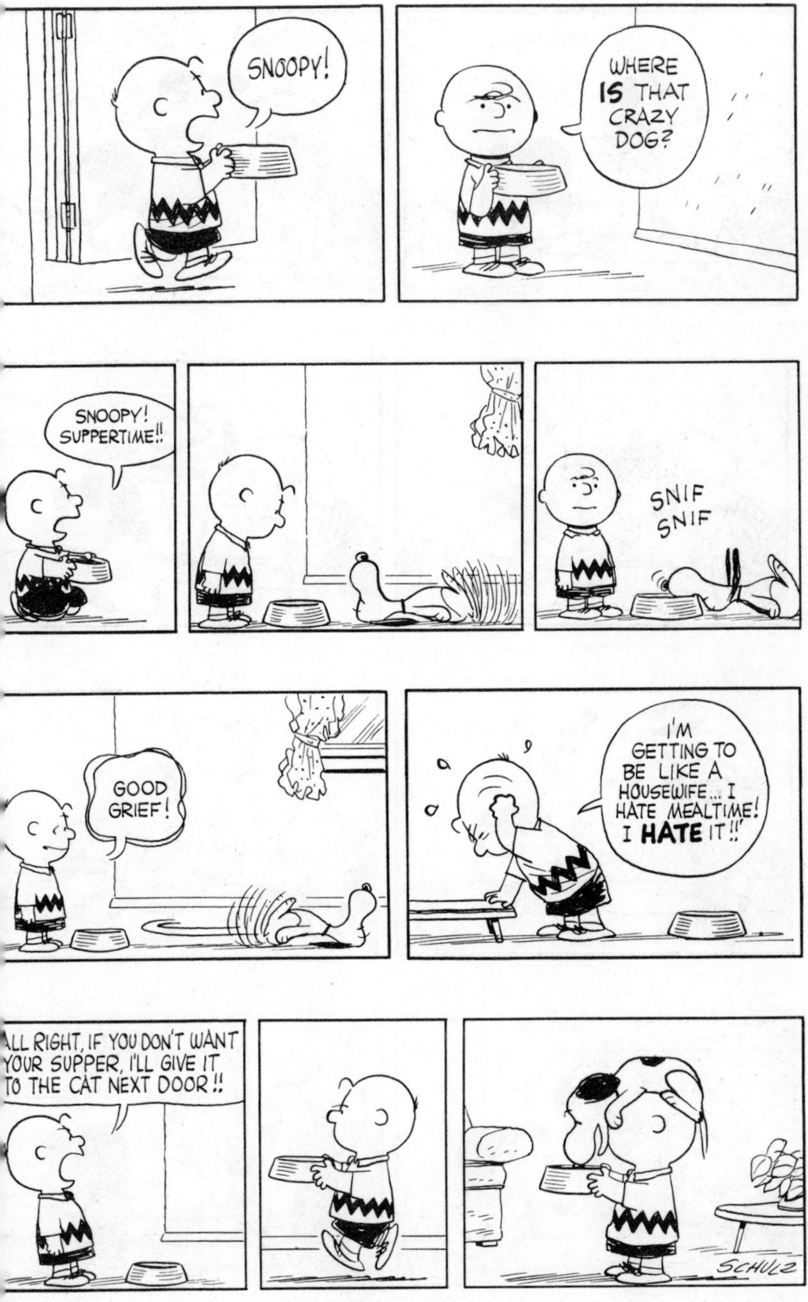
SNOOPY!
WHERE IS THAT CRAZY DOG?
SNOOPY! SUPPERTIME!!
SNIF SNIF
GOOD GRIEF!
I'M GETTING TO BE LIKE A HOUSEWIFE... I HATE MEALTIME! I HATE IT!!
ALL RIGHT, IF YOU DON'T WANT YOUR SUPPER, I'LL GIVE IT TO THE CAT NEXT DOOR!!
SCHULZ

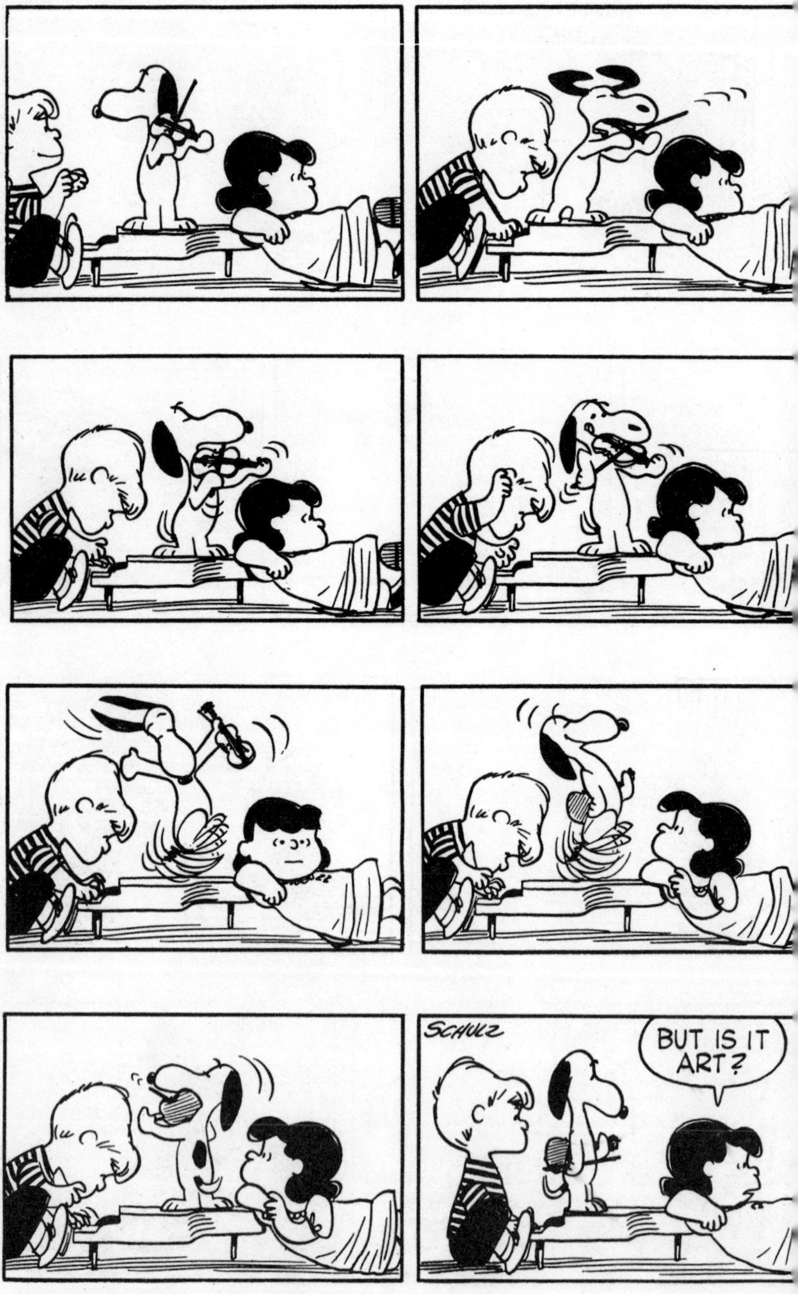
SCHULZ
BUT IS IT ART?

GOOD GRIEF, WHERE IS IT?
IF I EVER LOSE THAT BLANKET, I'LL CRACK UP FOR SURE!
WHERE'S THAT BLANKET OF MINE? I GOTTA HAVE THAT BLANKET..
HERE IT IS...HOT OUT OF THE DRYER!
WHOOP!!
WHOOP!
WHOOOP
WHOOP!
CLOMP
WHOOP
SCHULZ

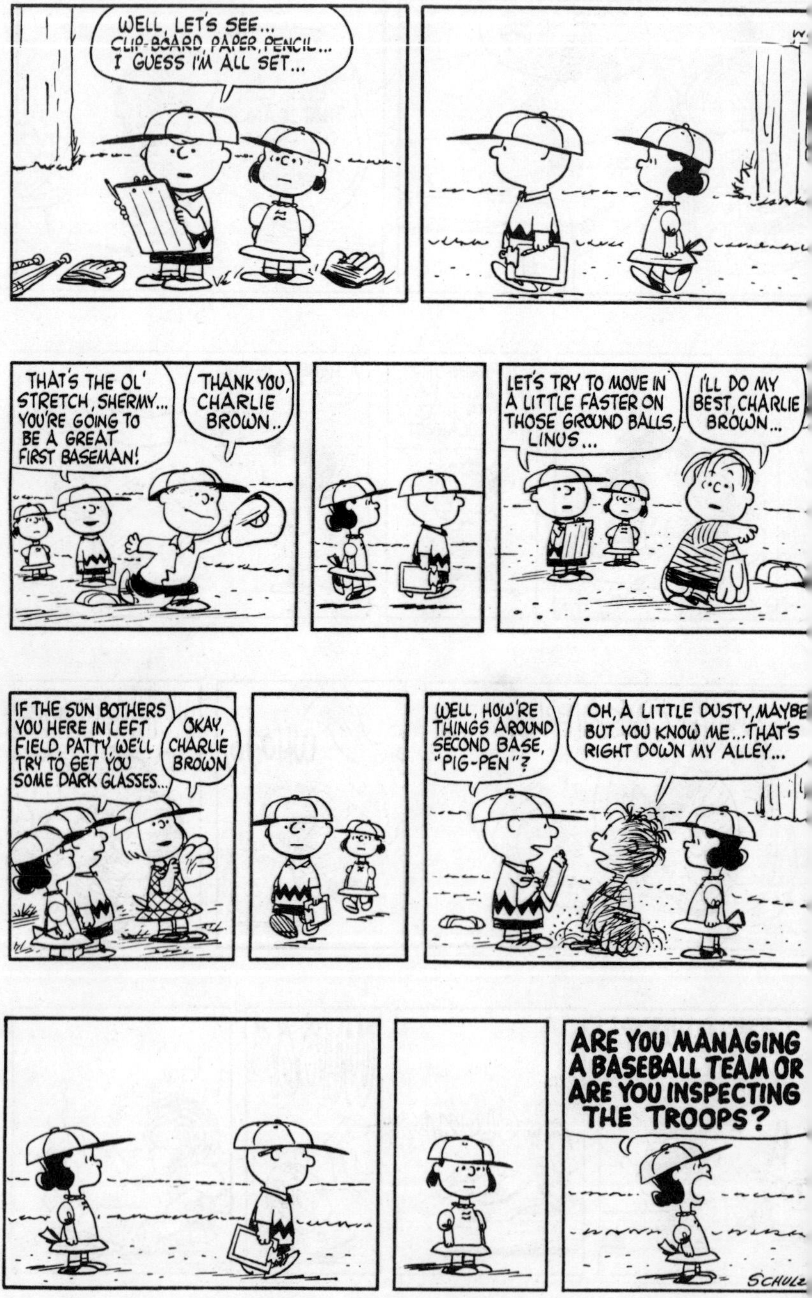
WELL, LET'S SEE... CLIP-BOARD, PAPER, PENCIL... I GUESS I'M ALL SET...
THAT'S THE OL' STRETCH, SHERMY... YOU'RE GOING TO BE A GREAT FIRST BASEMAN!
THANK YOU, CHARLIE BROWN..
LET'S TRY TO MOVE IN A LITTLE FASTER ON THOSE GROUND BALLS, LINUS...
I'LL DO MY BEST, CHARLIE BROWN...
IF THE SUN BOTHERS YOU HERE IN LEFT FIELD, PATTY, WE'LL TRY TO GET YOU SOME DARK GLASSES...
OKAY, CHARLIE BROWN
WELL, HOW'RE THINGS AROUND SECOND BASE, "PIG-PEN"?
OH, A LITTLE DUSTY, MAYBE BUT YOU KNOW ME... THAT'S RIGHT DOWN MY ALLEY...
ARE YOU MANAGING A BASEBALL TEAM OR ARE YOU INSPECTING THE TROOPS?
SCHULZ

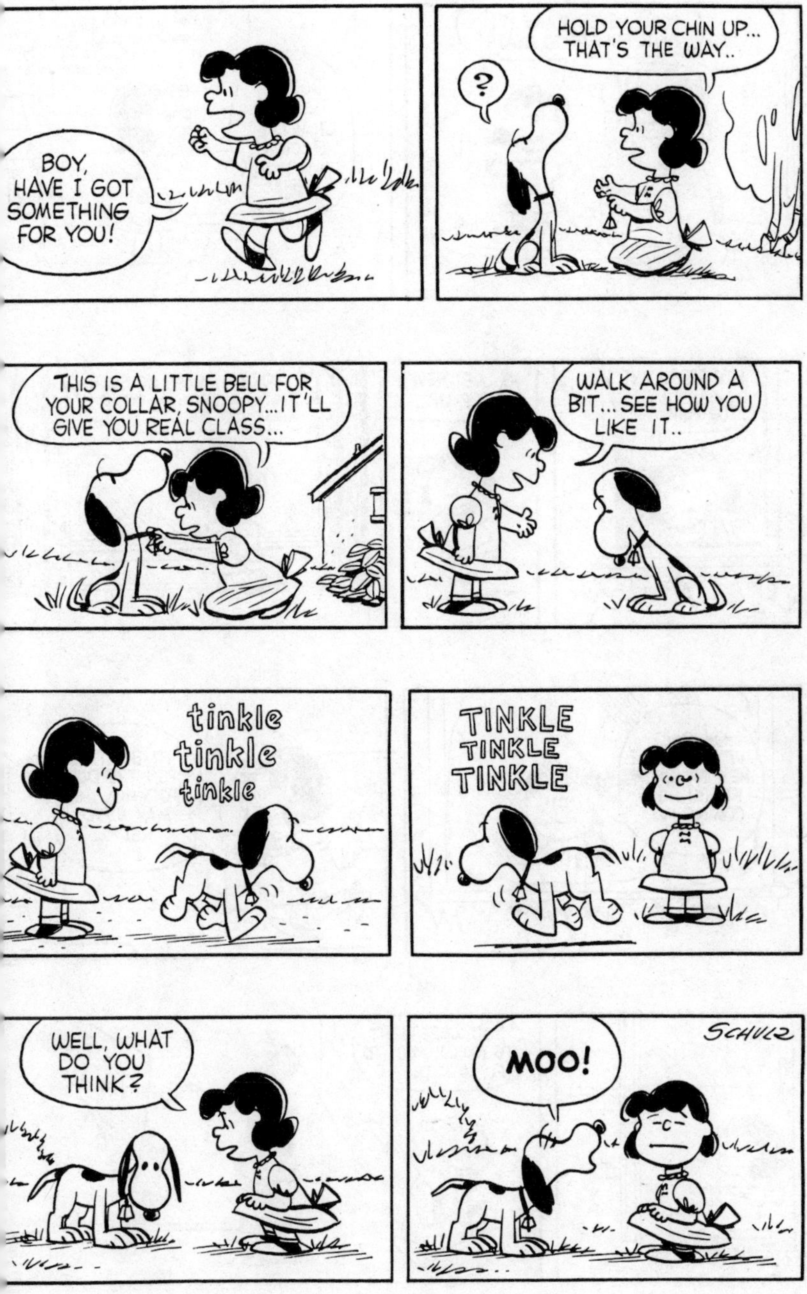
BOY, HAVE I GOT SOMETHING FOR YOU!
HOLD YOUR CHIN UP... THAT'S THE WAY..
?
THIS IS A LITTLE BELL FOR YOUR COLLAR, SNOOPY... IT'LL GIVE YOU REAL CLASS...
WALK AROUND A BIT... SEE HOW YOU LIKE IT..
tinkle tinkle tinkle
TINKLE TINKLE TINKLE
WELL, WHAT DO YOU THINK?
SCHULZ
MOO!

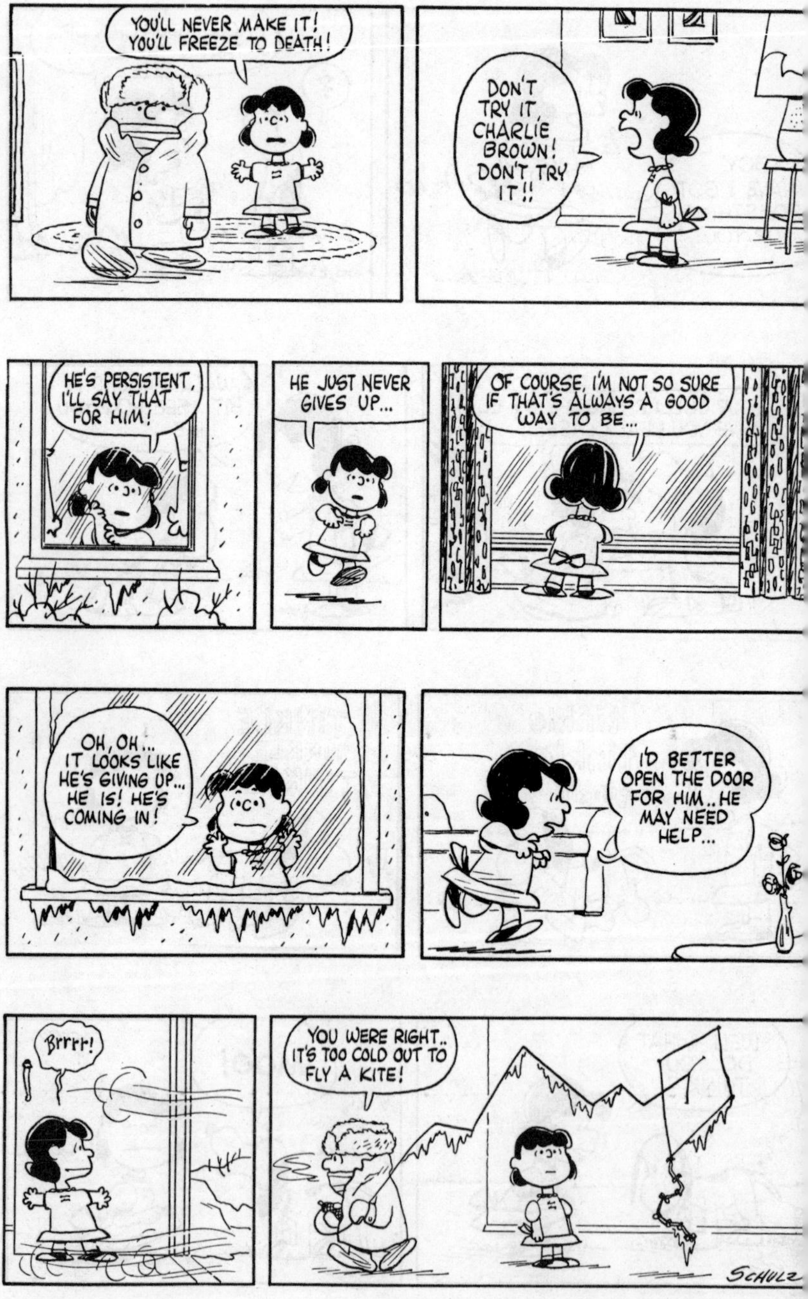
YOU'LL NEVER MAKE IT! YOU'LL FREEZE TO DEATH!
DON'T TRY IT, CHARLIE BROWN! DON'T TRY IT!!
HE'S PERSISTENT, I'LL SAY THAT FOR HIM!
HE JUST NEVER GIVES UP...
OF COURSE, I'M NOT SO SURE IF THAT'S ALWAYS A GOOD WAY TO BE...
OH, OH... IT LOOKS LIKE HE'S GIVING UP... HE IS! HE'S COMING IN!
I'D BETTER OPEN THE DOOR FOR HIM.. HE MAY NEED HELP...
Brrrr!
YOU WERE RIGHT.. IT'S TOO COLD OUT TO FLY A KITE!
SCHULZ

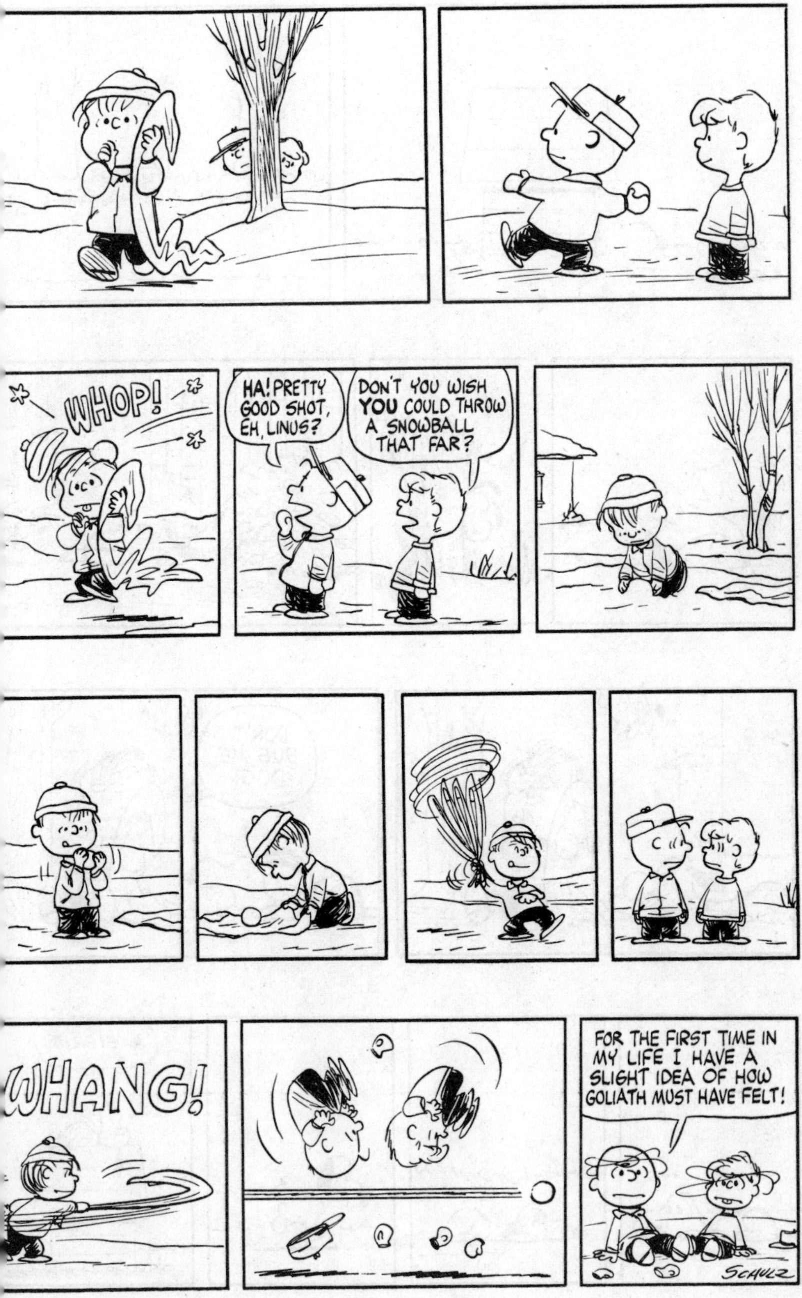
WHOP!
HA! PRETTY GOOD SHOT, EH, LINUS?
DON'T YOU WISH YOU COULD THROW A SNOWBALL THAT FAR?
WHANG!
FOR THE FIRST TIME IN MY LIFE I HAVE A SLIGHT IDEA OF HOW GOLIATH MUST HAVE FELT!
SCHULZ

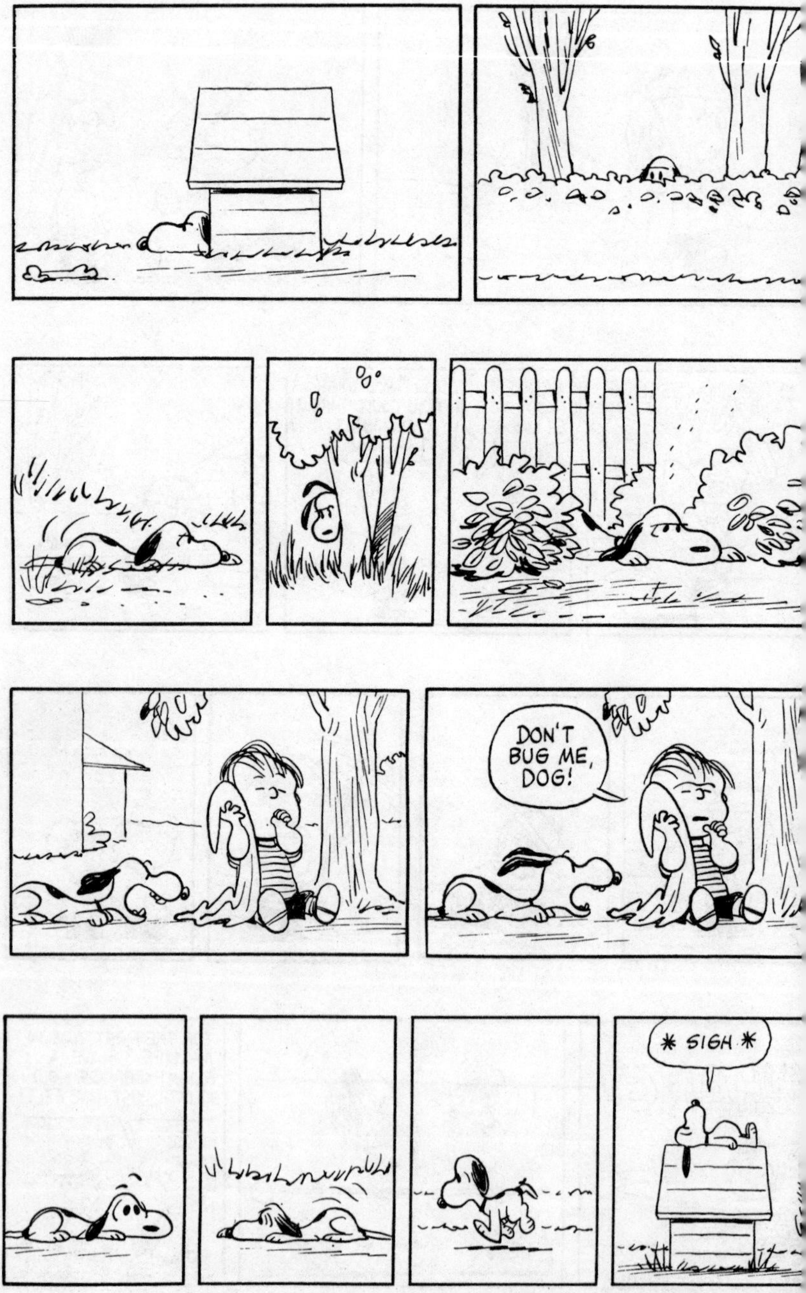
DON'T BUG ME, DOG!
* SIGH *

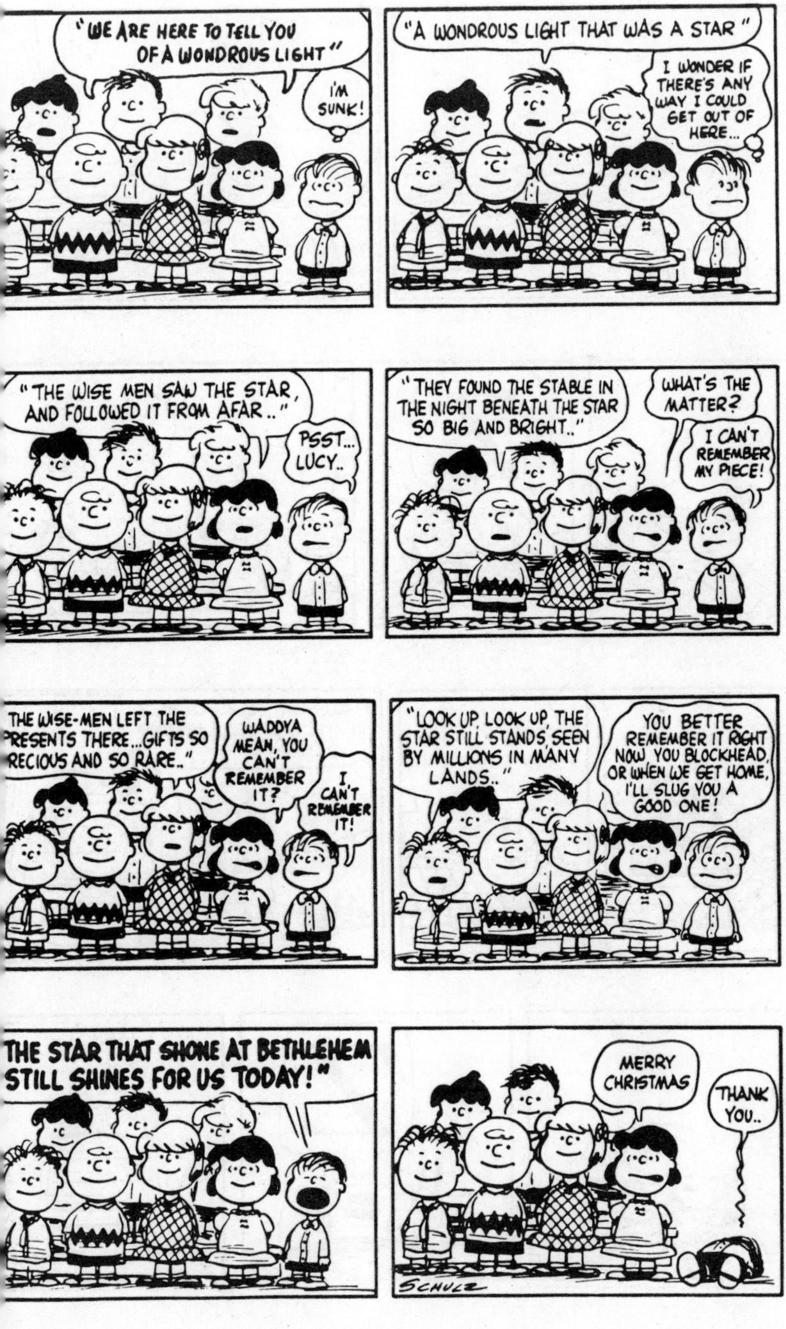
"WE ARE HERE TO TELL YOU OF A WONDROUS LIGHT"
I'M SUNK!
"A WONDROUS LIGHT THAT WAS A STAR"
I WONDER IF THERE'S ANY WAY I COULD GET OUT OF HERE...
"THE WISE MEN SAW THE STAR, AND FOLLOWED IT FROM AFAR.."
PSST... LUCY..
"THEY FOUND THE STABLE IN THE NIGHT BENEATH THE STAR SO BIG AND BRIGHT.."
WHAT'S THE MATTER?
I CAN'T REMEMBER MY PIECE!
THE WISE-MEN LEFT THE PRESENTS THERE...GIFTS SO RECIOUS AND SO RARE.."
WADDYA MEAN, YOU CAN'T REMEMBER IT?
I, CAN'T REMEMBER IT!
"LOOK UP, LOOK UP, THE STAR STILL STANDS, SEEN BY MILLIONS IN MANY LANDS.."
YOU BETTER REMEMBER IT RIGHT NOW, YOU BLOCKHEAD, OR WHEN WE GET HOME, I'LL SLUG YOU A GOOD ONE!
THE STAR THAT SHONE AT BETHLEHEM STILL SHINES FOR US TODAY!"
MERRY CHRISTMAS
THANK YOU..
SCHULZ

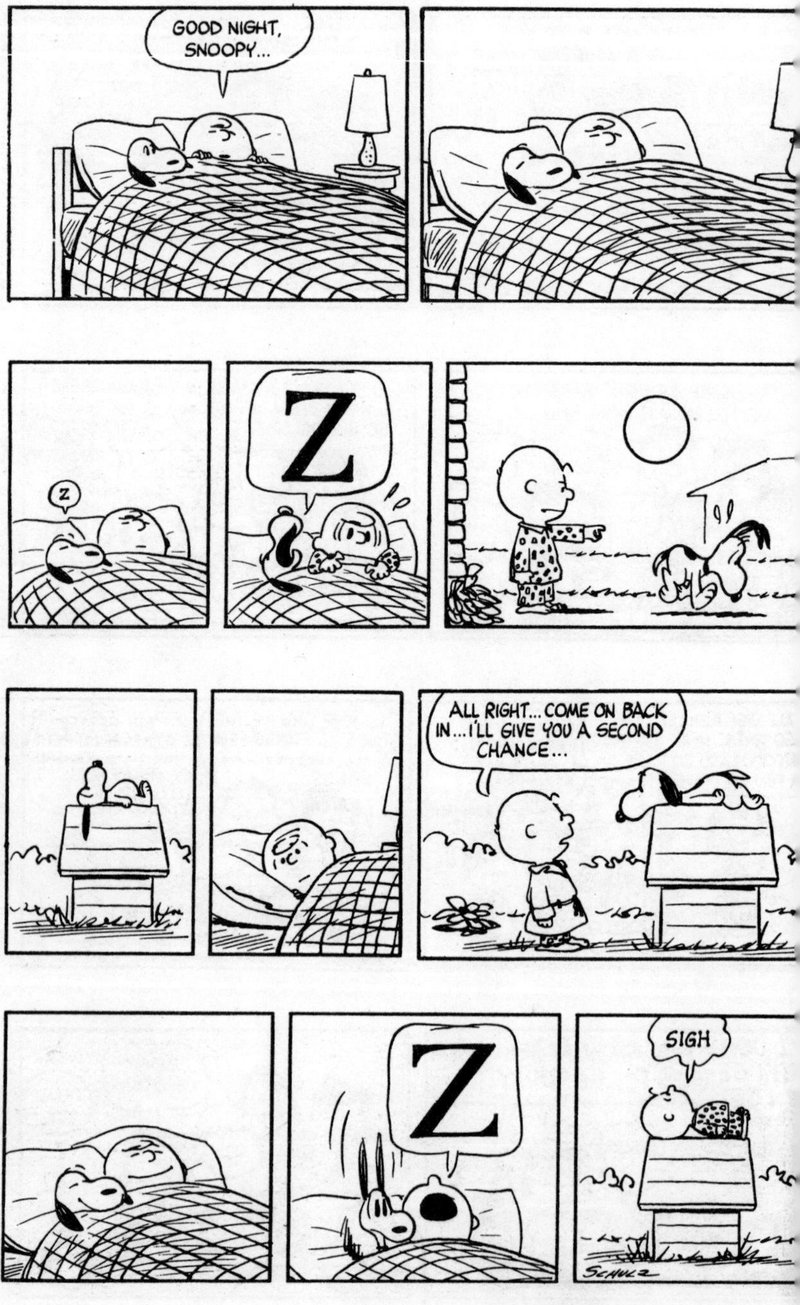
GOOD NIGHT, SNOOPY...
Z
Z
ALL RIGHT... COME ON BACK IN... I'LL GIVE YOU A SECOND CHANCE...
Z
SIGH
SCHULZ

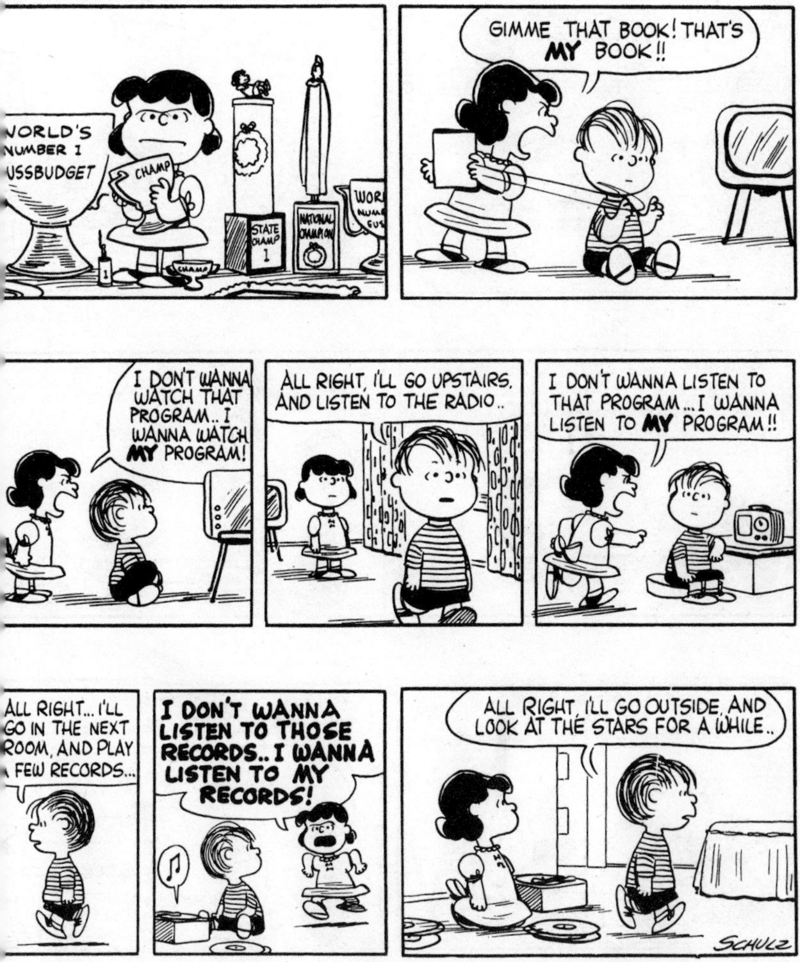
CHAMP
STATE CHAMP 1
NATIONAL CHAMPION
GIMME THAT BOOK! THAT'S **MY** BOOK!!
I DON'T WANNA WATCH THAT PROGRAM.. I WANNA WATCH **MY** PROGRAM!
ALL RIGHT, I'LL GO UPSTAIRS, AND LISTEN TO THE RADIO..
I DON'T WANNA LISTEN TO THAT PROGRAM... I WANNA LISTEN TO **MY** PROGRAM!!
ALL RIGHT... I'LL GO IN THE NEXT ROOM, AND PLAY A FEW RECORDS...
I DON'T WANNA LISTEN TO THOSE RECORDS.. I WANNA LISTEN TO MY RECORDS!
ALL RIGHT, I'LL GO OUTSIDE, AND LOOK AT THE STARS FOR A WHILE..
SCHULZ

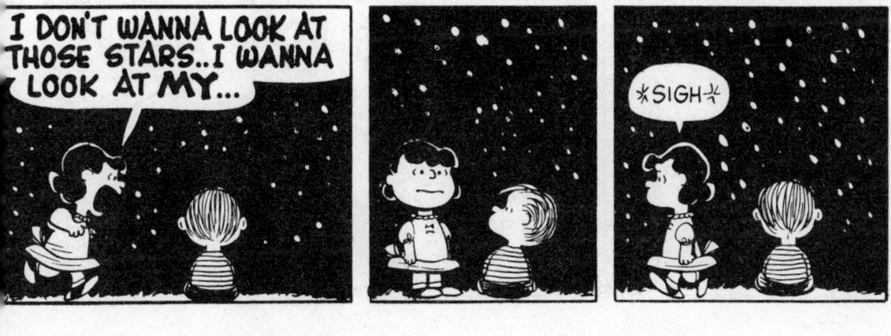
I DON'T WANNA LOOK AT THOSE STARS.. I WANNA LOOK AT MY...
SIGH

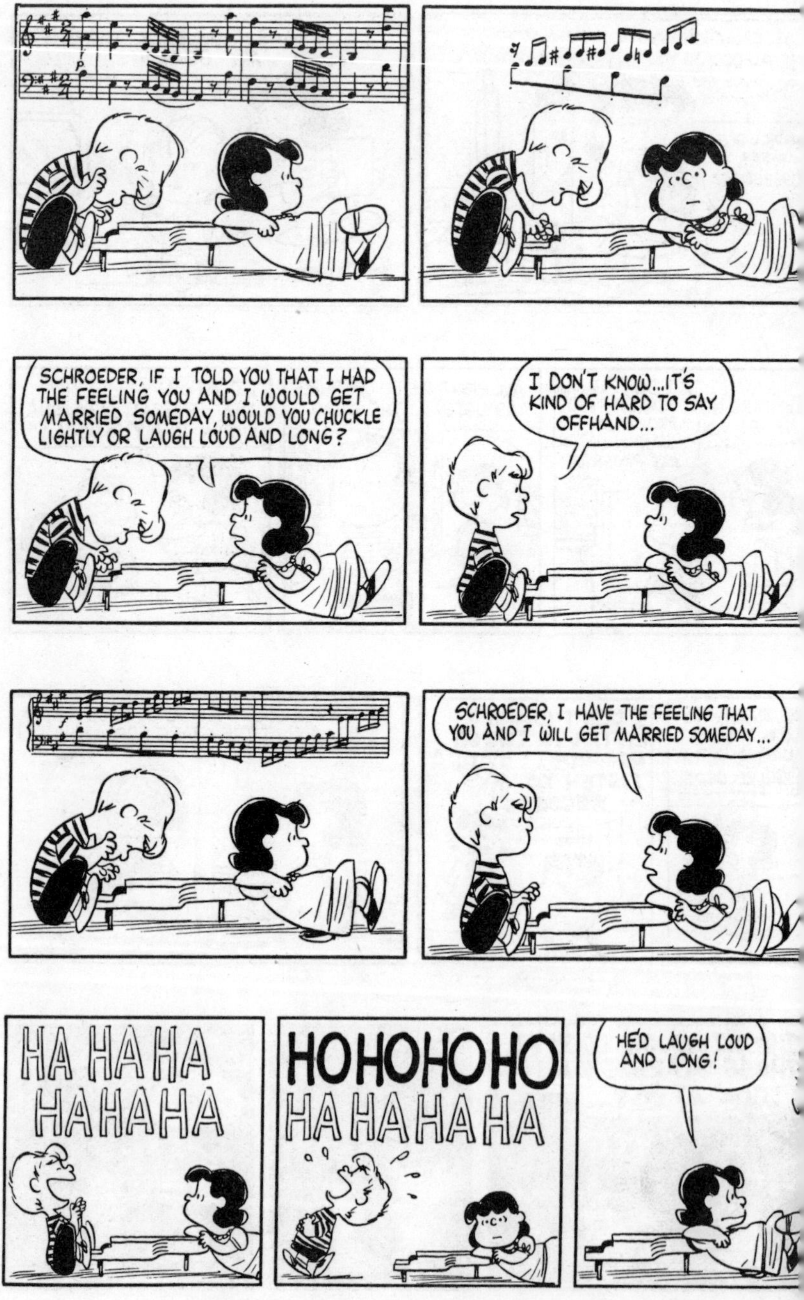
SCHROEDER, IF I TOLD YOU THAT I HAD THE FEELING YOU AND I WOULD GET MARRIED SOMEDAY, WOULD YOU CHUCKLE LIGHTLY OR LAUGH LOUD AND LONG?
I DON'T KNOW...IT'S KIND OF HARD TO SAY OFFHAND...
SCHROEDER, I HAVE THE FEELING THAT YOU AND I WILL GET MARRIED SOMEDAY...
HA HA HA HA HAHA
HOHOHOHO HA HA HA HA HA
HE'D LAUGH LOUD AND LONG!

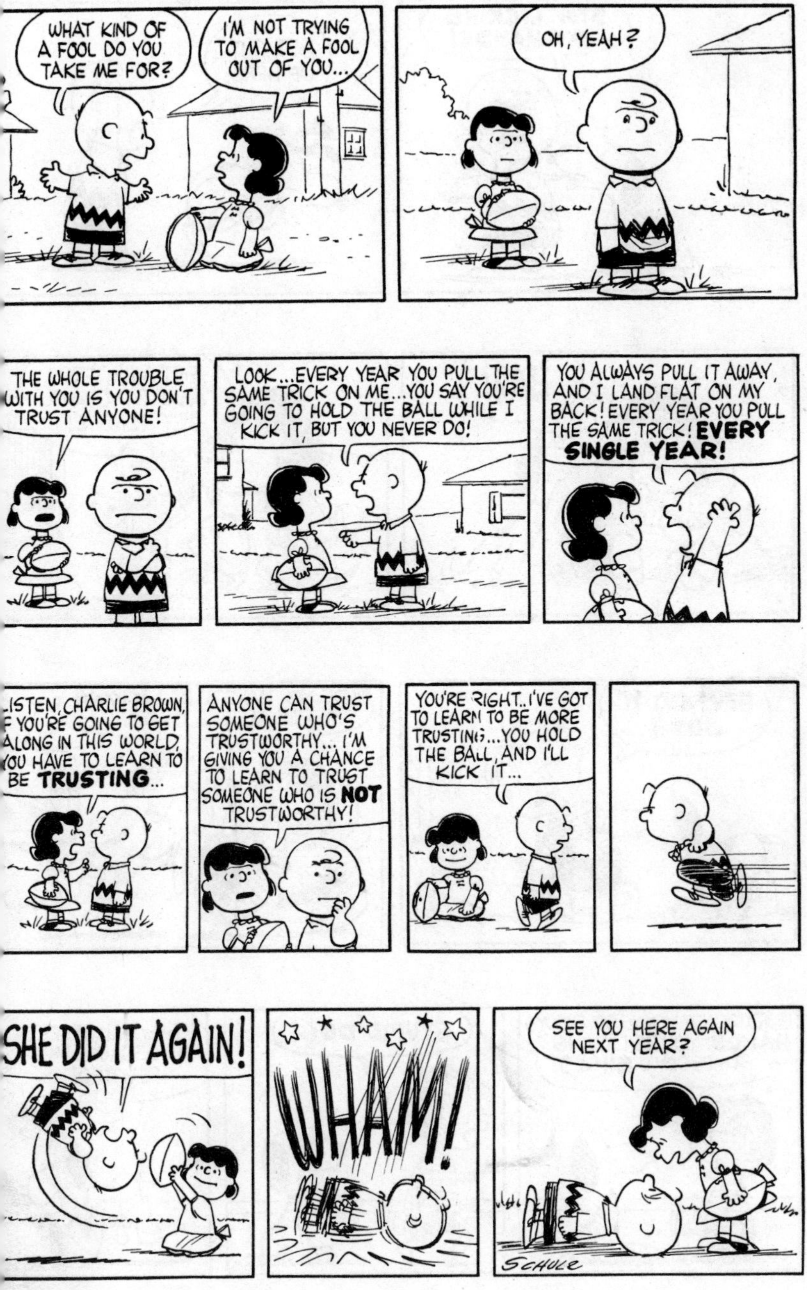

WHAT KIND OF A FOOL DO YOU TAKE ME FOR?
I'M NOT TRYING TO MAKE A FOOL OUT OF YOU...
OH, YEAH?
THE WHOLE TROUBLE WITH YOU IS YOU DON'T TRUST ANYONE!
LOOK...EVERY YEAR YOU PULL THE SAME TRICK ON ME...YOU SAY YOU'RE GOING TO HOLD THE BALL WHILE I KICK IT, BUT YOU NEVER DO!
YOU ALWAYS PULL IT AWAY, AND I LAND FLAT ON MY BACK! EVERY YEAR YOU PULL THE SAME TRICK! EVERY SINGLE YEAR!
LISTEN, CHARLIE BROWN, IF YOU'RE GOING TO GET ALONG IN THIS WORLD, YOU HAVE TO LEARN TO BE TRUSTING...
ANYONE CAN TRUST SOMEONE WHO'S TRUSTWORTHY... I'M GIVING YOU A CHANCE TO LEARN TO TRUST SOMEONE WHO IS NOT TRUSTWORTHY!
YOU'RE RIGHT...I'VE GOT TO LEARN TO BE MORE TRUSTING...YOU HOLD THE BALL, AND I'LL KICK IT...
SHE DID IT AGAIN!
WHAM!
SEE YOU HERE AGAIN NEXT YEAR?
SCHULZ

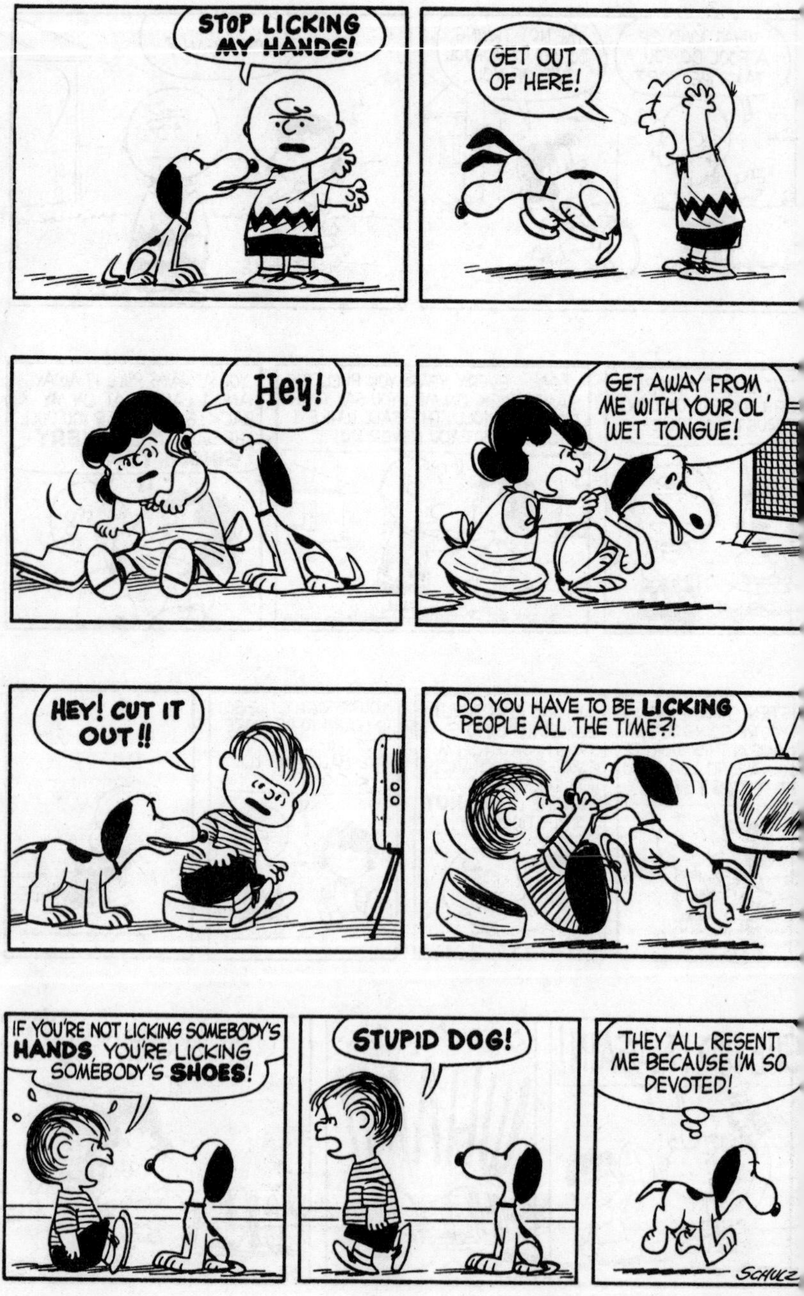
STOP LICKING MY HANDS!
GET OUT OF HERE!
Hey!
GET AWAY FROM ME WITH YOUR OL' WET TONGUE!
HEY! CUT IT OUT!!
DO YOU HAVE TO BE LICKING PEOPLE ALL THE TIME?!
IF YOU'RE NOT LICKING SOMEBODY'S HANDS, YOU'RE LICKING SOMEBODY'S SHOES!
STUPID DOG!
THEY ALL RESENT ME BECAUSE I'M SO DEVOTED!
SCHULZ

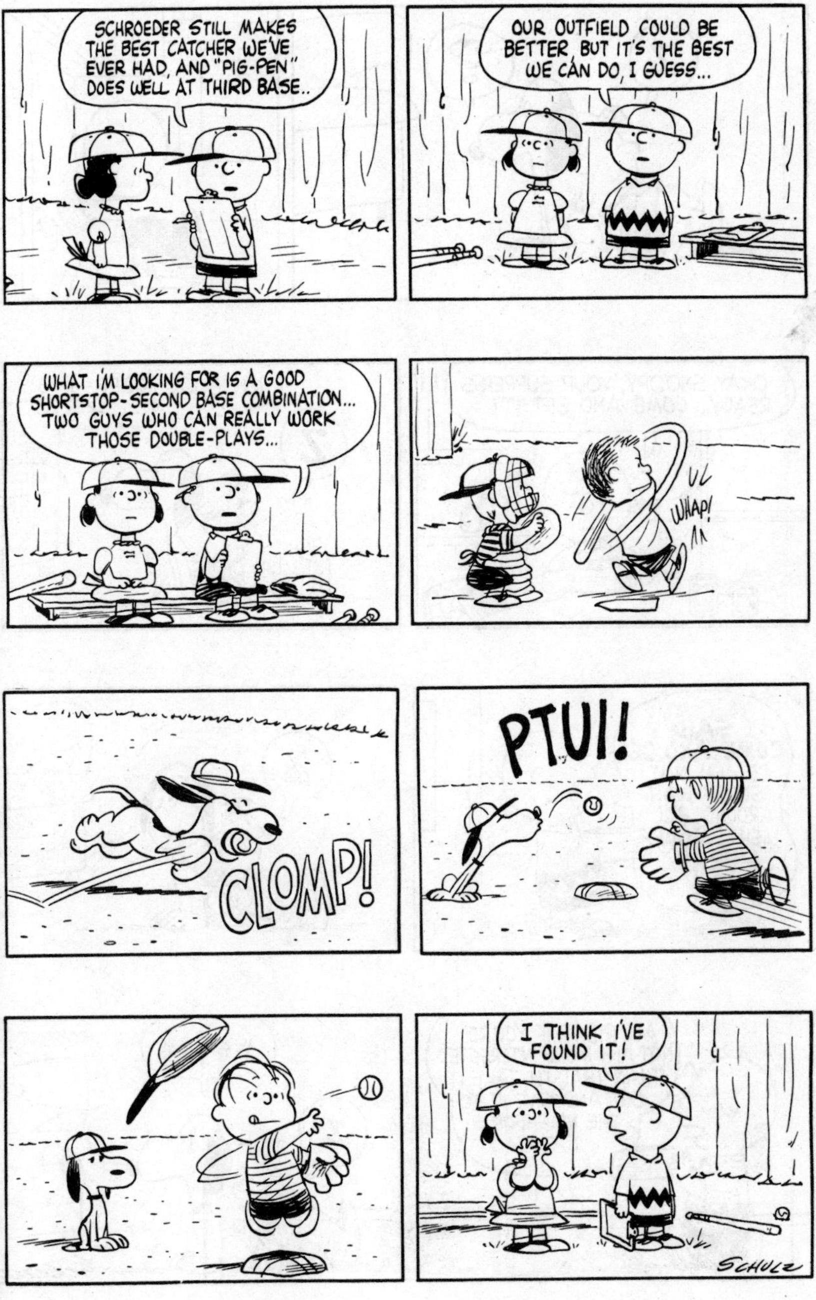
SCHROEDER STILL MAKES THE BEST CATCHER WE'VE EVER HAD, AND "PIG-PEN" DOES WELL AT THIRD BASE..
OUR OUTFIELD COULD BE BETTER, BUT IT'S THE BEST WE CAN DO, I GUESS...
WHAT I'M LOOKING FOR IS A GOOD SHORTSTOP-SECOND BASE COMBINATION... TWO GUYS WHO CAN REALLY WORK THOSE DOUBLE-PLAYS...
WHAP!
CLOMP!
PTUI!
I THINK I'VE FOUND IT!
SCHULZ

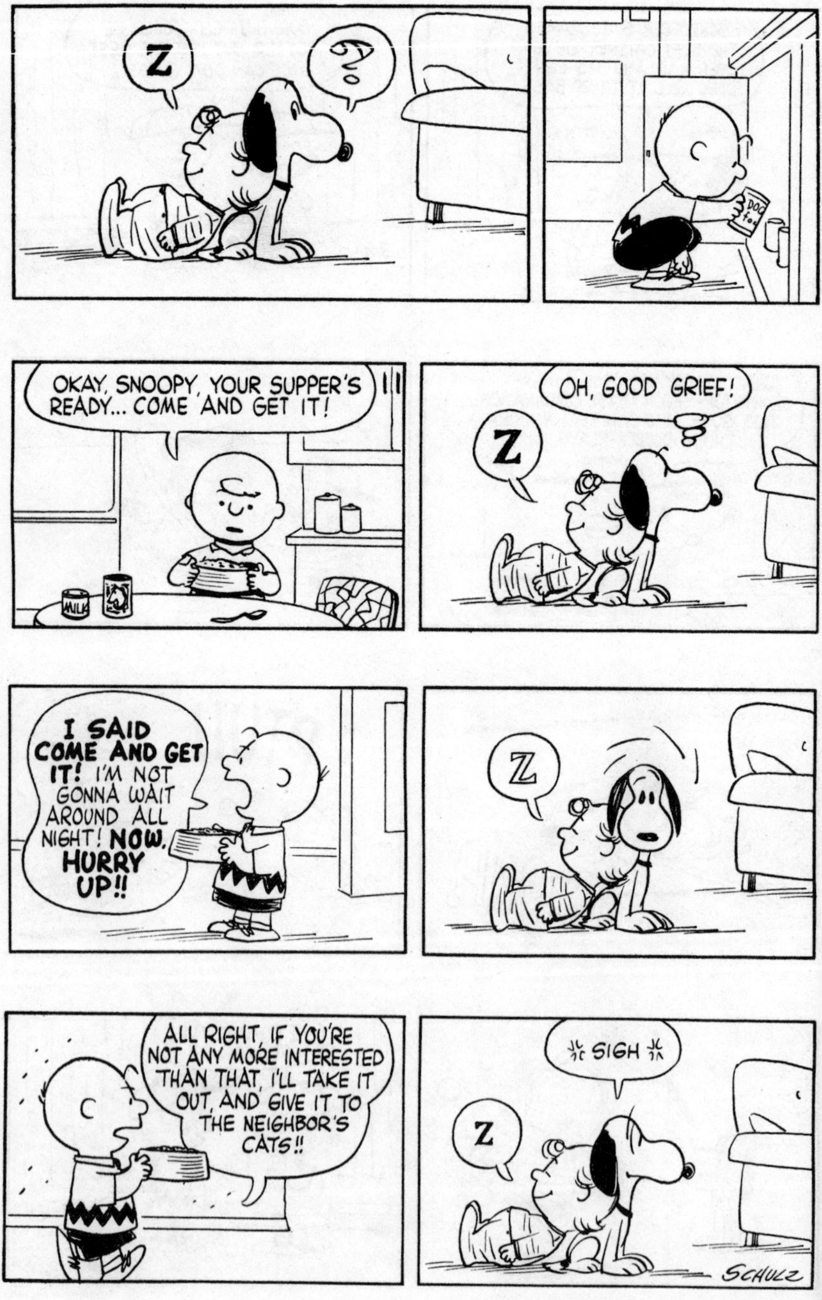
Z
?
DOG food
OKAY, SNOOPY, YOUR SUPPER'S READY... COME AND GET IT!
MILK
Z
OH, GOOD GRIEF!
I SAID COME AND GET IT! I'M NOT GONNA WAIT AROUND ALL NIGHT! NOW, HURRY UP!!
Z
ALL RIGHT, IF YOU'RE NOT ANY MORE INTERESTED THAN THAT, I'LL TAKE IT OUT, AND GIVE IT TO THE NEIGHBOR'S CATS!!
SIGH
Z
SCHULZ

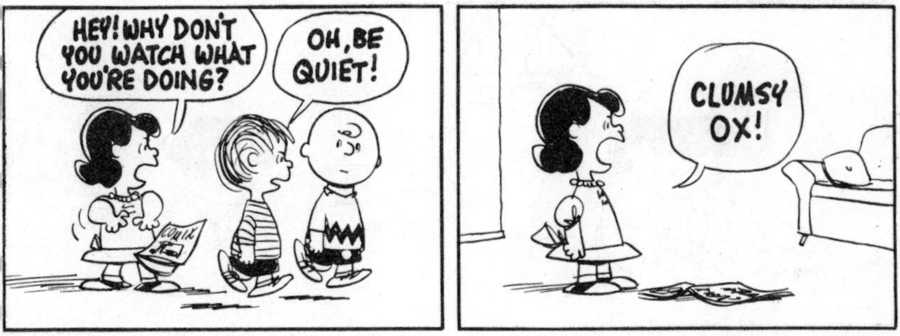
HEY! WHY DON'T YOU WATCH WHAT YOU'RE DOING?
OH, BE QUIET!
CLUMSY OX!

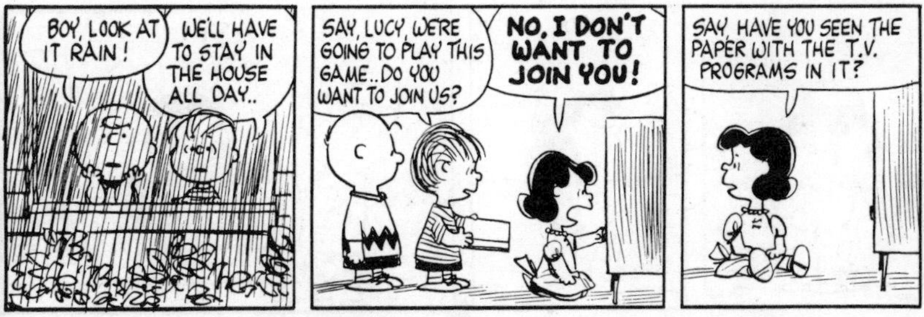
BOY, LOOK AT IT RAIN!
WE'LL HAVE TO STAY IN THE HOUSE ALL DAY..
SAY, LUCY, WE'RE GOING TO PLAY THIS GAME..DO YOU WANT TO JOIN US?
NO, I DON'T WANT TO JOIN YOU!
SAY, HAVE YOU SEEN THE PAPER WITH THE T.V. PROGRAMS IN IT?

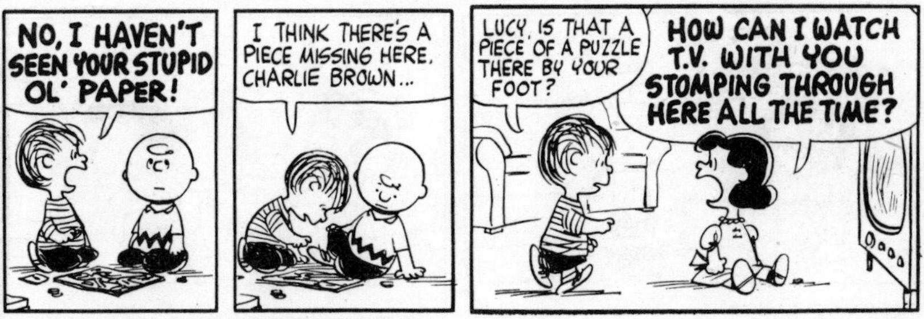
NO, I HAVEN'T SEEN YOUR STUPID OL' PAPER!
I THINK THERE'S A PIECE MISSING HERE, CHARLIE BROWN...
LUCY, IS THAT A PIECE OF A PUZZLE THERE BY YOUR FOOT?
HOW CAN I WATCH T.V. WITH YOU STOMPING THROUGH HERE ALL THE TIME?

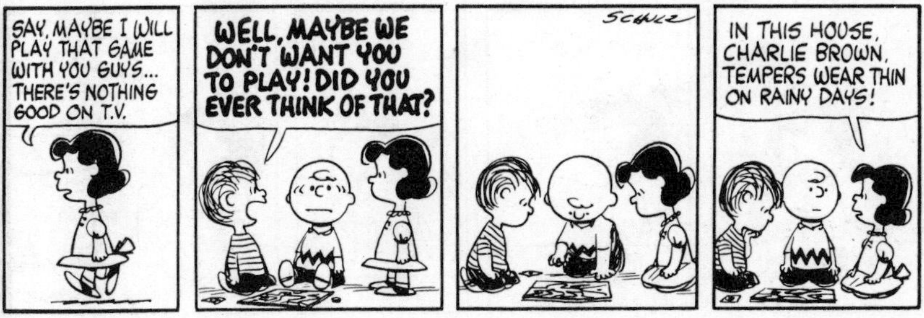
SAY, MAYBE I WILL PLAY THAT GAME WITH YOU GUYS... THERE'S NOTHING GOOD ON T.V.
WELL, MAYBE WE DON'T WANT YOU TO PLAY! DID YOU EVER THINK OF THAT?
SCHULZ
IN THIS HOUSE, CHARLIE BROWN, TEMPERS WEAR THIN ON RAINY DAYS!

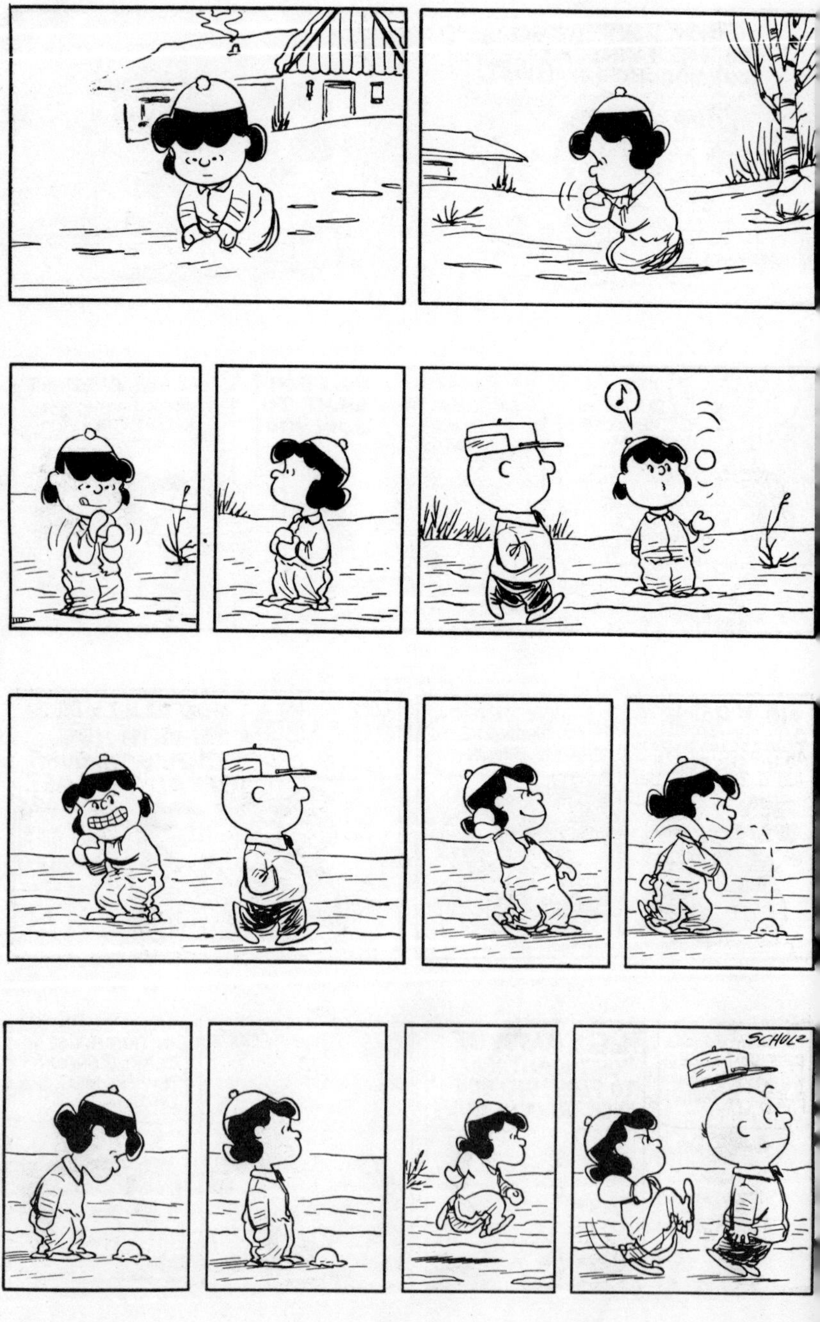
SCHULZ

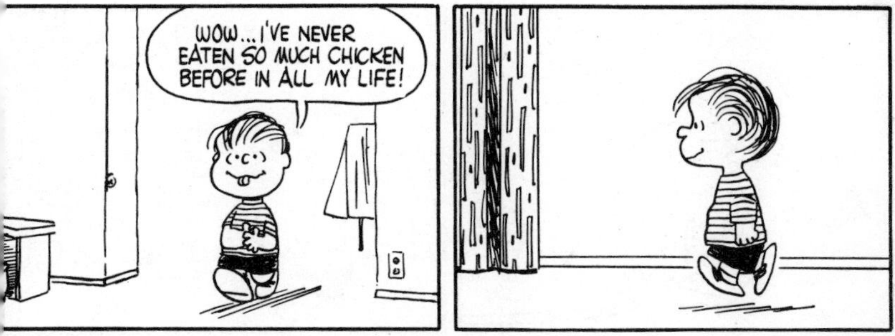
WOW... I'VE NEVER EATEN SO MUCH CHICKEN BEFORE IN ALL MY LIFE!

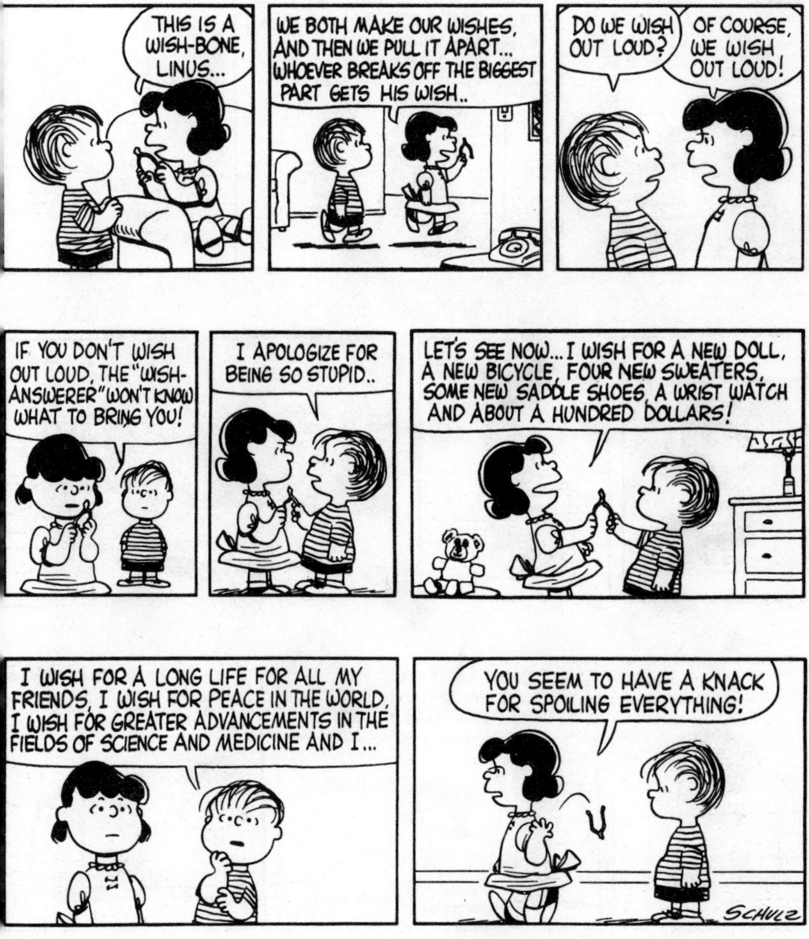
THIS IS A WISH-BONE, LINUS...
WE BOTH MAKE OUR WISHES, AND THEN WE PULL IT APART... WHOEVER BREAKS OFF THE BIGGEST PART GETS HIS WISH..
DO WE WISH OUT LOUD?
OF COURSE, WE WISH OUT LOUD!
IF YOU DON'T WISH OUT LOUD, THE "WISH-ANSWERER" WON'T KNOW WHAT TO BRING YOU!
I APOLOGIZE FOR BEING SO STUPID..
LET'S SEE NOW... I WISH FOR A NEW DOLL, A NEW BICYCLE, FOUR NEW SWEATERS, SOME NEW SADDLE SHOES, A WRIST WATCH AND ABOUT A HUNDRED DOLLARS!
I WISH FOR A LONG LIFE FOR ALL MY FRIENDS, I WISH FOR PEACE IN THE WORLD, I WISH FOR GREATER ADVANCEMENTS IN THE FIELDS OF SCIENCE AND MEDICINE AND I...
YOU SEEM TO HAVE A KNACK FOR SPOILING EVERYTHING!
SCHULZ

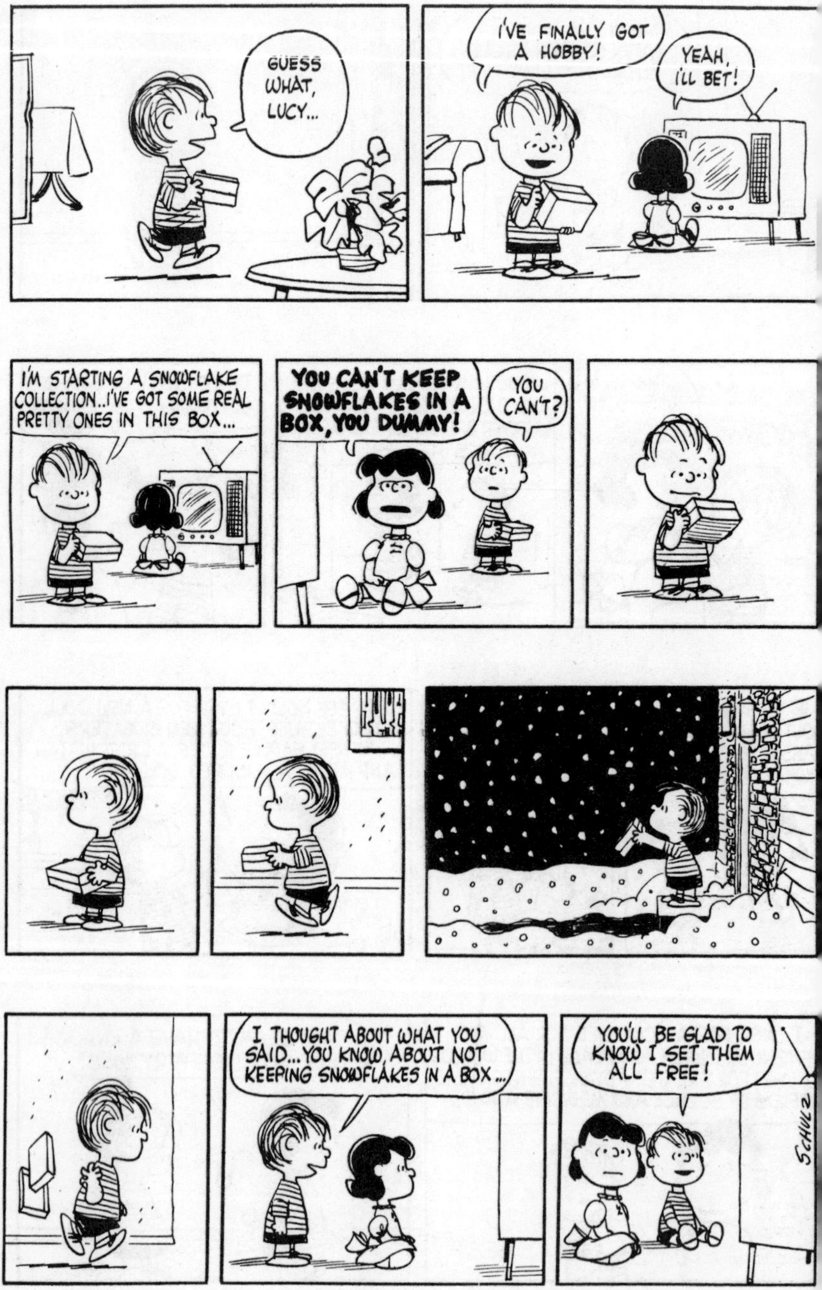
GUESS WHAT, LUCY...
I'VE FINALLY GOT A HOBBY!
YEAH, I'LL BET!
I'M STARTING A SNOWFLAKE COLLECTION..I'VE GOT SOME REAL PRETTY ONES IN THIS BOX...
YOU CAN'T KEEP SNOWFLAKES IN A BOX, YOU DUMMY!
YOU CAN'T?
I THOUGHT ABOUT WHAT YOU SAID...YOU KNOW, ABOUT NOT KEEPING SNOWFLAKES IN A BOX...
YOU'LL BE GLAD TO KNOW I SET THEM ALL FREE!
SCHULZ

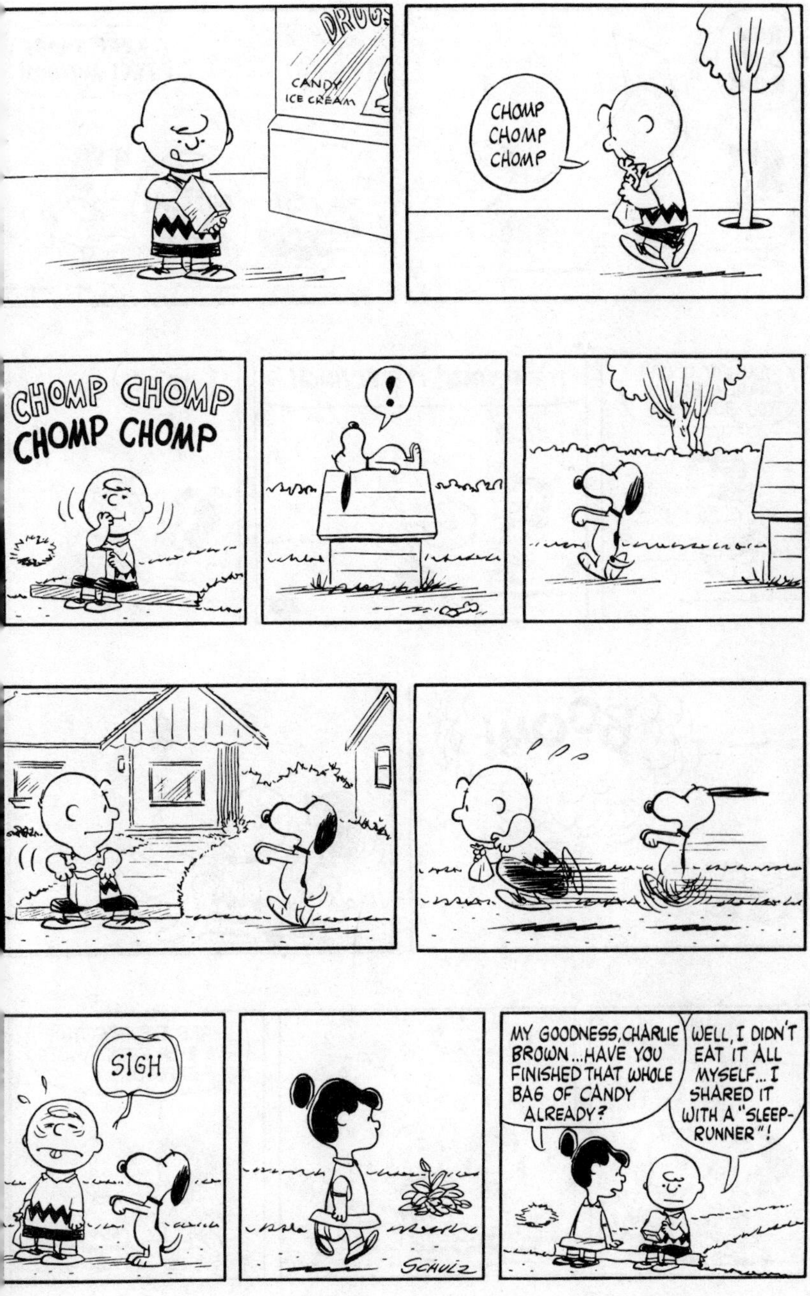
DRUGS
CANDY
ICE CREAM
CHOMP CHOMP CHOMP
CHOMP CHOMP
CHOMP CHOMP
!
SIGH
SCHULZ
MY GOODNESS, CHARLIE BROWN...HAVE YOU FINISHED THAT WHOLE BAG OF CANDY ALREADY?
WELL, I DIDN'T EAT IT ALL MYSELF... I SHARED IT WITH A "SLEEP-RUNNER"!

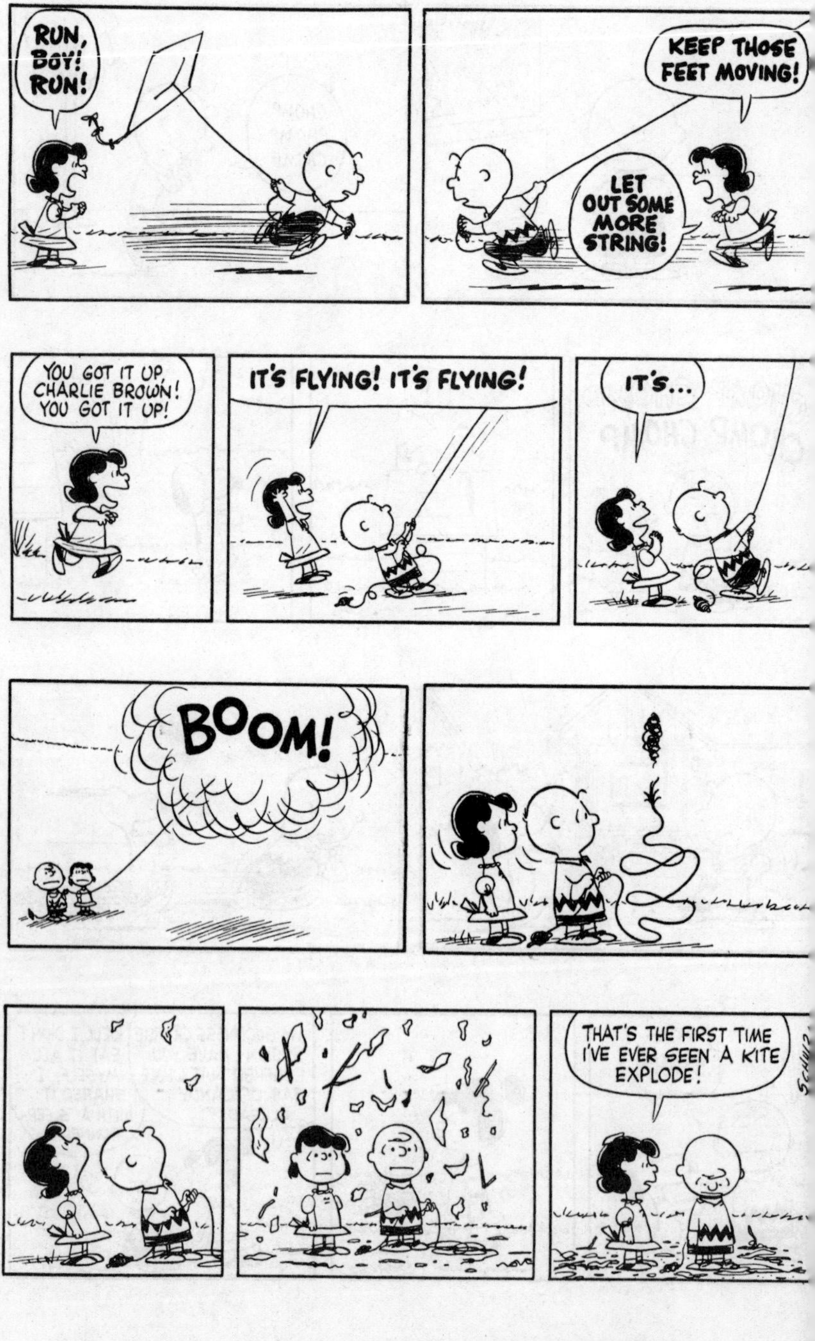
RUN, BOY! RUN!
KEEP THOSE FEET MOVING!
LET OUT SOME MORE STRING!
YOU GOT IT UP, CHARLIE BROWN! YOU GOT IT UP!
IT'S FLYING! IT'S FLYING!
IT'S...
BOOM!
THAT'S THE FIRST TIME I'VE EVER SEEN A KITE EXPLODE!
SCHULZ

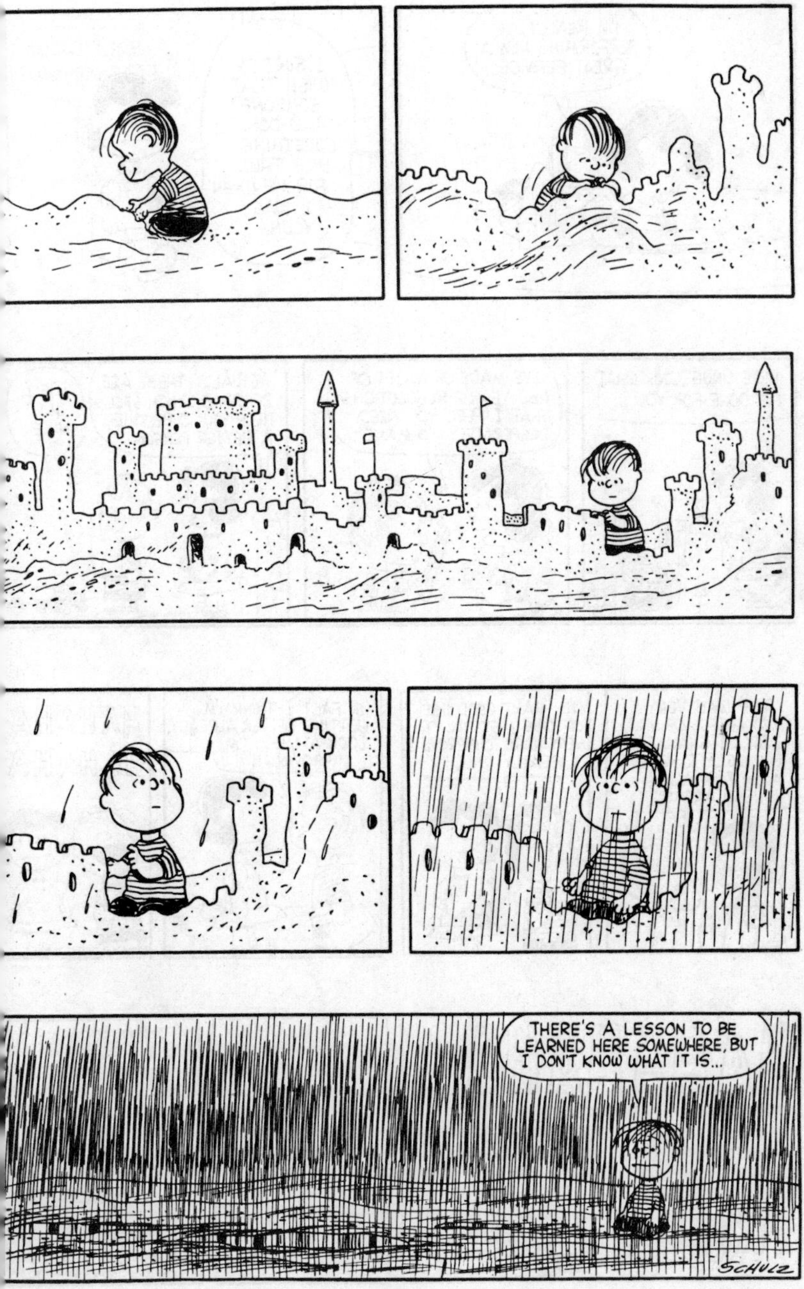
THERE'S A LESSON TO BE LEARNED HERE SOMEWHERE, BUT I DON'T KNOW WHAT IT IS...
SCHULZ

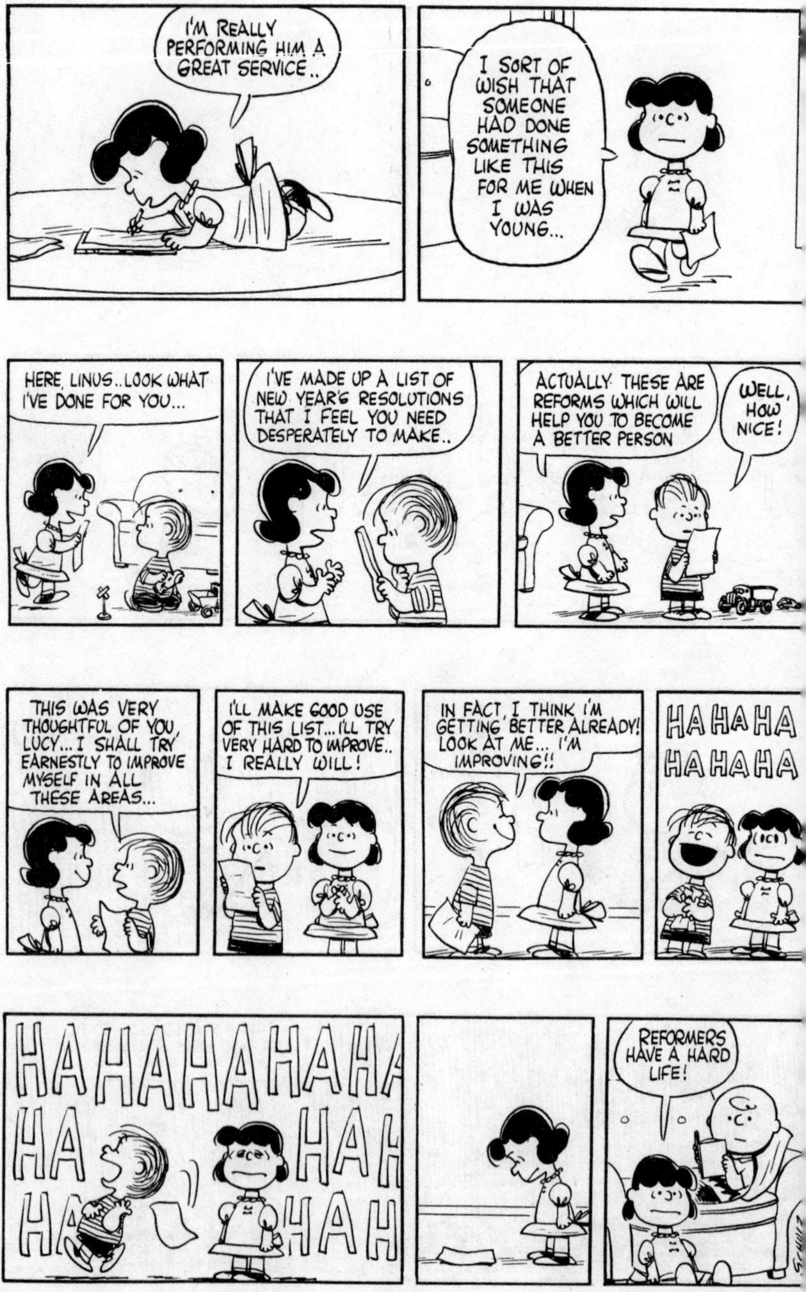

I'M REALLY PERFORMING HIM A GREAT SERVICE..
I SORT OF WISH THAT SOMEONE HAD DONE SOMETHING LIKE THIS FOR ME WHEN I WAS YOUNG...
HERE, LINUS..LOOK WHAT I'VE DONE FOR YOU...
I'VE MADE UP A LIST OF NEW YEAR'S RESOLUTIONS THAT I FEEL YOU NEED DESPERATELY TO MAKE..
ACTUALLY THESE ARE REFORMS WHICH WILL HELP YOU TO BECOME A BETTER PERSON
WELL, HOW NICE!
THIS WAS VERY THOUGHTFUL OF YOU, LUCY... I SHALL TRY EARNESTLY TO IMPROVE MYSELF IN ALL THESE AREAS...
I'LL MAKE GOOD USE OF THIS LIST... I'LL TRY VERY HARD TO IMPROVE.. I REALLY WILL!
IN FACT, I THINK I'M GETTING BETTER ALREADY! LOOK AT ME... I'M IMPROVING!!
HAHAHA HAHAHA
HAHAHAHAHAHAHA HA HAH HA HAH
REFORMERS HAVE A HARD LIFE!
SCHULZ

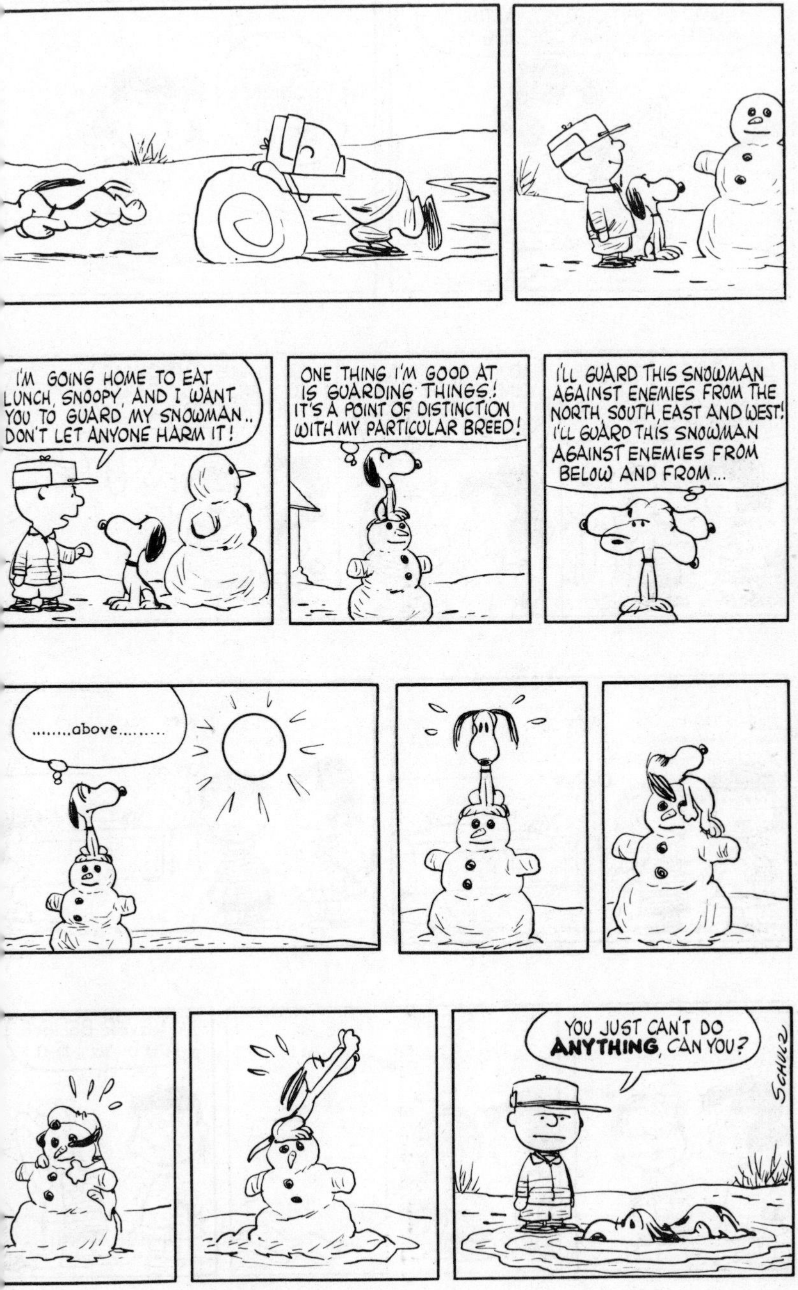
I'M GOING HOME TO EAT LUNCH, SNOOPY, AND I WANT YOU TO GUARD MY SNOWMAN.. DON'T LET ANYONE HARM IT!
ONE THING I'M GOOD AT IS GUARDING THINGS! IT'S A POINT OF DISTINCTION WITH MY PARTICULAR BREED!
I'LL GUARD THIS SNOWMAN AGAINST ENEMIES FROM THE NORTH, SOUTH, EAST AND WEST! I'LL GUARD THIS SNOWMAN AGAINST ENEMIES FROM BELOW AND FROM...
........above.........
YOU JUST CAN'T DO **ANYTHING**, CAN YOU?
SCHULZ

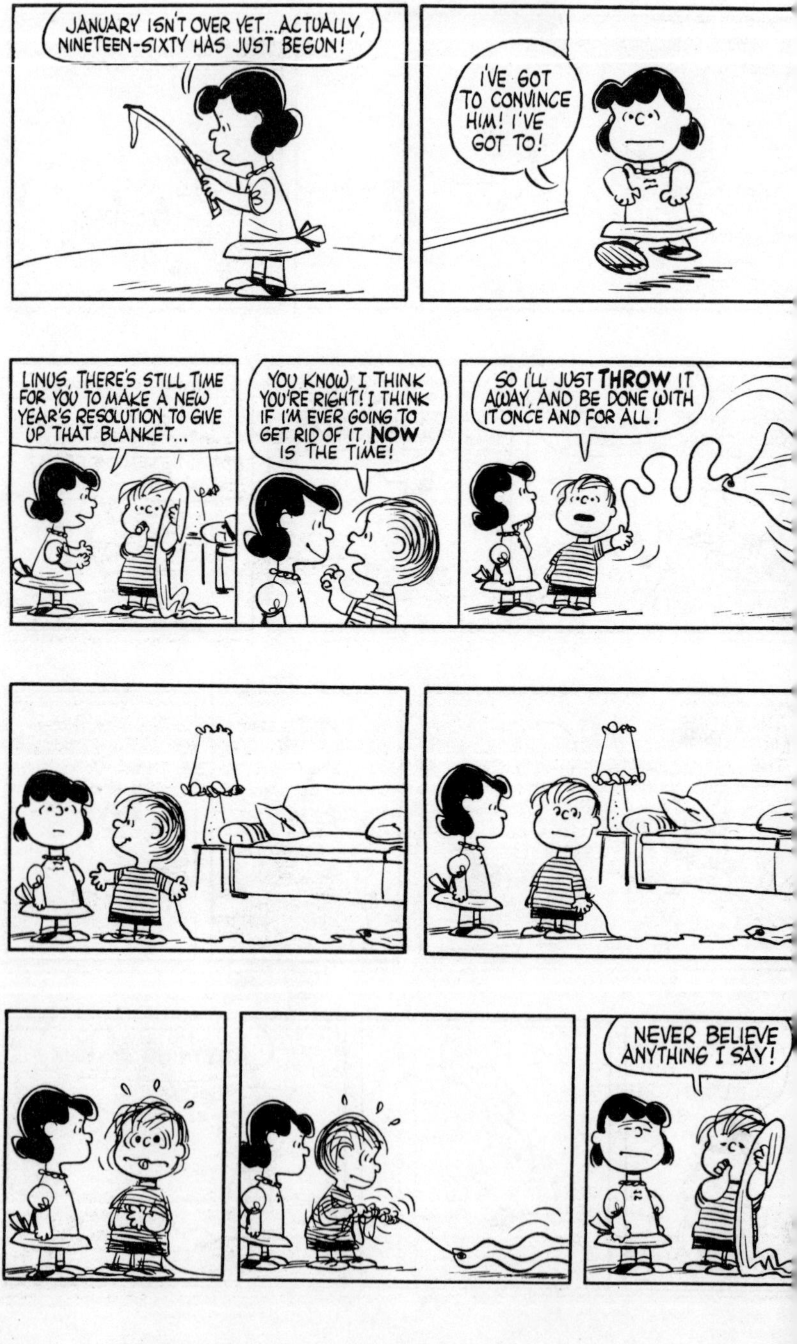
JANUARY ISN'T OVER YET...ACTUALLY, NINETEEN-SIXTY HAS JUST BEGUN!
I'VE GOT TO CONVINCE HIM! I'VE GOT TO!
LINUS, THERE'S STILL TIME FOR YOU TO MAKE A NEW YEAR'S RESOLUTION TO GIVE UP THAT BLANKET...
YOU KNOW, I THINK YOU'RE RIGHT! I THINK IF I'M EVER GOING TO GET RID OF IT, NOW IS THE TIME!
SO I'LL JUST THROW IT AWAY, AND BE DONE WITH IT ONCE AND FOR ALL!
NEVER BELIEVE ANYTHING I SAY!

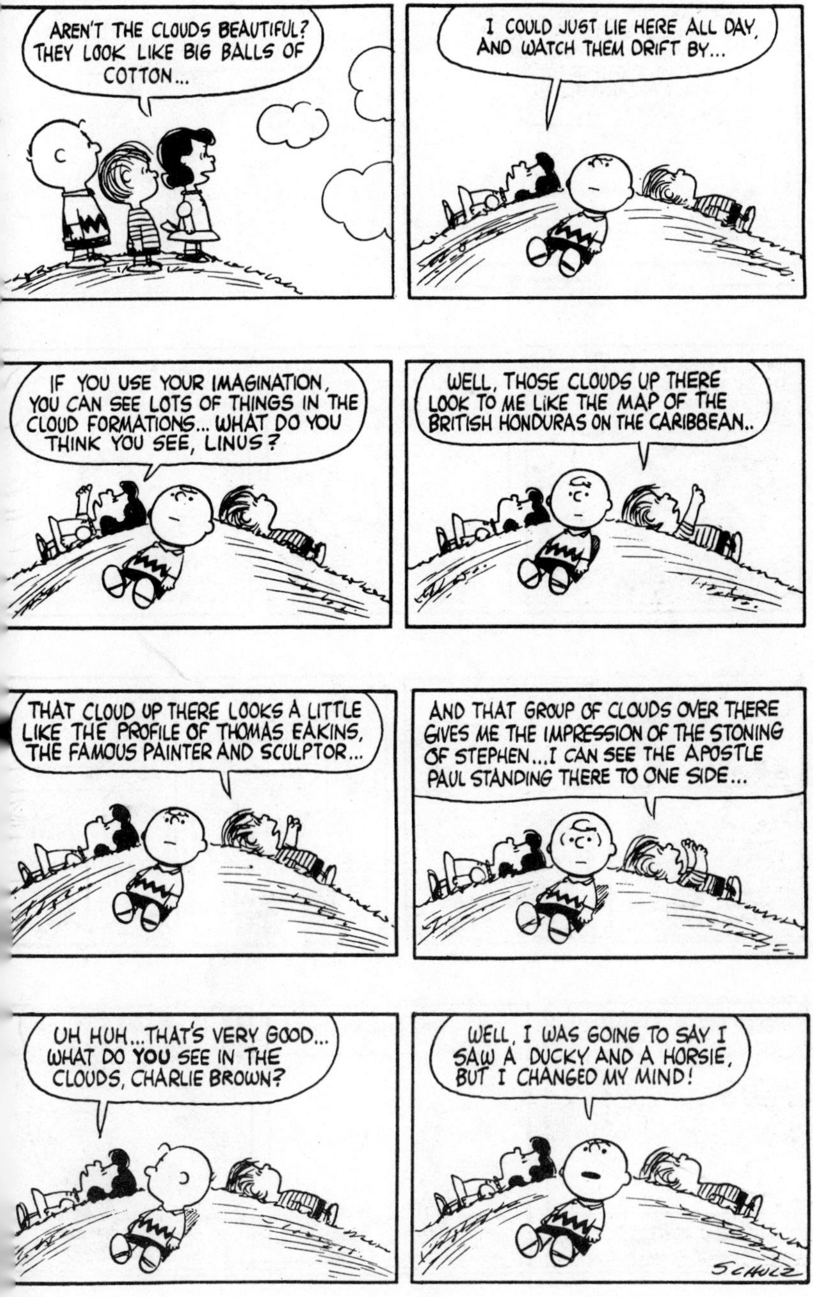
AREN'T THE CLOUDS BEAUTIFUL? THEY LOOK LIKE BIG BALLS OF COTTON...
I COULD JUST LIE HERE ALL DAY, AND WATCH THEM DRIFT BY...
IF YOU USE YOUR IMAGINATION, YOU CAN SEE LOTS OF THINGS IN THE CLOUD FORMATIONS... WHAT DO YOU THINK YOU SEE, LINUS?
WELL, THOSE CLOUDS UP THERE LOOK TO ME LIKE THE MAP OF THE BRITISH HONDURAS ON THE CARIBBEAN..
THAT CLOUD UP THERE LOOKS A LITTLE LIKE THE PROFILE OF THOMAS EAKINS, THE FAMOUS PAINTER AND SCULPTOR...
AND THAT GROUP OF CLOUDS OVER THERE GIVES ME THE IMPRESSION OF THE STONING OF STEPHEN...I CAN SEE THE APOSTLE PAUL STANDING THERE TO ONE SIDE...
UH HUH...THAT'S VERY GOOD... WHAT DO YOU SEE IN THE CLOUDS, CHARLIE BROWN?
WELL, I WAS GOING TO SAY I SAW A DUCKY AND A HORSIE, BUT I CHANGED MY MIND!
SCHULZ

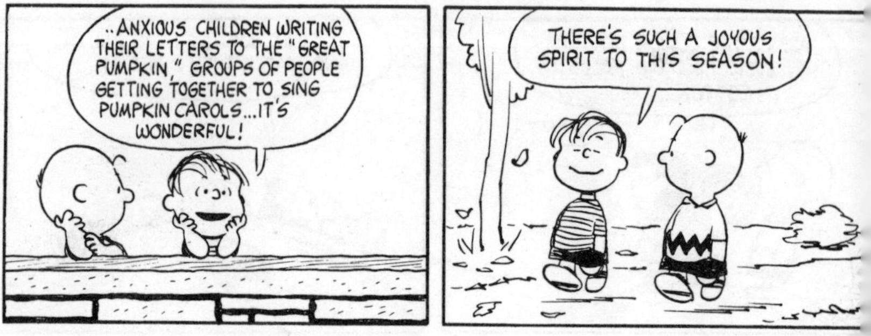
..ANXIOUS CHILDREN WRITING THEIR LETTERS TO THE "GREAT PUMPKIN," GROUPS OF PEOPLE GETTING TOGETHER TO SING PUMPKIN CAROLS...IT'S WONDERFUL!
THERE'S SUCH A JOYOUS SPIRIT TO THIS SEASON!

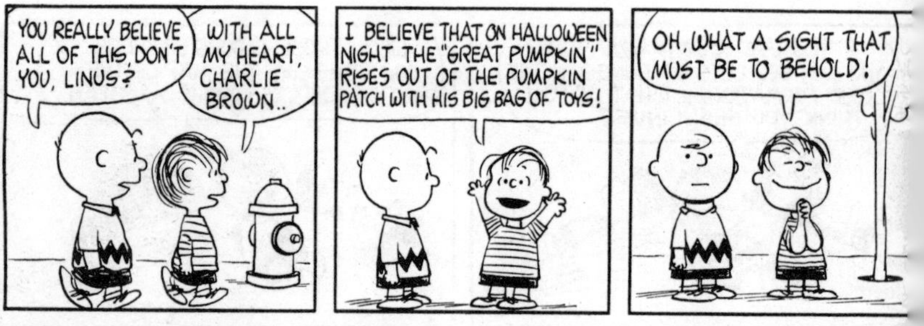
YOU REALLY BELIEVE ALL OF THIS, DON'T YOU, LINUS?
WITH ALL MY HEART, CHARLIE BROWN..
I BELIEVE THAT ON HALLOWEEN NIGHT THE "GREAT PUMPKIN" RISES OUT OF THE PUMPKIN PATCH WITH HIS BIG BAG OF TOYS!
OH, WHAT A SIGHT THAT MUST BE TO BEHOLD!

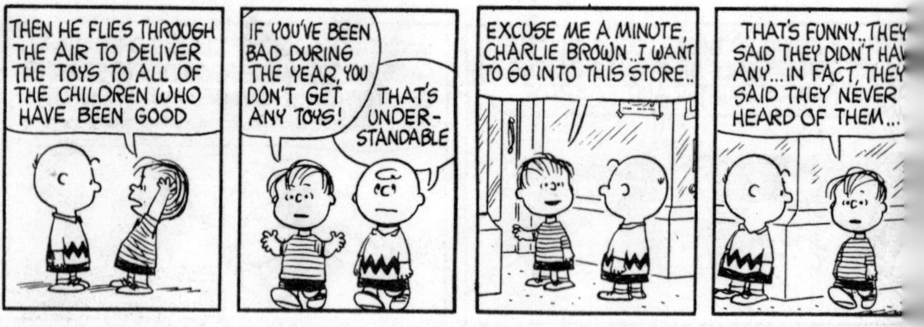
THEN HE FLIES THROUGH THE AIR TO DELIVER THE TOYS TO ALL OF THE CHILDREN WHO HAVE BEEN GOOD
IF YOU'VE BEEN BAD DURING THE YEAR, YOU DON'T GET ANY TOYS!
THAT'S UNDER-STANDABLE
EXCUSE ME A MINUTE, CHARLIE BROWN..I WANT TO GO INTO THIS STORE..
THAT'S FUNNY..THEY SAID THEY DIDN'T HAV ANY...IN FACT, THEY SAID THEY NEVER HEARD OF THEM...

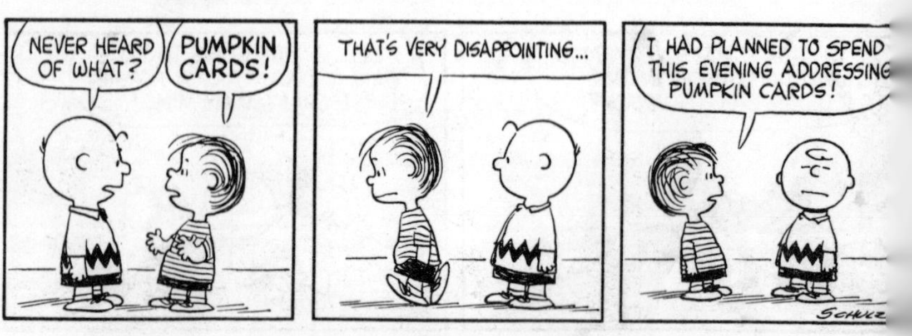
NEVER HEARD OF WHAT?
PUMPKIN CARDS!
THAT'S VERY DISAPPOINTING...
I HAD PLANNED TO SPEND THIS EVENING ADDRESSING PUMPKIN CARDS!
SCHULZ

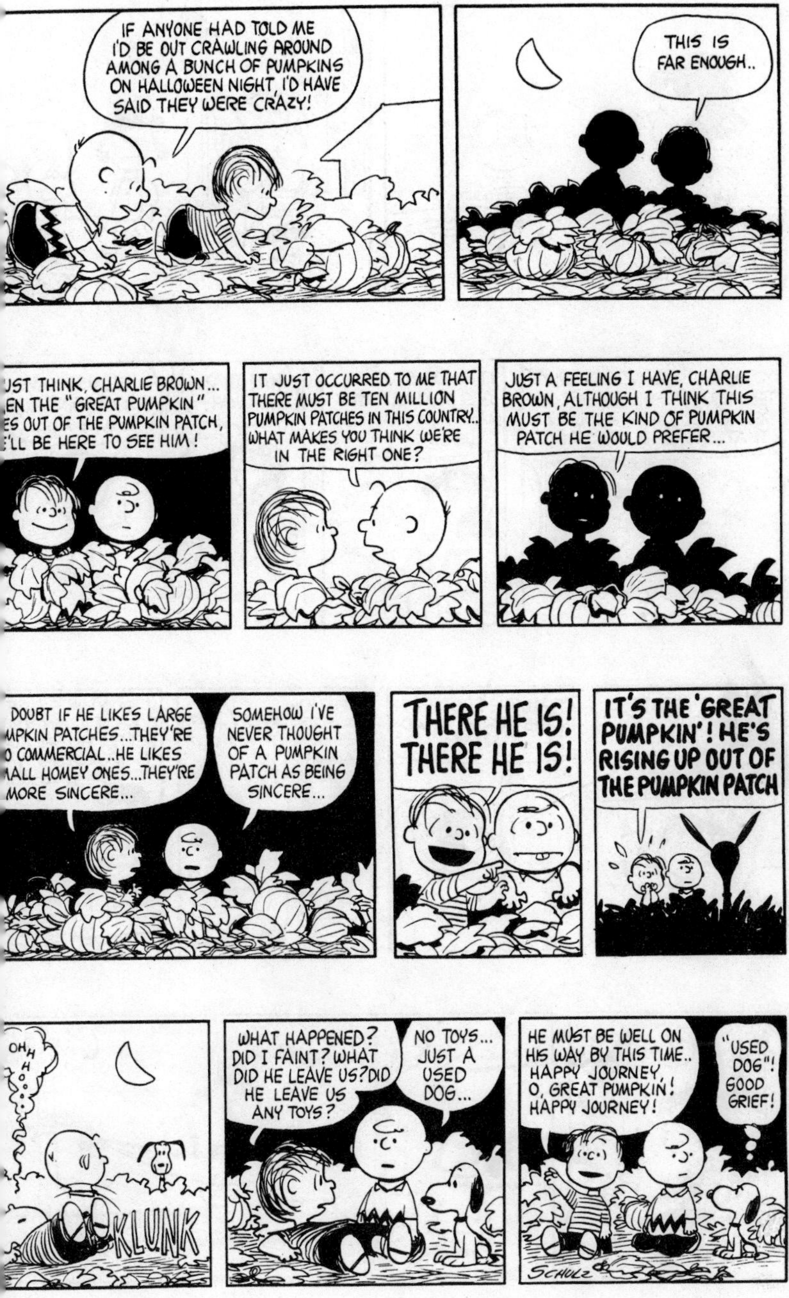

IF ANYONE HAD TOLD ME I'D BE OUT CRAWLING AROUND AMONG A BUNCH OF PUMPKINS ON HALLOWEEN NIGHT, I'D HAVE SAID THEY WERE CRAZY!
THIS IS FAR ENOUGH..
UST THINK, CHARLIE BROWN... EN THE "GREAT PUMPKIN" ES OUT OF THE PUMPKIN PATCH, 'LL BE HERE TO SEE HIM!
IT JUST OCCURRED TO ME THAT THERE MUST BE TEN MILLION PUMPKIN PATCHES IN THIS COUNTRY.. WHAT MAKES YOU THINK WE'RE IN THE RIGHT ONE?
JUST A FEELING I HAVE, CHARLIE BROWN, ALTHOUGH I THINK THIS MUST BE THE KIND OF PUMPKIN PATCH HE WOULD PREFER...
DOUBT IF HE LIKES LARGE MPKIN PATCHES...THEY'RE O COMMERCIAL..HE LIKES MALL HOMEY ONES...THEY'RE MORE SINCERE...
SOMEHOW I'VE NEVER THOUGHT OF A PUMPKIN PATCH AS BEING SINCERE...
THERE HE IS! THERE HE IS!
IT'S THE 'GREAT PUMPKIN'! HE'S RISING UP OUT OF THE PUMPKIN PATCH
KLUNK
WHAT HAPPENED? DID I FAINT? WHAT DID HE LEAVE US? DID HE LEAVE US ANY TOYS?
NO TOYS... JUST A USED DOG...
HE MUST BE WELL ON HIS WAY BY THIS TIME.. HAPPY JOURNEY, O, GREAT PUMPKIN! HAPPY JOURNEY!
"USED DOG"! GOOD GRIEF!
SCHULZ

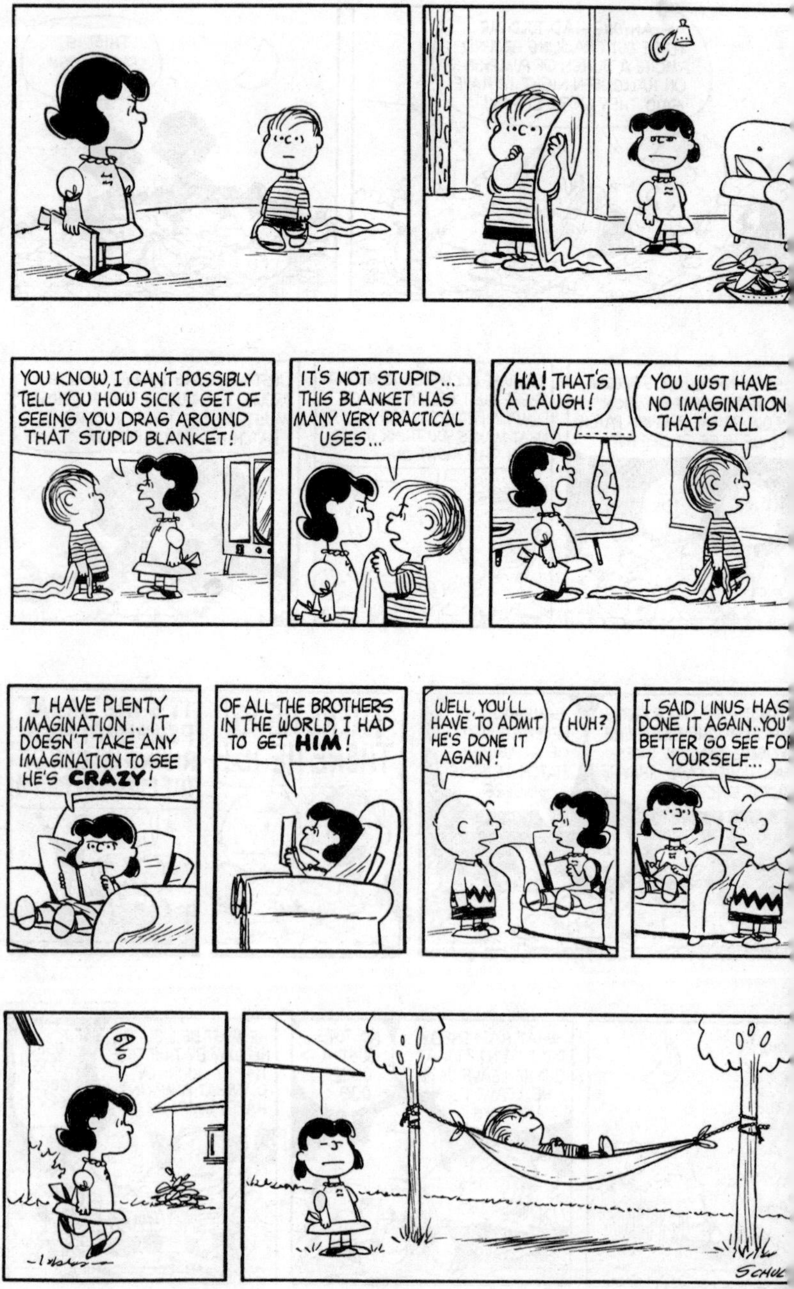
YOU KNOW, I CAN'T POSSIBLY TELL YOU HOW SICK I GET OF SEEING YOU DRAG AROUND THAT STUPID BLANKET!
IT'S NOT STUPID... THIS BLANKET HAS MANY VERY PRACTICAL USES...
HA! THAT'S A LAUGH!
YOU JUST HAVE NO IMAGINATION THAT'S ALL
I HAVE PLENTY IMAGINATION... IT DOESN'T TAKE ANY IMAGINATION TO SEE HE'S CRAZY!
OF ALL THE BROTHERS IN THE WORLD, I HAD TO GET HIM!
WELL, YOU'LL HAVE TO ADMIT HE'S DONE IT AGAIN!
HUH?
I SAID LINUS HAS DONE IT AGAIN..YOU' BETTER GO SEE FO YOURSELF...
?

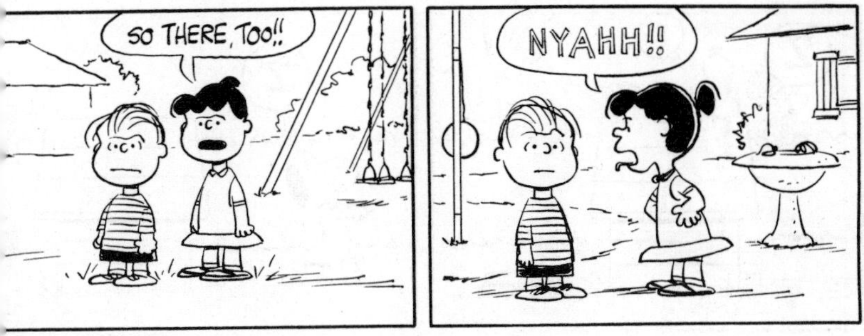
SO THERE, TOO!!
NYAHH!!

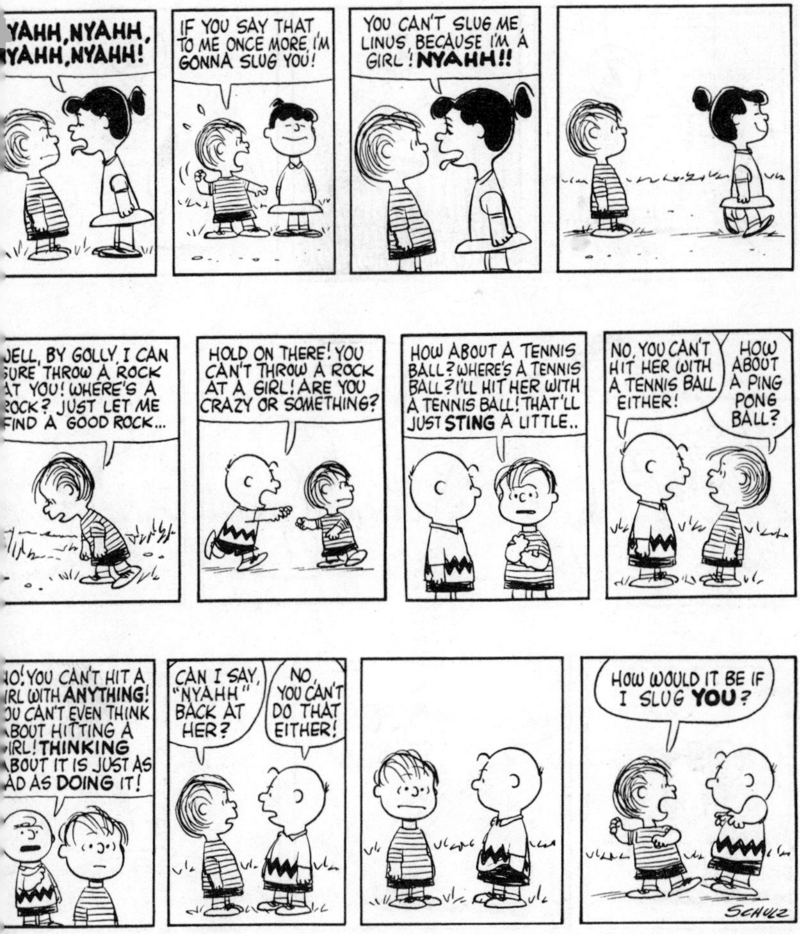
YAHH, NYAHH, YAHH, NYAHH!
IF YOU SAY THAT TO ME ONCE MORE, I'M GONNA SLUG YOU!
YOU CAN'T SLUG ME, LINUS, BECAUSE I'M A GIRL! NYAHH!!
JELL, BY GOLLY, I CAN SURE THROW A ROCK AT YOU! WHERE'S A ROCK? JUST LET ME FIND A GOOD ROCK...
HOLD ON THERE! YOU CAN'T THROW A ROCK AT A GIRL! ARE YOU CRAZY OR SOMETHING?
HOW ABOUT A TENNIS BALL? WHERE'S A TENNIS BALL? I'LL HIT HER WITH A TENNIS BALL! THAT'LL JUST STING A LITTLE..
NO, YOU CAN'T HIT HER WITH A TENNIS BALL EITHER!
HOW ABOUT A PING PONG BALL?
O! YOU CAN'T HIT A IRL WITH ANYTHING! OU CAN'T EVEN THINK BOUT HITTING A IRL! THINKING BOUT IT IS JUST AS AD AS DOING IT!
CAN I SAY, "NYAHH" BACK AT HER?
NO, YOU CAN'T DO THAT EITHER!
HOW WOULD IT BE IF I SLUG YOU?
SCHULZ

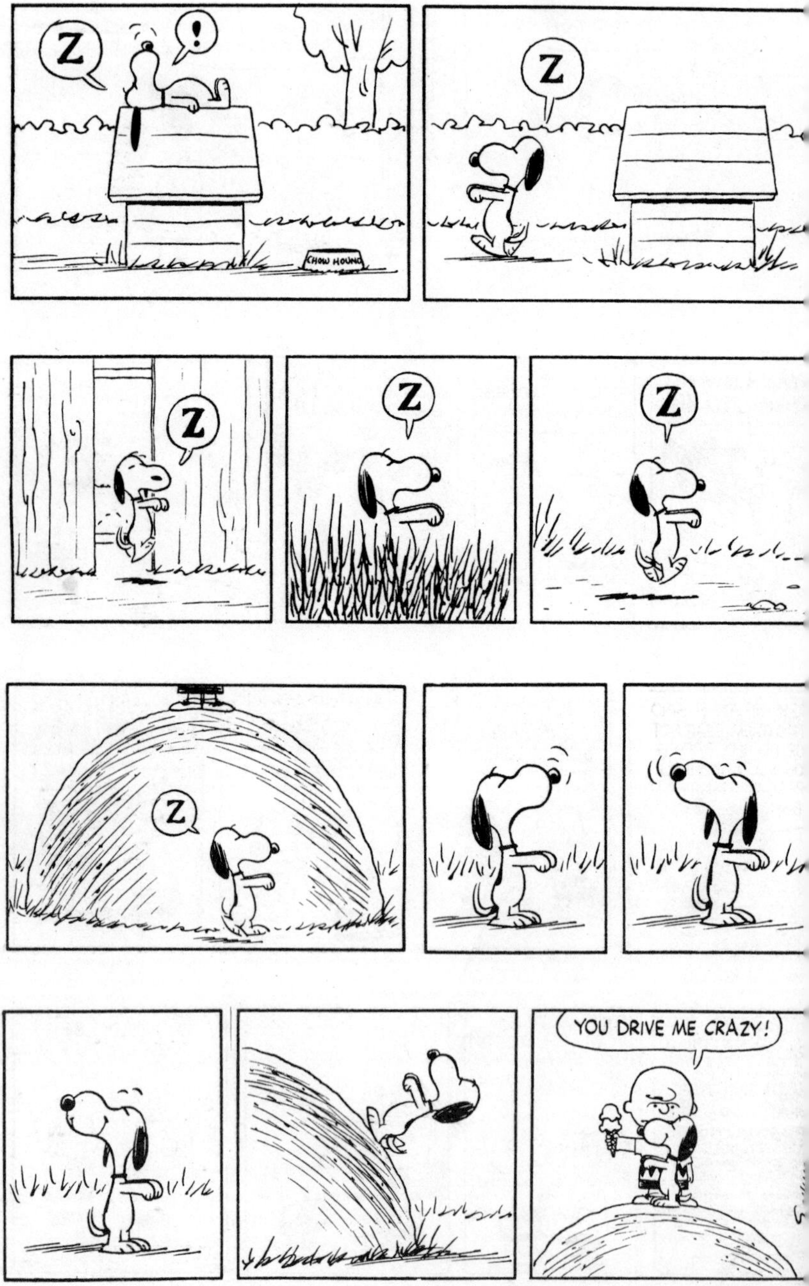

Z
!
CHOW HOUND
Z
Z
Z
Z
Z
YOU DRIVE ME CRAZY!

YES, SIR... LONG PANTS SURE DO MAKE THE MAN!

WELL, HOW DO I LOOK?

FINE...IT'S THE FIRST TIME I'VE SEEN YOU IN A WHITE SHIRT IN SIX MONTHS!

NOW ARE YOU SURE YOU KNOW YOUR PIECE FOR THE CHRISTMAS PROGRAM?

I KNOW IT BACKWARDS AND FORWARDS AND SIDEWAYS AND UPSIDE DOWN! I COULD SAY IT IN MY SLEEP!

YEAH, WELL, I REMEMBER **LAST** YEAR..YOU ALMOST GOOFED THE WHOLE PROGRAM!

WELL, THIS IS **THIS** YEAR, AND **THIS** YEAR I WON'T FORGET!

AND THE ANGEL SAID UNTO THEM, FEAR NOT: FOR, BEHOLD, I BRING YOU GOOD TIDINGS OF GREAT JOY WHICH SHALL BE TO ALL PEOPLE."

SAY, THAT'S PRETTY GOOD..

I **TOLD** YOU I KNEW IT.. I HAVE A MEMORY LIKE THE PROVERBIAL ELEPHANT!

WELL, I'M GOING ON AHEAD TO THE CHURCH...I'LL SEE YOU THERE...

...FOR, BEHOLD, I BRING YOU GOOD TIDINGS OF GREAT JOY WHICH SHALL BE TO ALL PEOPLE." WHAT A MEMORY!!!

WHAT IN THE WORLD? I THOUGHT YOU JUST LEFT?

I DID, BUT I CAME BACK..

I FORGOT WHERE THE CHURCH IS!

SCHULZ

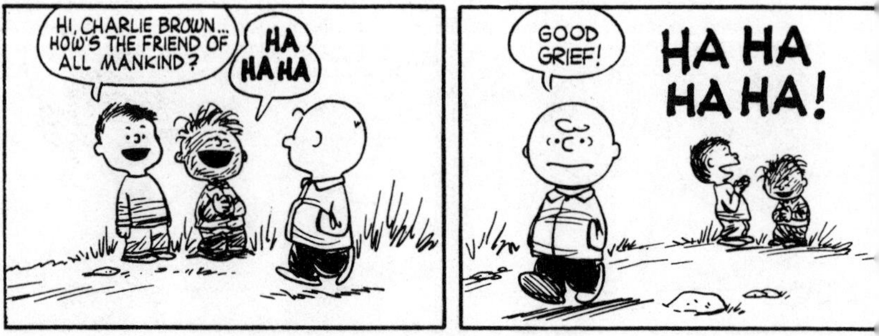
HI, CHARLIE BROWN... HOW'S THE FRIEND OF ALL MANKIND?
HA HA HA
GOOD GRIEF!
HA HA HA HA!

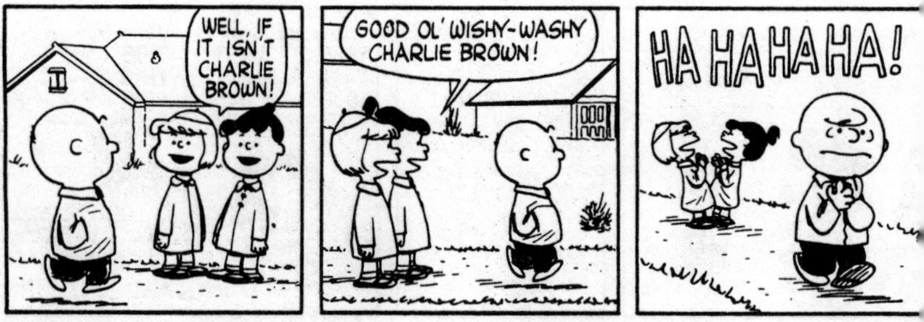
WELL, IF IT ISN'T CHARLIE BROWN!
GOOD OL' WISHY-WASHY CHARLIE BROWN!
HA HA HA HA HA!

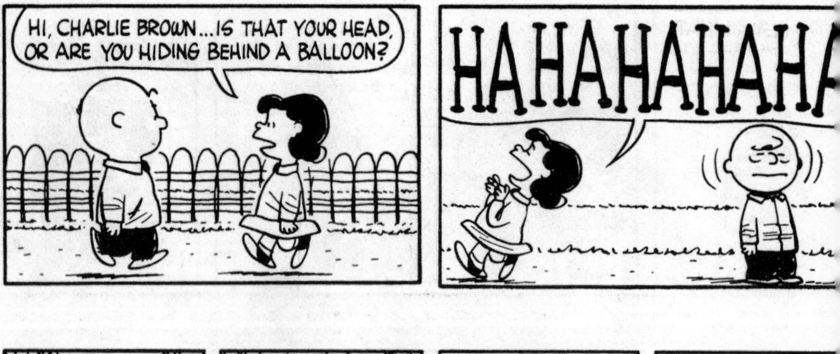
HI, CHARLIE BROWN...IS THAT YOUR HEAD, OR ARE YOU HIDING BEHIND A BALLOON?
HAHAHAHAHA

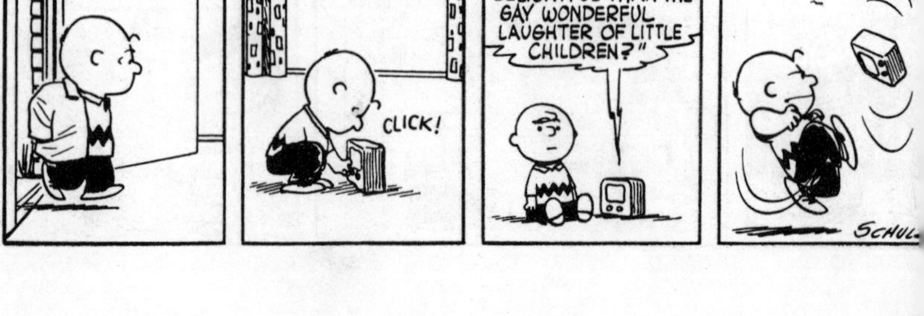
CLICK!
"...AND WHAT, IN ALL THIS WORLD, IS MORE DELIGHTFUL THAN THE GAY WONDERFUL LAUGHTER OF LITTLE CHILDREN?"

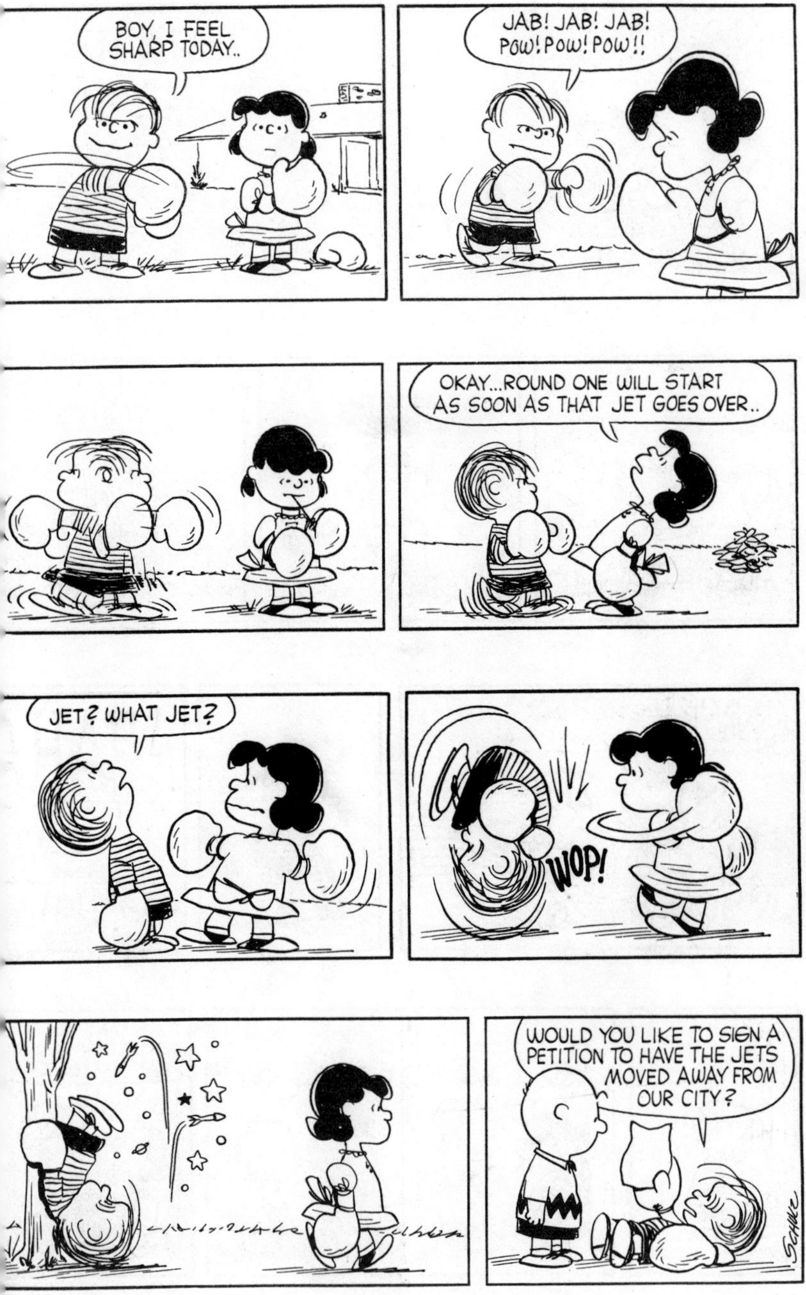
BOY, I FEEL SHARP TODAY..
JAB! JAB! JAB! POW! POW! POW!!
OKAY...ROUND ONE WILL START AS SOON AS THAT JET GOES OVER..
JET? WHAT JET?
WOP!
WOULD YOU LIKE TO SIGN A PETITION TO HAVE THE JETS MOVED AWAY FROM OUR CITY?

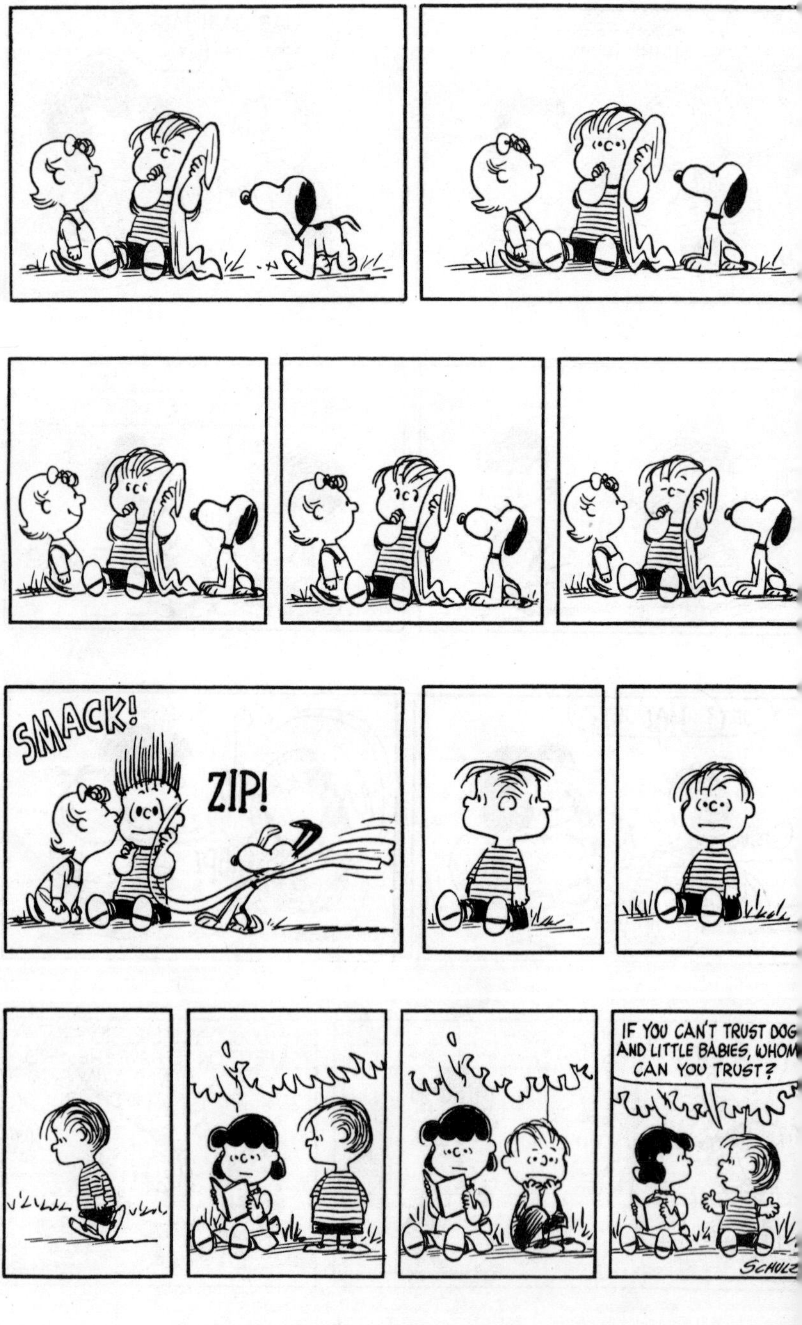
SMACK!
ZIP!
IF YOU CAN'T TRUST DOG
AND LITTLE BABIES, WHOM
CAN YOU TRUST?
SCHULZ

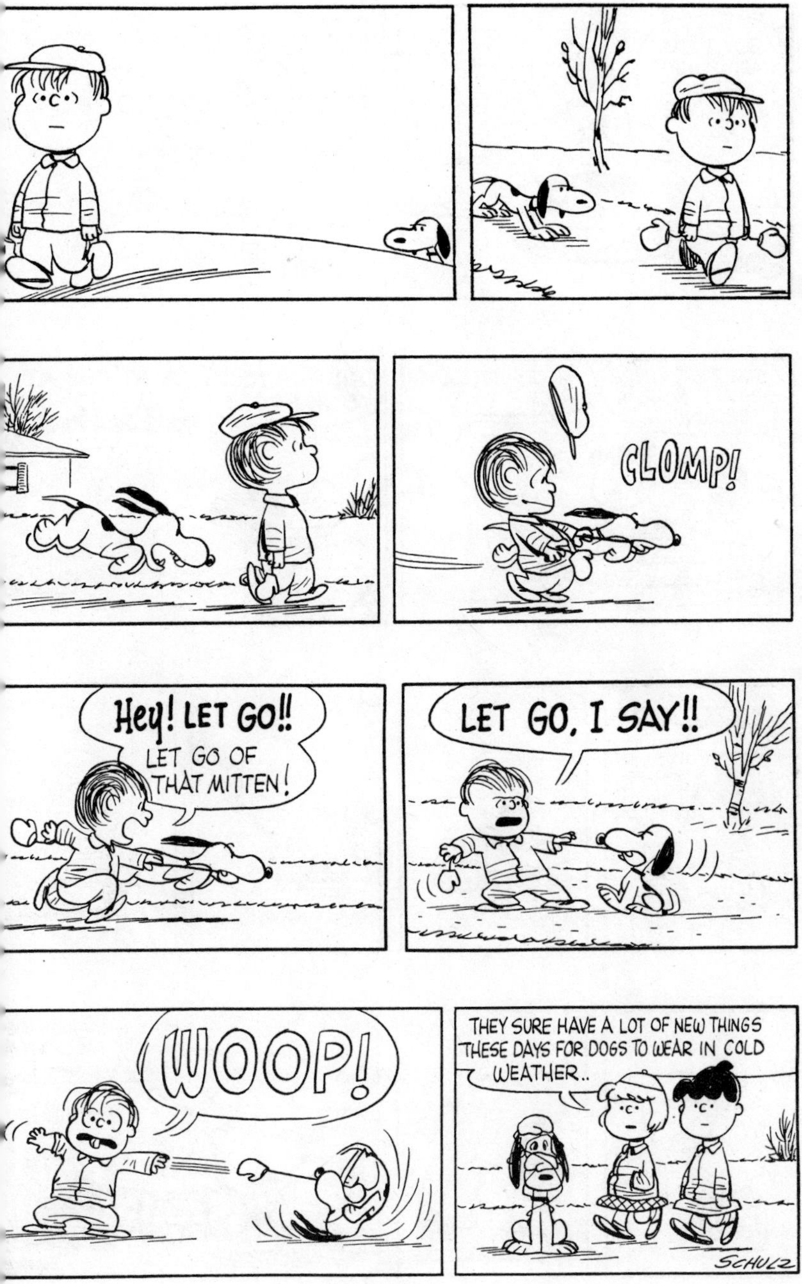
CLOMP!
Hey! LET GO!!
LET GO OF THAT MITTEN!
LET GO, I SAY!!
WOOP!
THEY SURE HAVE A LOT OF NEW THINGS THESE DAYS FOR DOGS TO WEAR IN COLD WEATHER..
SCHULZ

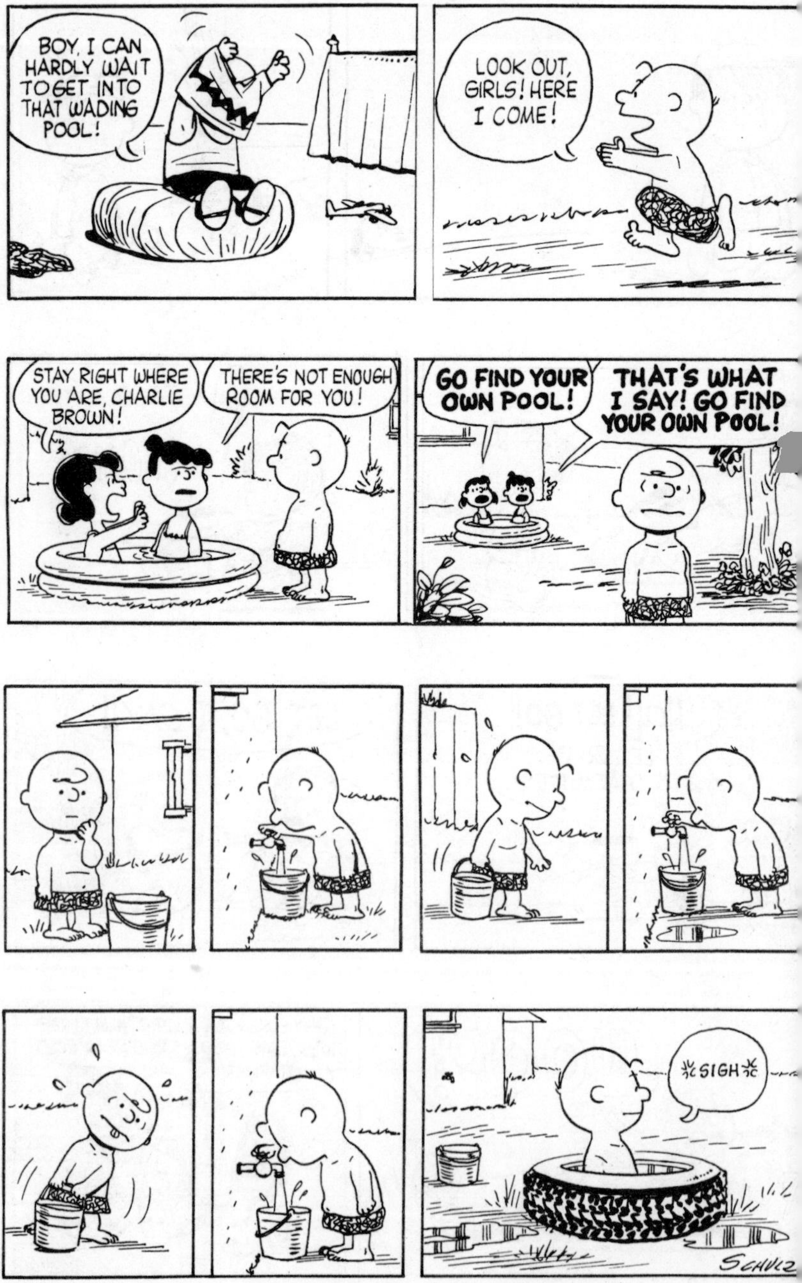

BOY, I CAN HARDLY WAIT TO GET INTO THAT WADING POOL!
LOOK OUT, GIRLS! HERE I COME!
STAY RIGHT WHERE YOU ARE, CHARLIE BROWN!
THERE'S NOT ENOUGH ROOM FOR YOU!
GO FIND YOUR OWN POOL!
THAT'S WHAT I SAY! GO FIND YOUR OWN POOL!
SIGH
SCHULZ

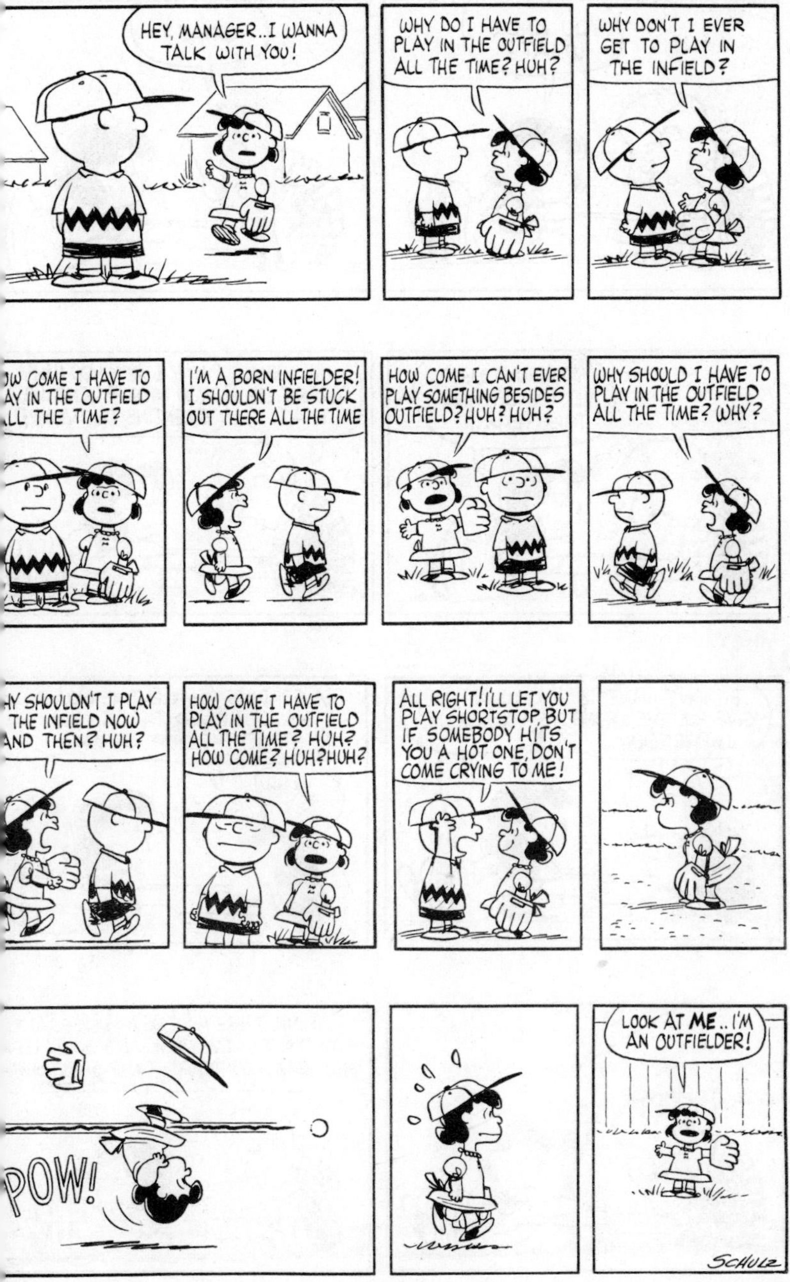
HEY, MANAGER..I WANNA TALK WITH YOU!
WHY DO I HAVE TO PLAY IN THE OUTFIELD ALL THE TIME? HUH?
WHY DON'T I EVER GET TO PLAY IN THE INFIELD?
)W COME I HAVE TO AY IN THE OUTFIELD LL THE TIME?
I'M A BORN INFIELDER! I SHOULDN'T BE STUCK OUT THERE ALL THE TIME
HOW COME I CAN'T EVER PLAY SOMETHING BESIDES OUTFIELD? HUH? HUH?
WHY SHOULD I HAVE TO PLAY IN THE OUTFIELD ALL THE TIME? WHY?
HY SHOULDN'T I PLAY THE INFIELD NOW AND THEN? HUH?
HOW COME I HAVE TO PLAY IN THE OUTFIELD ALL THE TIME? HUH? HOW COME? HUH?HUH?
ALL RIGHT! I'LL LET YOU PLAY SHORTSTOP, BUT IF SOMEBODY HITS YOU A HOT ONE, DON'T COME CRYING TO ME!
POW!
LOOK AT **ME**.. I'M AN OUTFIELDER!
SCHULZ

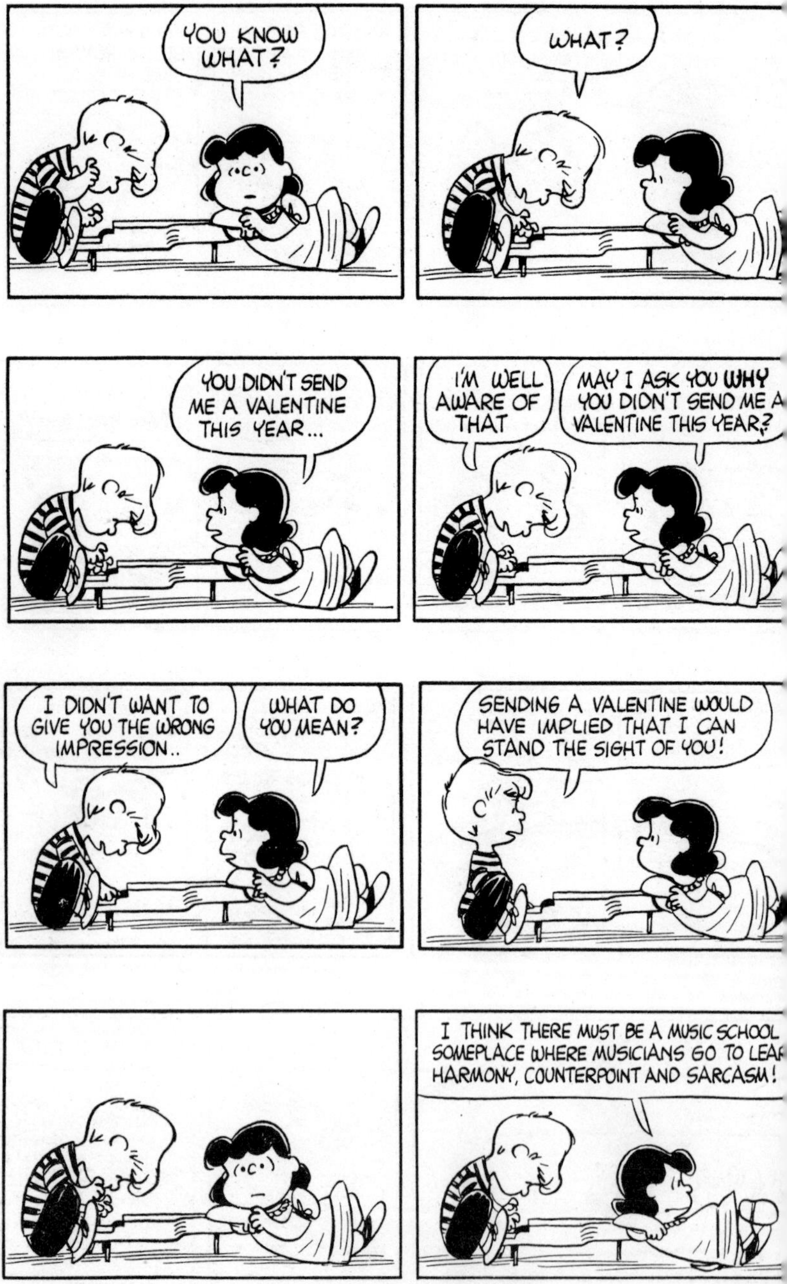

YOU KNOW WHAT?
WHAT?
YOU DIDN'T SEND ME A VALENTINE THIS YEAR...
I'M WELL AWARE OF THAT
MAY I ASK YOU WHY YOU DIDN'T SEND ME A VALENTINE THIS YEAR?
I DIDN'T WANT TO GIVE YOU THE WRONG IMPRESSION..
WHAT DO YOU MEAN?
SENDING A VALENTINE WOULD HAVE IMPLIED THAT I CAN STAND THE SIGHT OF YOU!
I THINK THERE MUST BE A MUSIC SCHOOL SOMEPLACE WHERE MUSICIANS GO TO LEAR
HARMONY, COUNTERPOINT AND SARCASM!

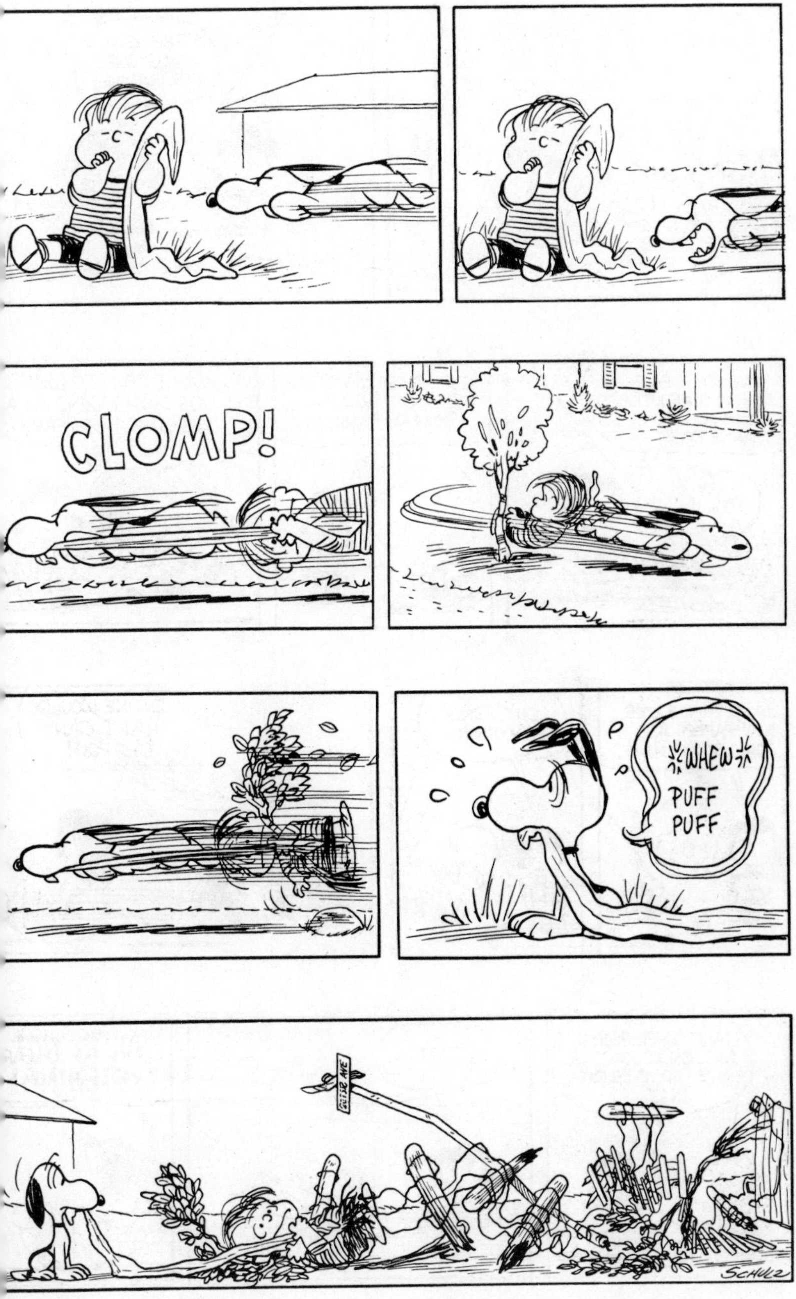
CLOMP!
WHEW
PUFF
PUFF
SCHULZ

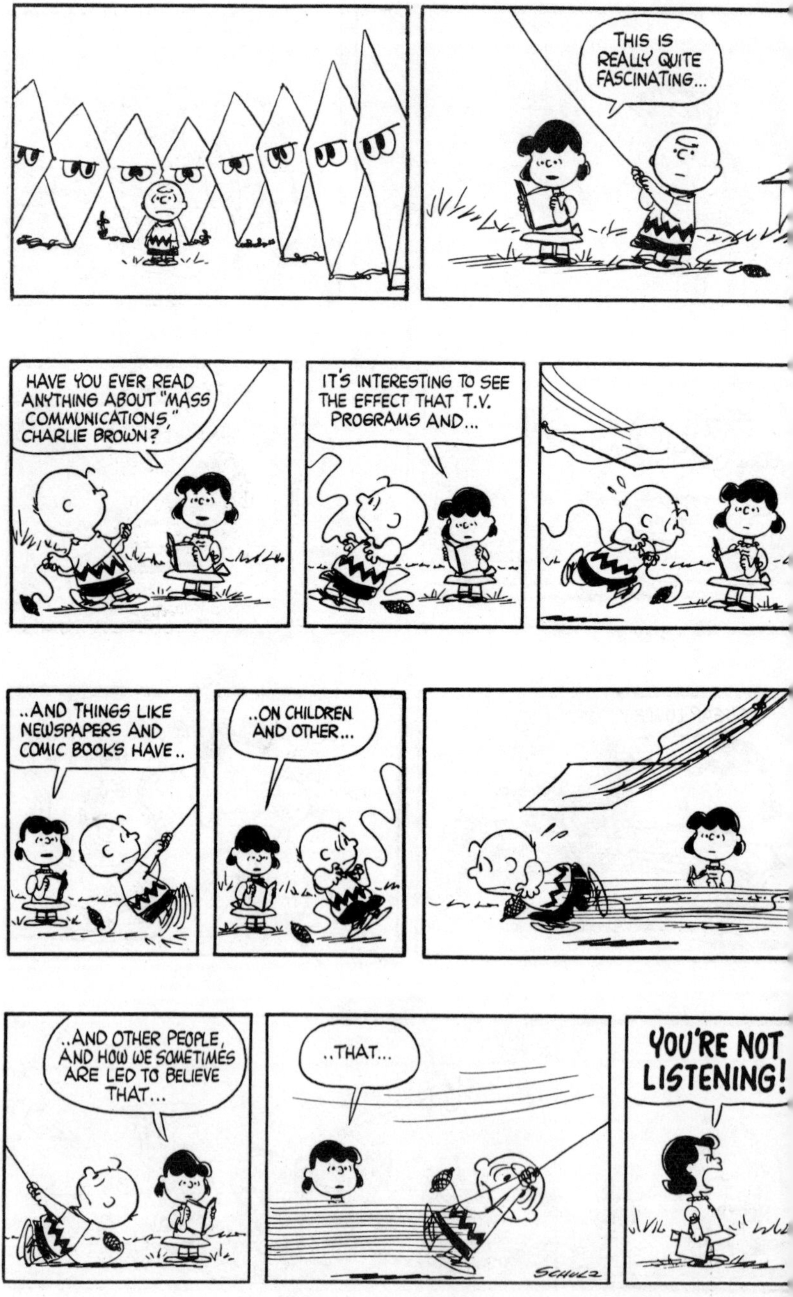
THIS IS REALLY QUITE FASCINATING...
HAVE YOU EVER READ ANYTHING ABOUT "MASS COMMUNICATIONS," CHARLIE BROWN?
IT'S INTERESTING TO SEE THE EFFECT THAT T.V. PROGRAMS AND...
..AND THINGS LIKE NEWSPAPERS AND COMIC BOOKS HAVE..
..ON CHILDREN AND OTHER...
..AND OTHER PEOPLE, AND HOW WE SOMETIMES ARE LED TO BELIEVE THAT...
..THAT...
SCHULZ
YOU'RE NOT LISTENING!

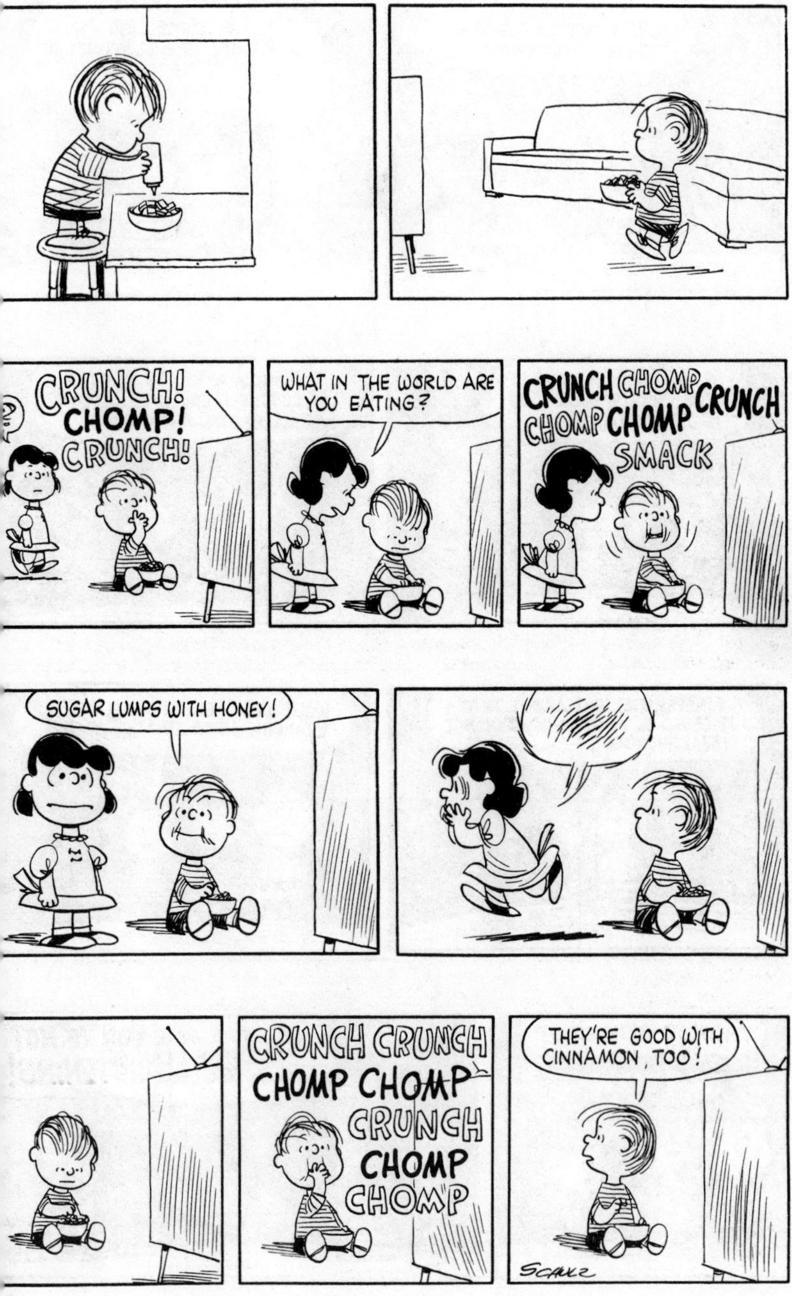
CRUNCH!
CHOMP!
CRUNCH!
WHAT IN THE WORLD ARE YOU EATING?
CRUNCH CHOMP CRUNCH
CHOMP CHOMP
SMACK
SUGAR LUMPS WITH HONEY!
CRUNCH CRUNCH
CHOMP CHOMP
CRUNCH
CHOMP
CHOMP
THEY'RE GOOD WITH CINNAMON, TOO!
SCHULZ

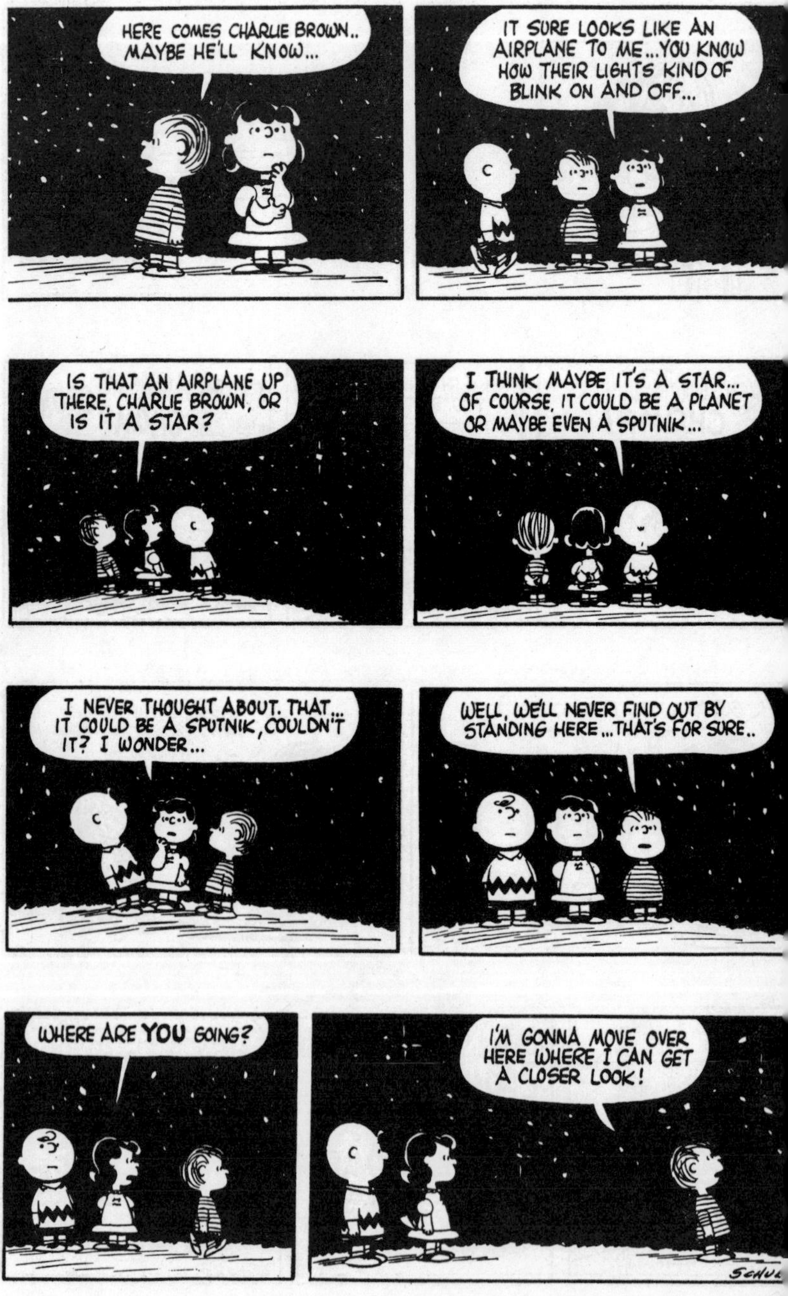
HERE COMES CHARLIE BROWN.. MAYBE HE'LL KNOW...
IT SURE LOOKS LIKE AN AIRPLANE TO ME...YOU KNOW HOW THEIR LIGHTS KIND OF BLINK ON AND OFF...
IS THAT AN AIRPLANE UP THERE, CHARLIE BROWN, OR IS IT A STAR?
I THINK MAYBE IT'S A STAR... OF COURSE, IT COULD BE A PLANET OR MAYBE EVEN A SPUTNIK...
I NEVER THOUGHT ABOUT. THAT... IT COULD BE A SPUTNIK, COULDN'T IT? I WONDER...
WELL, WE'LL NEVER FIND OUT BY STANDING HERE...THAT'S FOR SURE..
WHERE ARE YOU GOING?
I'M GONNA MOVE OVER HERE WHERE I CAN GET A CLOSER LOOK!

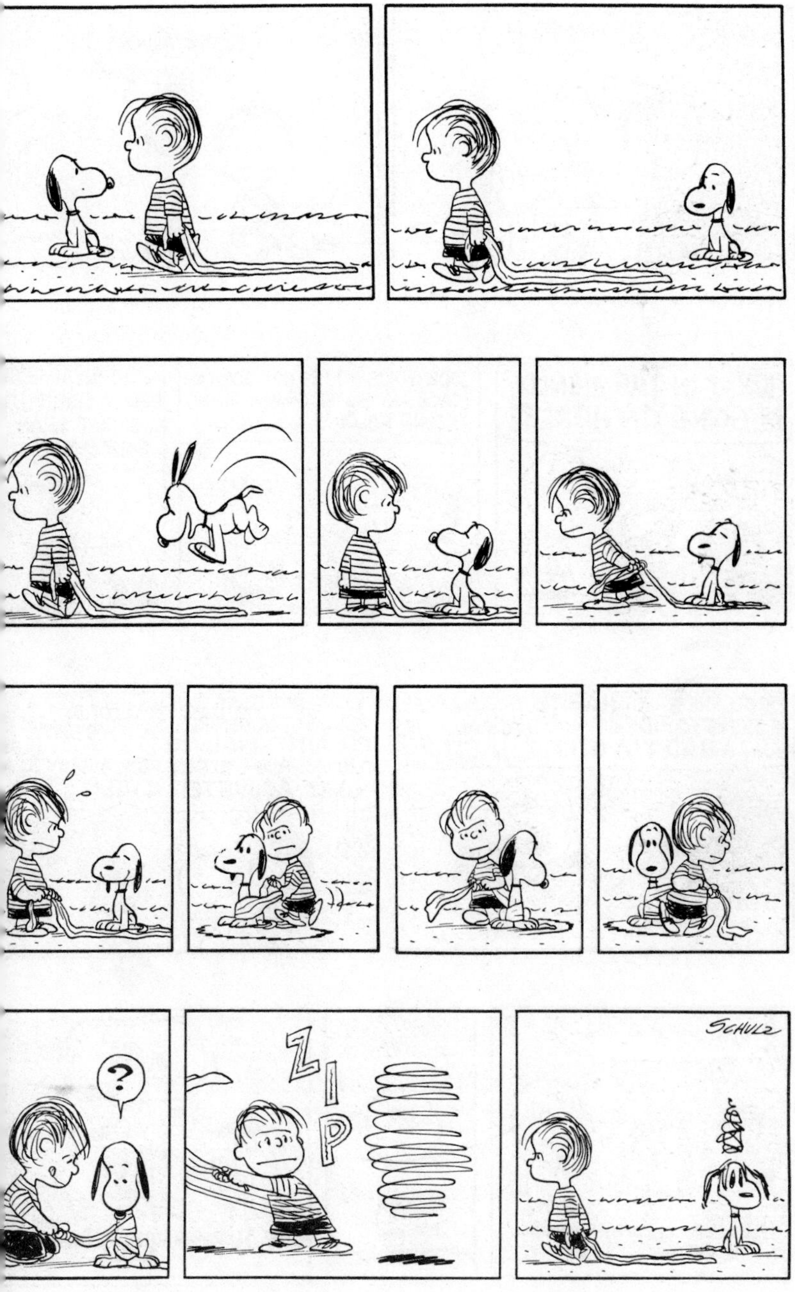
?
ZIP
SCHULZ

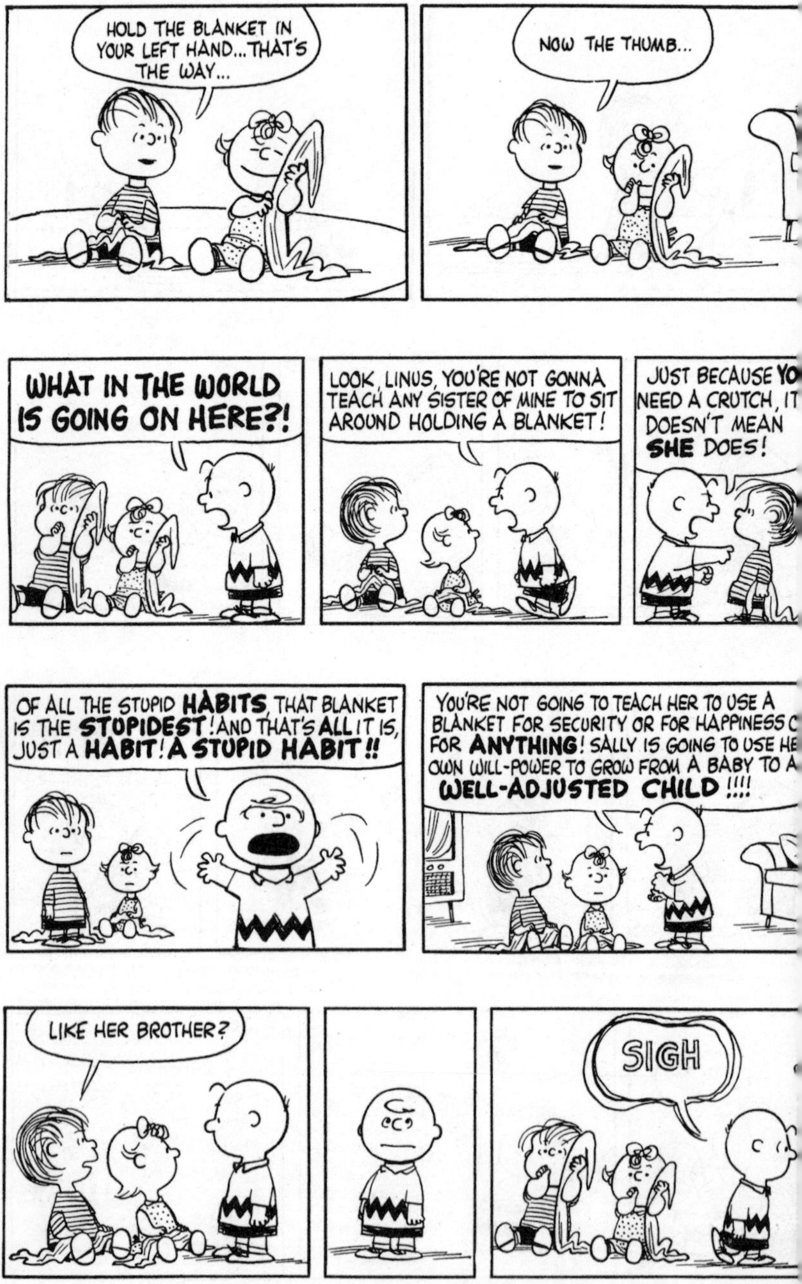
HOLD THE BLANKET IN YOUR LEFT HAND...THAT'S THE WAY...
NOW THE THUMB...
WHAT IN THE WORLD IS GOING ON HERE?!
LOOK, LINUS, YOU'RE NOT GONNA TEACH ANY SISTER OF MINE TO SIT AROUND HOLDING A BLANKET!
JUST BECAUSE YO
NEED A CRUTCH, IT
DOESN'T MEAN SHE DOES!
OF ALL THE STUPID HABITS, THAT BLANKET IS THE STOPIDEST! AND THAT'S ALL IT IS, JUST A HABIT! A STUPID HABIT!!
YOU'RE NOT GOING TO TEACH HER TO USE A BLANKET FOR SECURITY OR FOR HAPPINESS
FOR ANYTHING! SALLY IS GOING TO USE HE
OWN WILL-POWER TO GROW FROM A BABY TO A
WELL-ADJUSTED CHILD!!!!
LIKE HER BROTHER?
SIGH

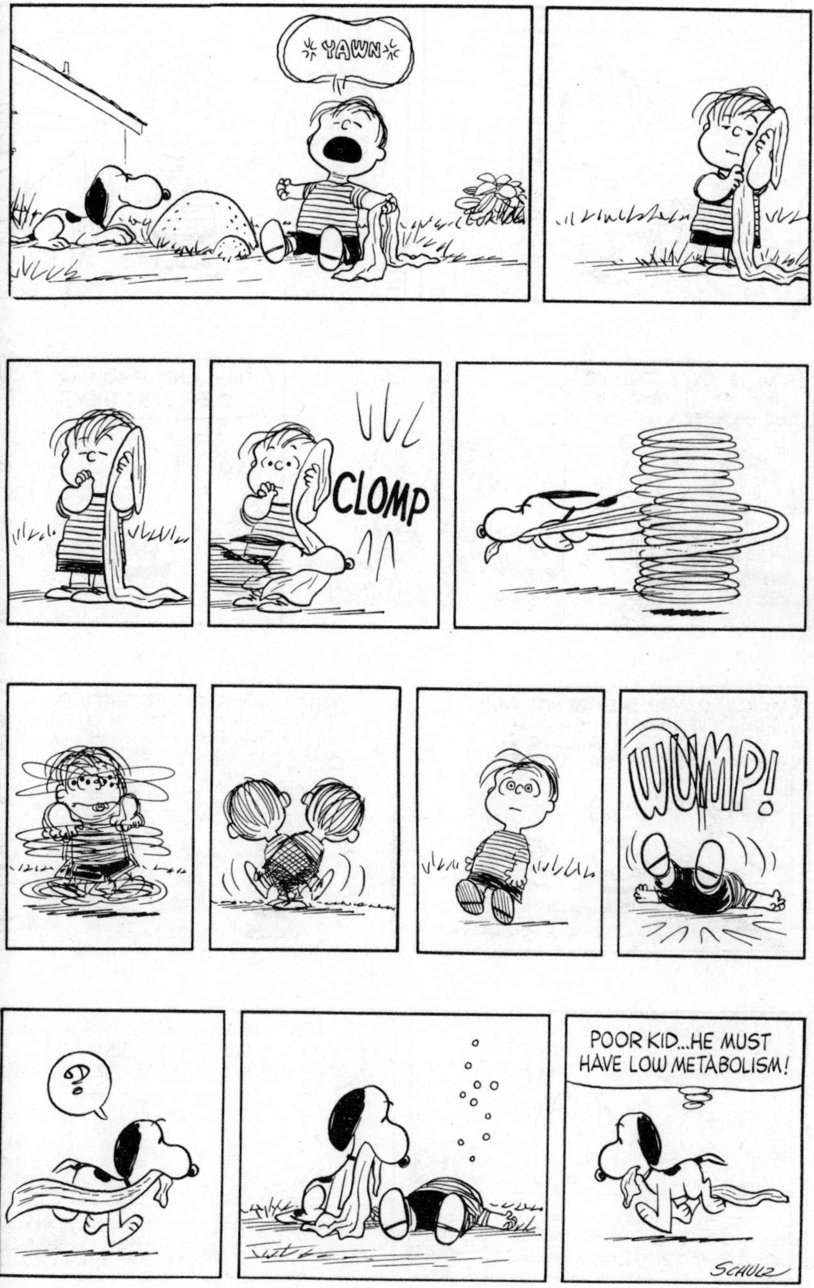
YAWN
CLOMP
WUMP!
?
POOR KID...HE MUST HAVE LOW METABOLISM!
SCHULZ

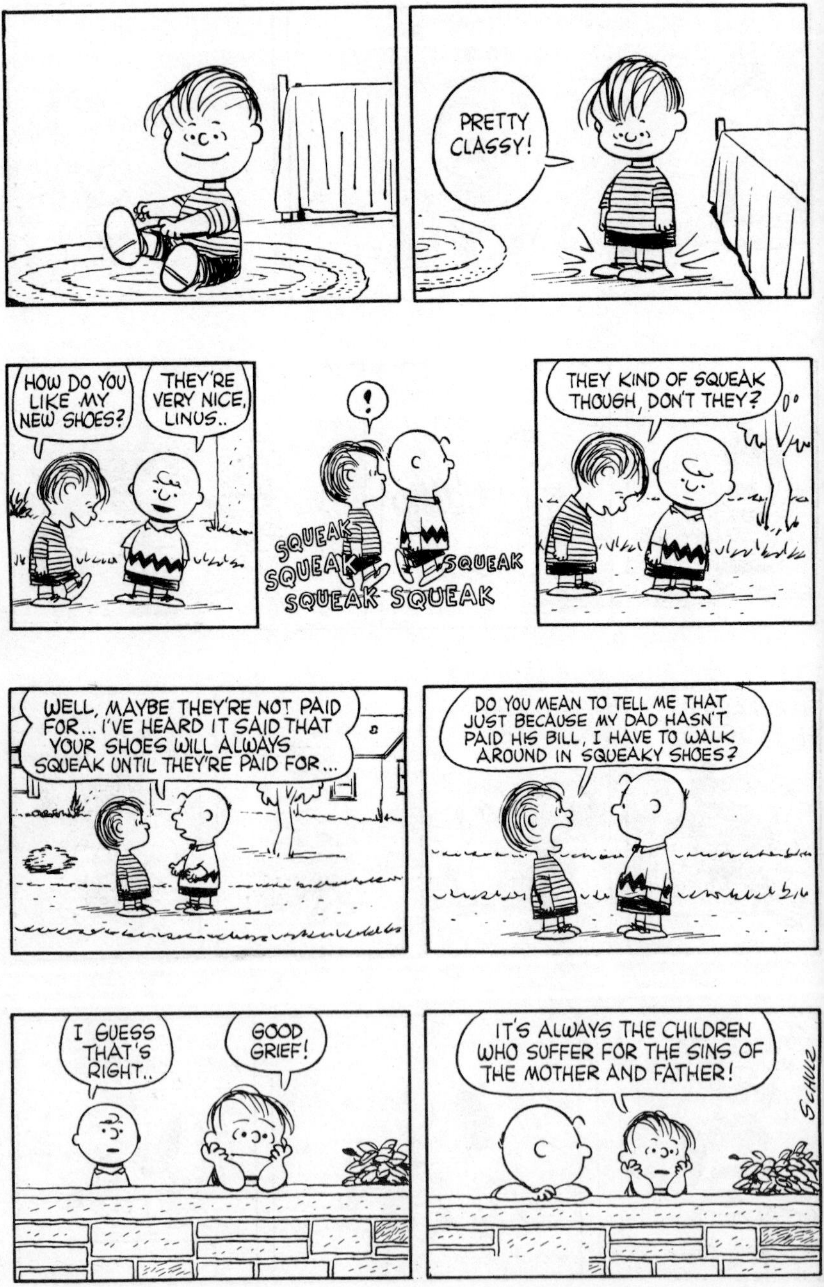

PRETTY CLASSY!
HOW DO YOU LIKE MY NEW SHOES?
THEY'RE VERY NICE, LINUS..
!
SQUEAK SQUEAK SQUEAK SQUEAK SQUEAK
THEY KIND OF SQUEAK THOUGH, DON'T THEY?
WELL, MAYBE THEY'RE NOT PAID FOR... I'VE HEARD IT SAID THAT YOUR SHOES WILL ALWAYS SQUEAK UNTIL THEY'RE PAID FOR...
DO YOU MEAN TO TELL ME THAT JUST BECAUSE MY DAD HASN'T PAID HIS BILL, I HAVE TO WALK AROUND IN SQUEAKY SHOES?
I GUESS THAT'S RIGHT..
GOOD GRIEF!
IT'S ALWAYS THE CHILDREN WHO SUFFER FOR THE SINS OF THE MOTHER AND FATHER!
SCHULZ

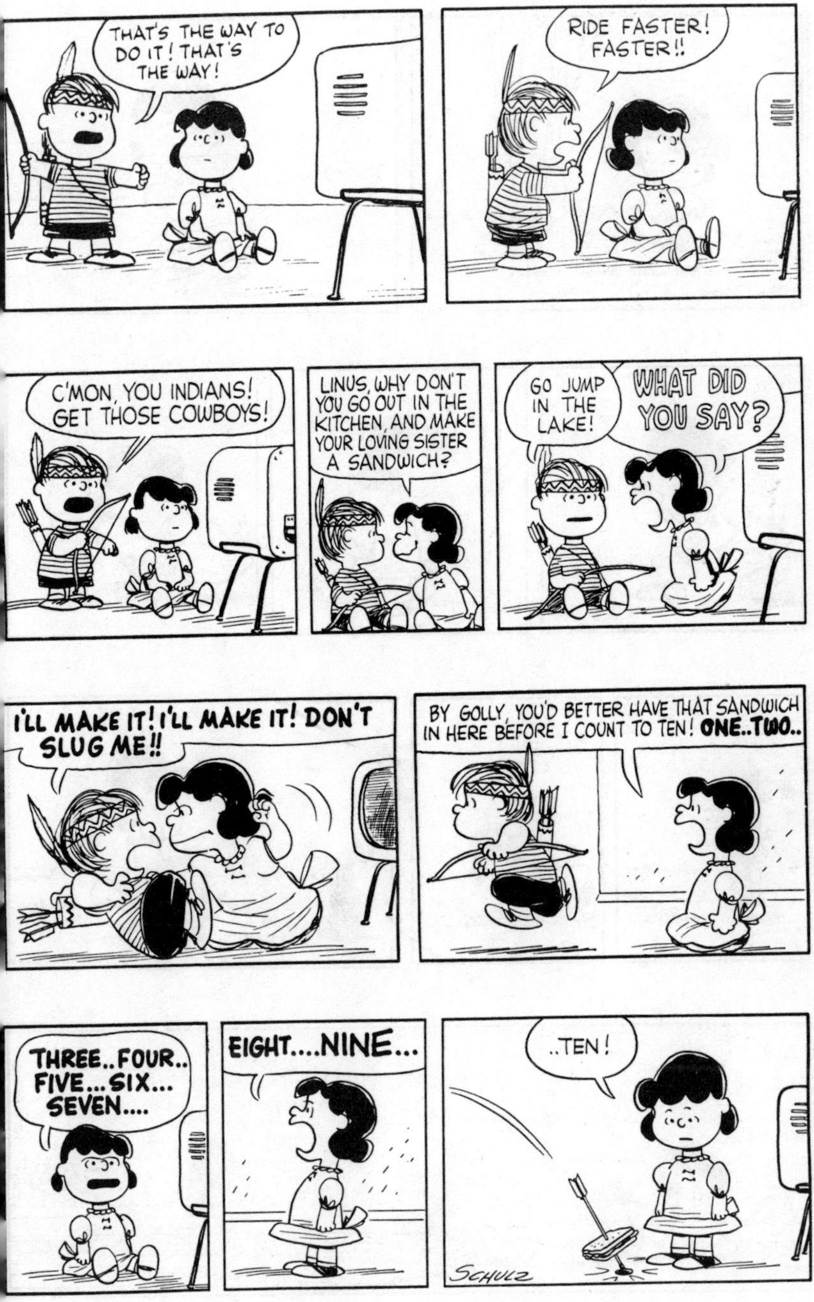

THAT'S THE WAY TO DO IT! THAT'S THE WAY!
RIDE FASTER! FASTER!!
C'MON, YOU INDIANS! GET THOSE COWBOYS!
LINUS, WHY DON'T YOU GO OUT IN THE KITCHEN, AND MAKE YOUR LOVING SISTER A SANDWICH?
GO JUMP IN THE LAKE!
WHAT DID YOU SAY?
I'LL MAKE IT! I'LL MAKE IT! DON'T SLUG ME!!
BY GOLLY, YOU'D BETTER HAVE THAT SANDWICH IN HERE BEFORE I COUNT TO TEN! ONE..TWO..
THREE..FOUR.. FIVE...SIX... SEVEN....
EIGHT....NINE...
..TEN!
SCHULZ

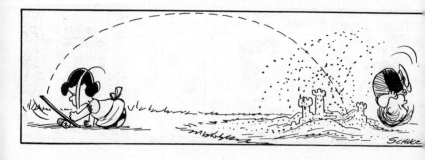

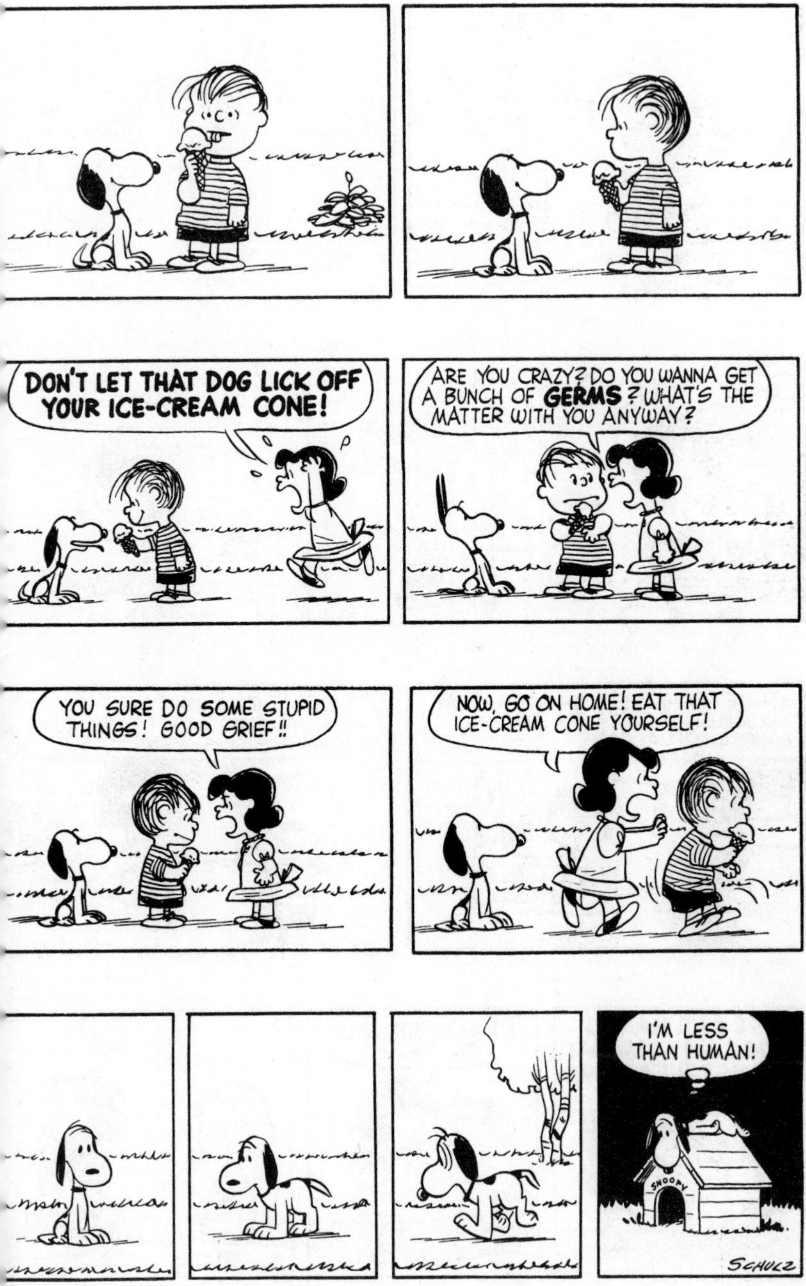
DON'T LET THAT DOG LICK OFF YOUR ICE-CREAM CONE!
ARE YOU CRAZY? DO YOU WANNA GET A BUNCH OF **GERMS**? WHAT'S THE MATTER WITH YOU ANYWAY?
YOU SURE DO SOME STUPID THINGS! GOOD GRIEF!!
NOW, GO ON HOME! EAT THAT ICE-CREAM CONE YOURSELF!
I'M LESS THAN HUMAN!
SNOOPY
SCHULZ

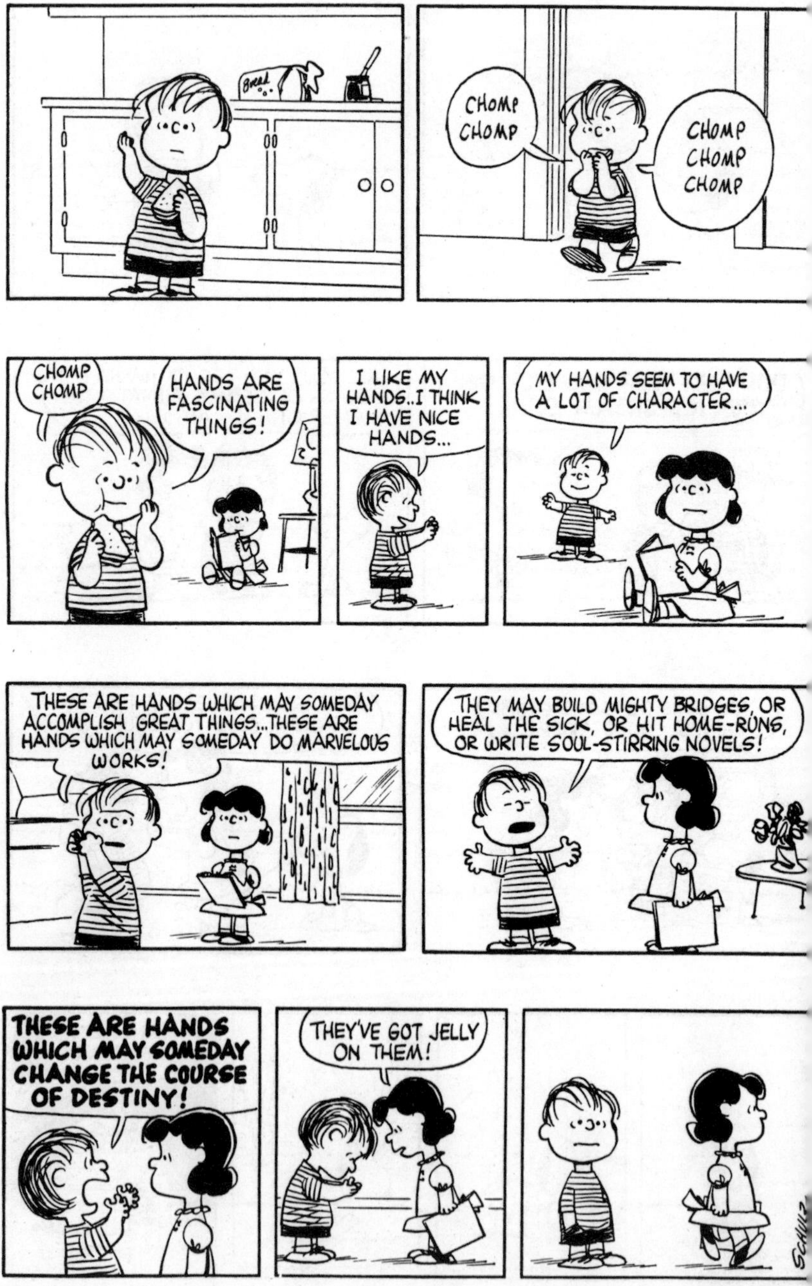
CHOMP CHOMP
CHOMP CHOMP CHOMP
CHOMP CHOMP
HANDS ARE FASCINATING THINGS!
I LIKE MY HANDS..I THINK I HAVE NICE HANDS...
MY HANDS SEEM TO HAVE A LOT OF CHARACTER...
THESE ARE HANDS WHICH MAY SOMEDAY ACCOMPLISH GREAT THINGS...THESE ARE HANDS WHICH MAY SOMEDAY DO MARVELOUS WORKS!
THEY MAY BUILD MIGHTY BRIDGES, OR HEAL THE SICK, OR HIT HOME-RUNS, OR WRITE SOUL-STIRRING NOVELS!
THESE ARE HANDS WHICH MAY SOMEDAY CHANGE THE COURSE OF DESTINY!
THEY'VE GOT JELLY ON THEM!
SCHULZ

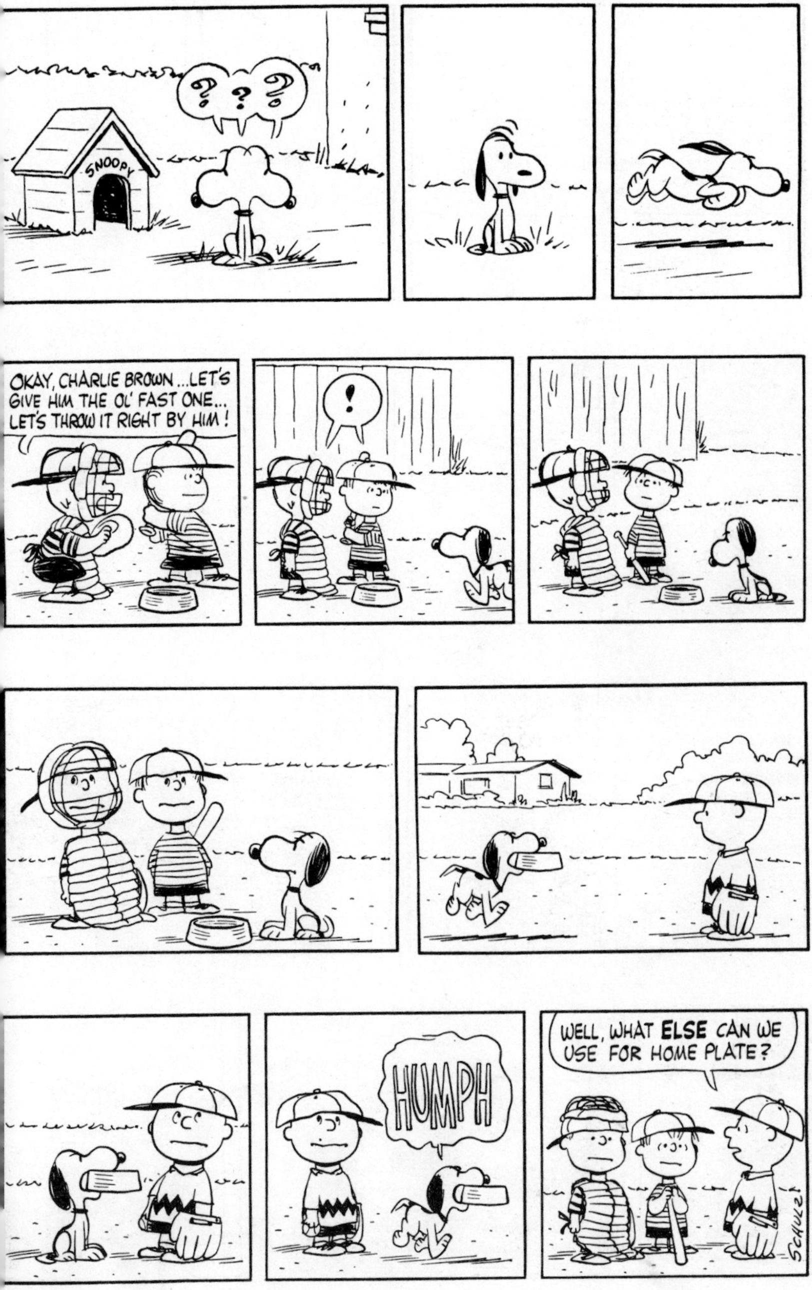

? ? ?
SNOOPY
OKAY, CHARLIE BROWN ...LET'S GIVE HIM THE OL' FAST ONE... LET'S THROW IT RIGHT BY HIM!
!
HUMPH
WELL, WHAT ELSE CAN WE USE FOR HOME PLATE?
SCHULZ

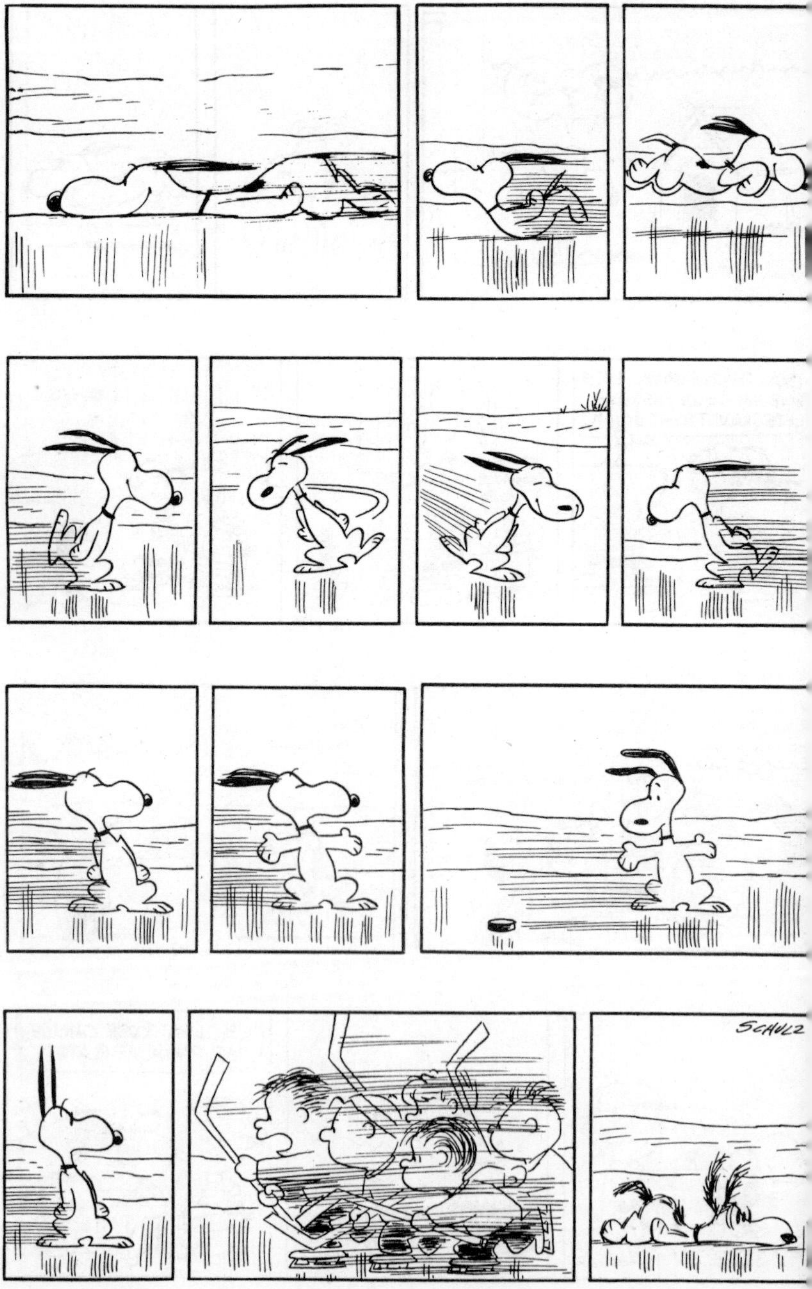
SCHULZ

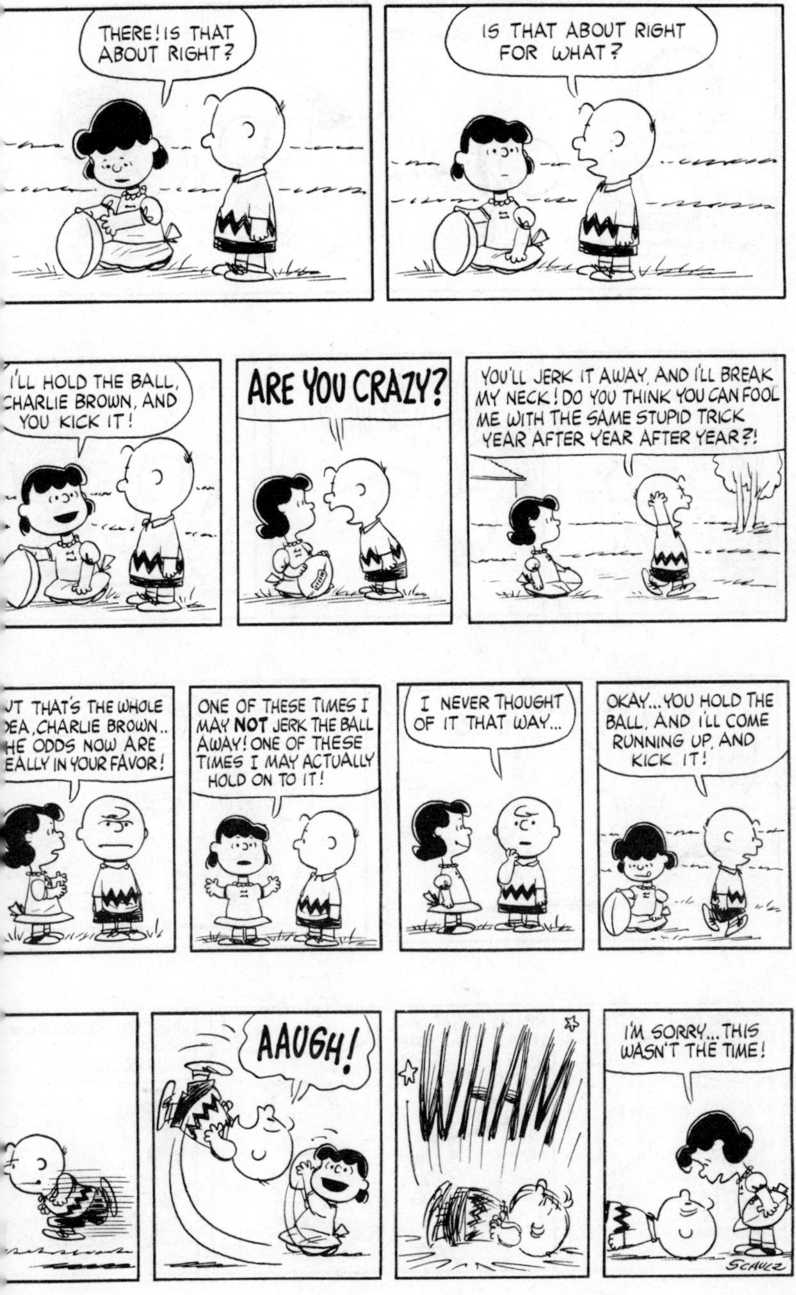
THERE! IS THAT ABOUT RIGHT?
IS THAT ABOUT RIGHT FOR WHAT?
I'LL HOLD THE BALL, CHARLIE BROWN, AND YOU KICK IT!
ARE YOU CRAZY?
YOU'LL JERK IT AWAY, AND I'LL BREAK MY NECK! DO YOU THINK YOU CAN FOOL ME WITH THE SAME STUPID TRICK YEAR AFTER YEAR AFTER YEAR?!
UT THAT'S THE WHOLE DEA, CHARLIE BROWN.. HE ODDS NOW ARE EALLY IN YOUR FAVOR!
ONE OF THESE TIMES I MAY NOT JERK THE BALL AWAY! ONE OF THESE TIMES I MAY ACTUALLY HOLD ON TO IT!
I NEVER THOUGHT OF IT THAT WAY...
OKAY... YOU HOLD THE BALL, AND I'LL COME RUNNING UP, AND KICK IT!
AAUGH!
WHAM
I'M SORRY... THIS WASN'T THE TIME!
SCHULZ

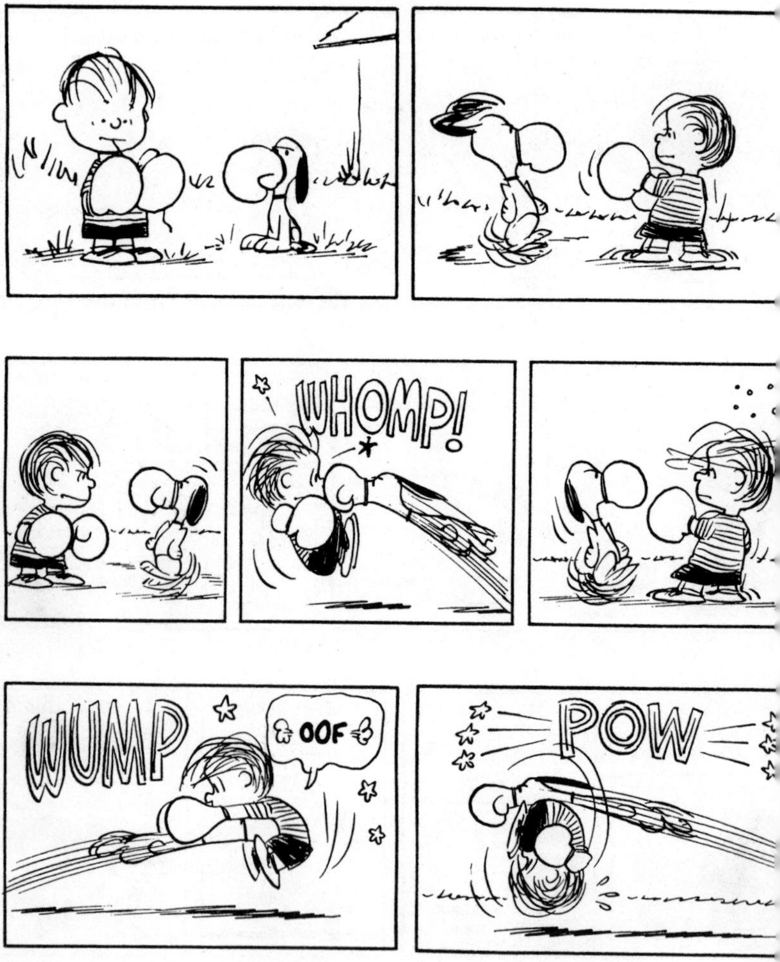
WHOMP!
WUMP
OOF
POW

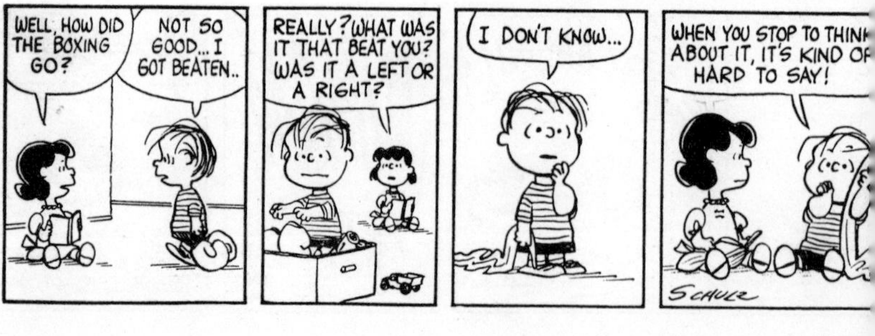
WELL, HOW DID THE BOXING GO?
NOT SO GOOD... I GOT BEATEN..
REALLY? WHAT WAS IT THAT BEAT YOU? WAS IT A LEFT OR A RIGHT?
I DON'T KNOW...
WHEN YOU STOP TO THINK ABOUT IT, IT'S KIND OF HARD TO SAY!
SCHULZ

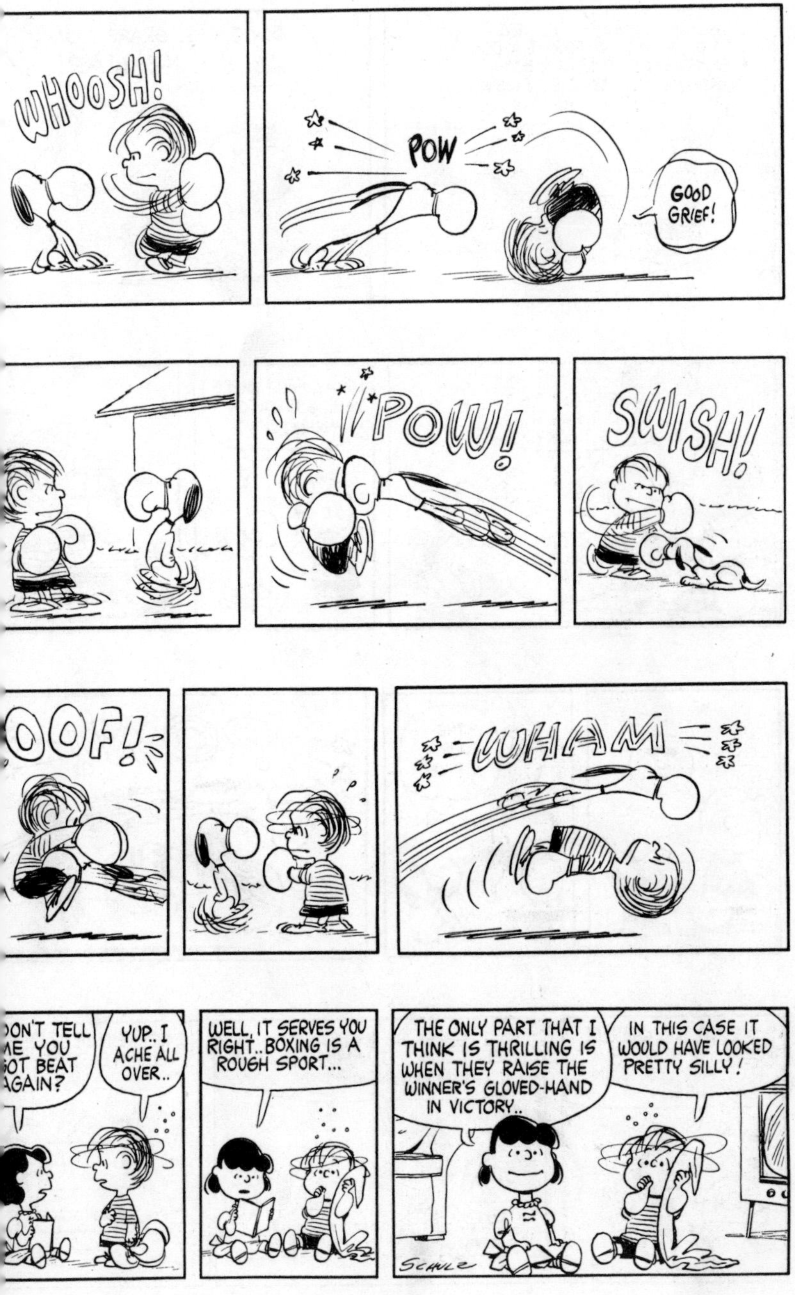
WHOOSH!
POW
GOOD GRIEF!
POW!
SWISH!
OOF!
WHAM
DON'T TELL ME YOU OT BEAT AGAIN?
YUP.. I ACHE ALL OVER..
WELL, IT SERVES YOU RIGHT.. BOXING IS A ROUGH SPORT...
THE ONLY PART THAT I THINK IS THRILLING IS WHEN THEY RAISE THE WINNER'S GLOVED-HAND IN VICTORY..
IN THIS CASE IT WOULD HAVE LOOKED PRETTY SILLY!
SCHULZ

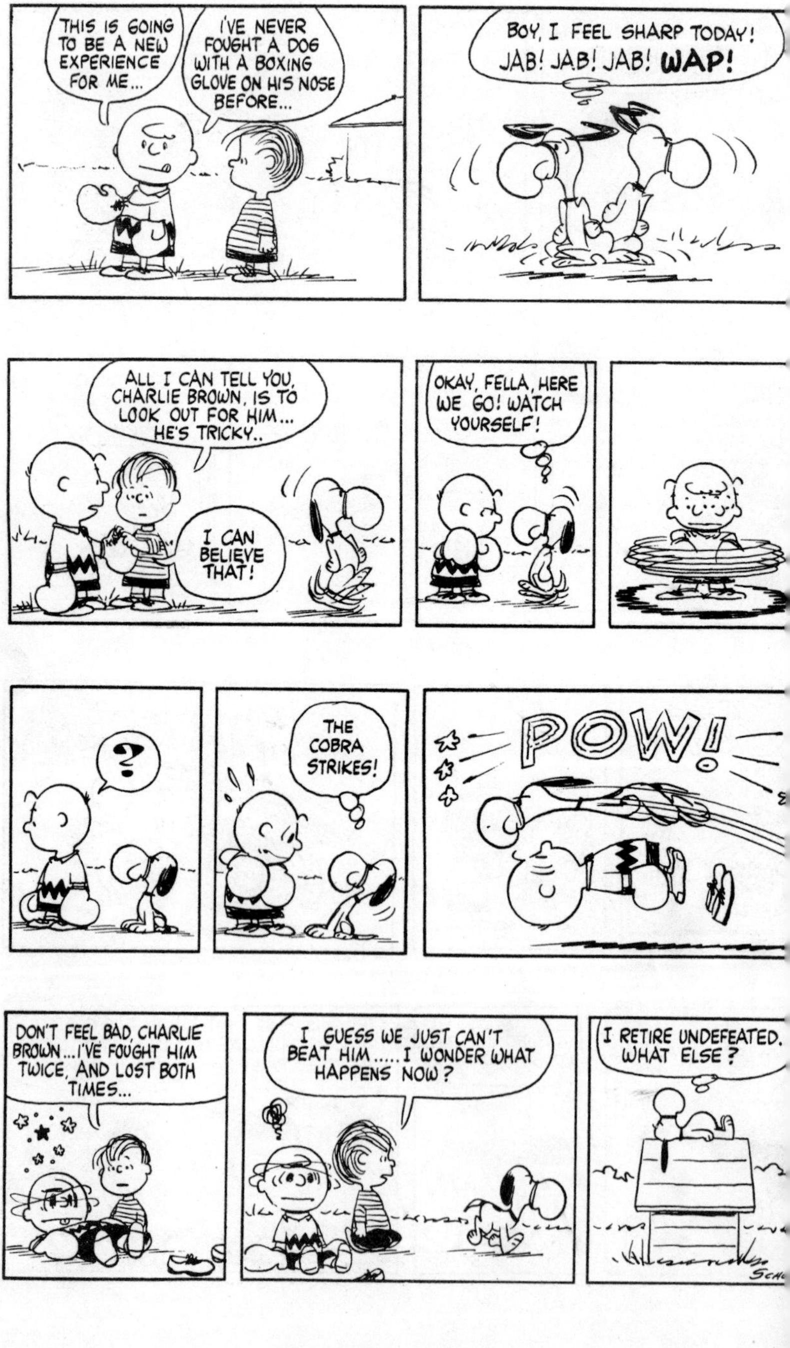
THIS IS GOING TO BE A NEW EXPERIENCE FOR ME...
I'VE NEVER FOUGHT A DOG WITH A BOXING GLOVE ON HIS NOSE BEFORE...
BOY, I FEEL SHARP TODAY! JAB! JAB! JAB! WAP!
ALL I CAN TELL YOU, CHARLIE BROWN, IS TO LOOK OUT FOR HIM... HE'S TRICKY..
I CAN BELIEVE THAT!
OKAY, FELLA, HERE WE GO! WATCH YOURSELF!
?
THE COBRA STRIKES!
POW!
DON'T FEEL BAD, CHARLIE BROWN...I'VE FOUGHT HIM TWICE, AND LOST BOTH TIMES...
I GUESS WE JUST CAN'T BEAT HIM.....I WONDER WHAT HAPPENS NOW?
I RETIRE UNDEFEATED. WHAT ELSE?

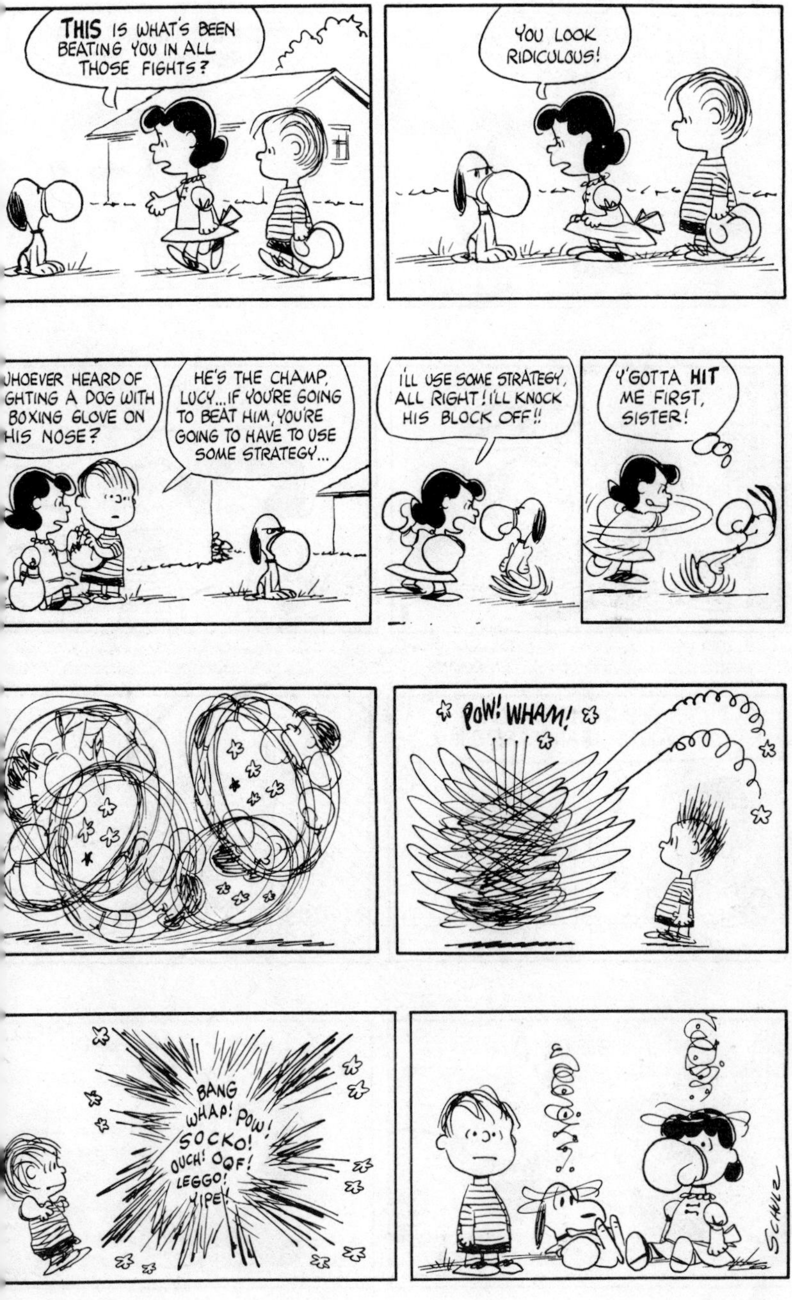

THIS IS WHAT'S BEEN BEATING YOU IN ALL THOSE FIGHTS?
YOU LOOK RIDICULOUS!
HOEVER HEARD OF GHTING A DOG WITH BOXING GLOVE ON HIS NOSE?
HE'S THE CHAMP, LUCY...IF YOU'RE GOING TO BEAT HIM, YOU'RE GOING TO HAVE TO USE SOME STRATEGY...
I'LL USE SOME STRATEGY, ALL RIGHT! I'LL KNOCK HIS BLOCK OFF!!
Y'GOTTA HIT ME FIRST, SISTER!
POW! WHAM!
BANG
WHAP! POW!
SOCKO!
OUCH! OOF!
LEGGO!
YIPE!
SCHULZ

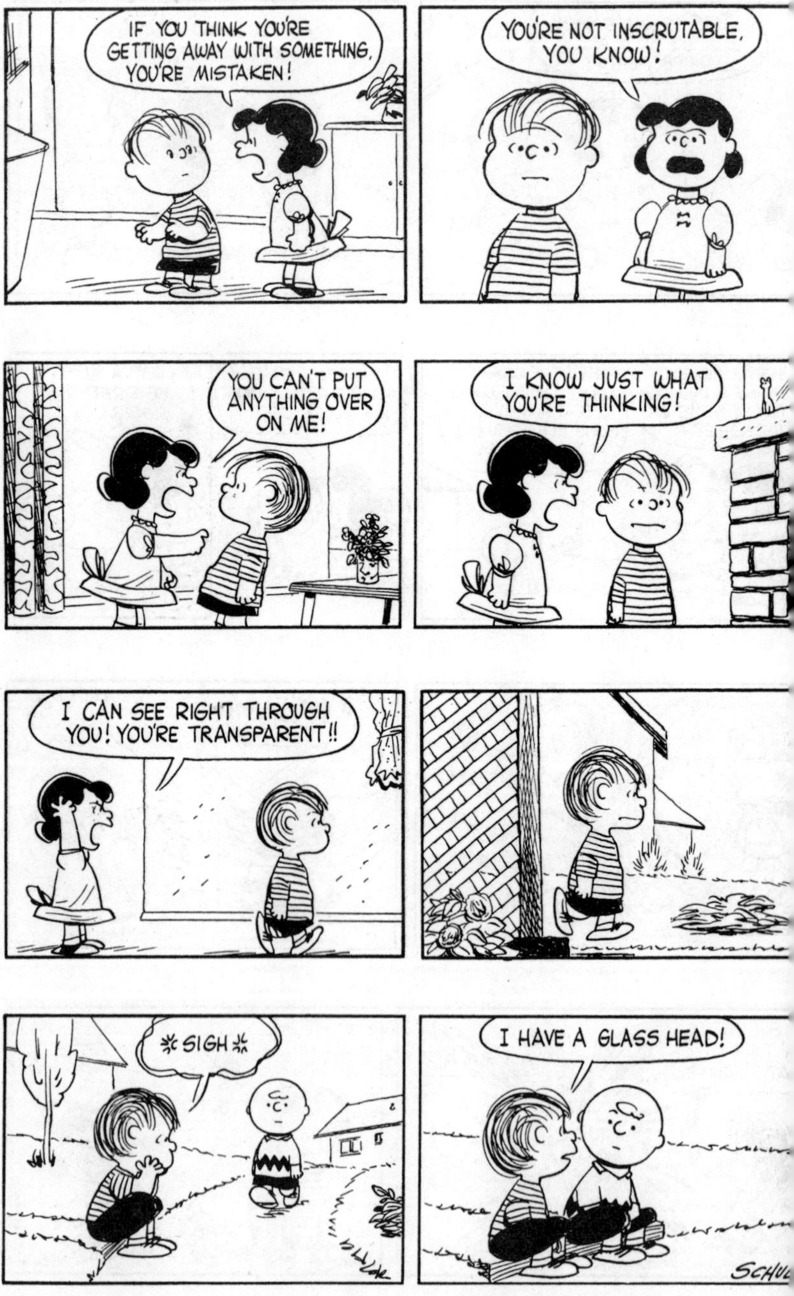
IF YOU THINK YOU'RE GETTING AWAY WITH SOMETHING, YOU'RE MISTAKEN!
YOU'RE NOT INSCRUTABLE, YOU KNOW!
YOU CAN'T PUT ANYTHING OVER ON ME!
I KNOW JUST WHAT YOU'RE THINKING!
I CAN SEE RIGHT THROUGH YOU! YOU'RE TRANSPARENT!!
SIGH
I HAVE A GLASS HEAD!

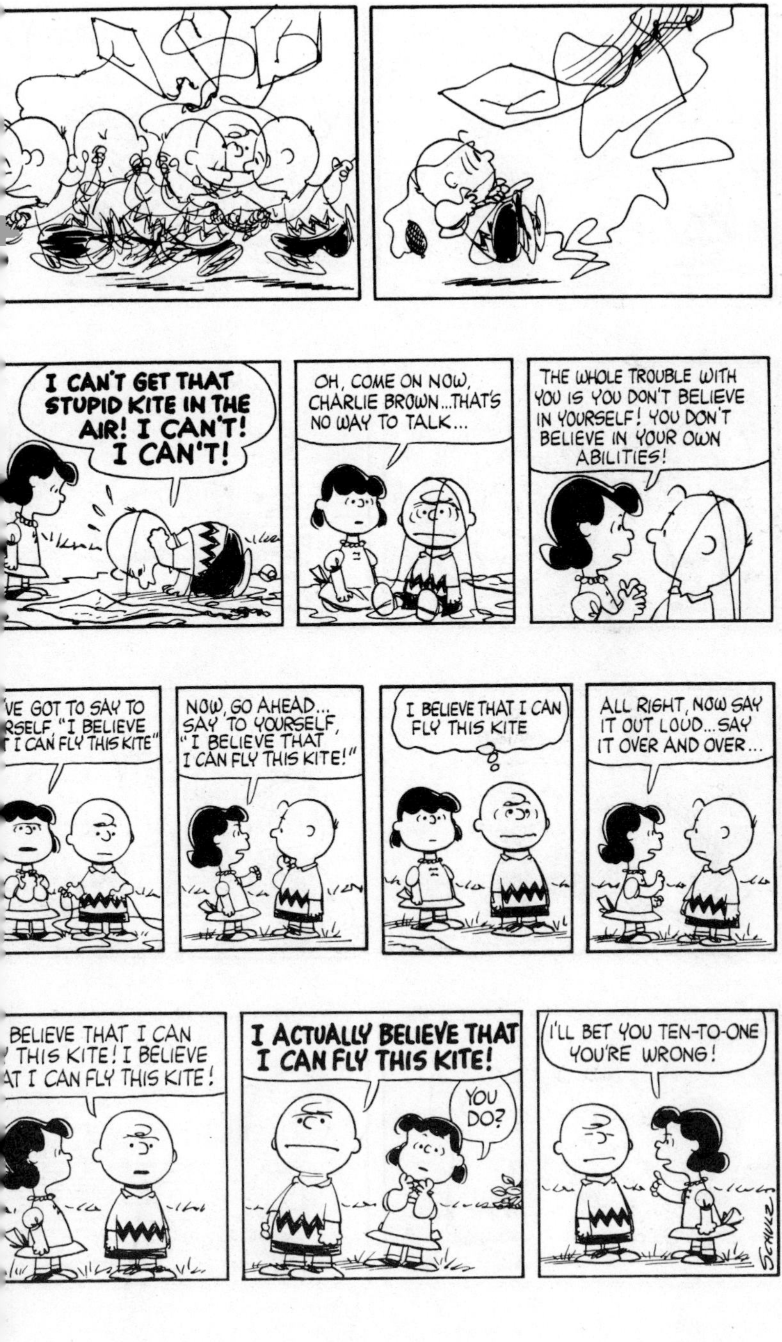
I CAN'T GET THAT STUPID KITE IN THE AIR! I CAN'T! I CAN'T!
OH, COME ON NOW, CHARLIE BROWN...THAT'S NO WAY TO TALK...
THE WHOLE TROUBLE WITH YOU IS YOU DON'T BELIEVE IN YOURSELF! YOU DON'T BELIEVE IN YOUR OWN ABILITIES!
'VE GOT TO SAY TO RSELF, "I BELIEVE T I CAN FLY THIS KITE"
NOW, GO AHEAD... SAY TO YOURSELF, "I BELIEVE THAT I CAN FLY THIS KITE!"
I BELIEVE THAT I CAN FLY THIS KITE
ALL RIGHT, NOW SAY IT OUT LOUD...SAY IT OVER AND OVER...
BELIEVE THAT I CAN THIS KITE! I BELIEVE AT I CAN FLY THIS KITE!
I ACTUALLY BELIEVE THAT I CAN FLY THIS KITE!
YOU DO?
I'LL BET YOU TEN-TO-ONE YOU'RE WRONG!
SCHULZ

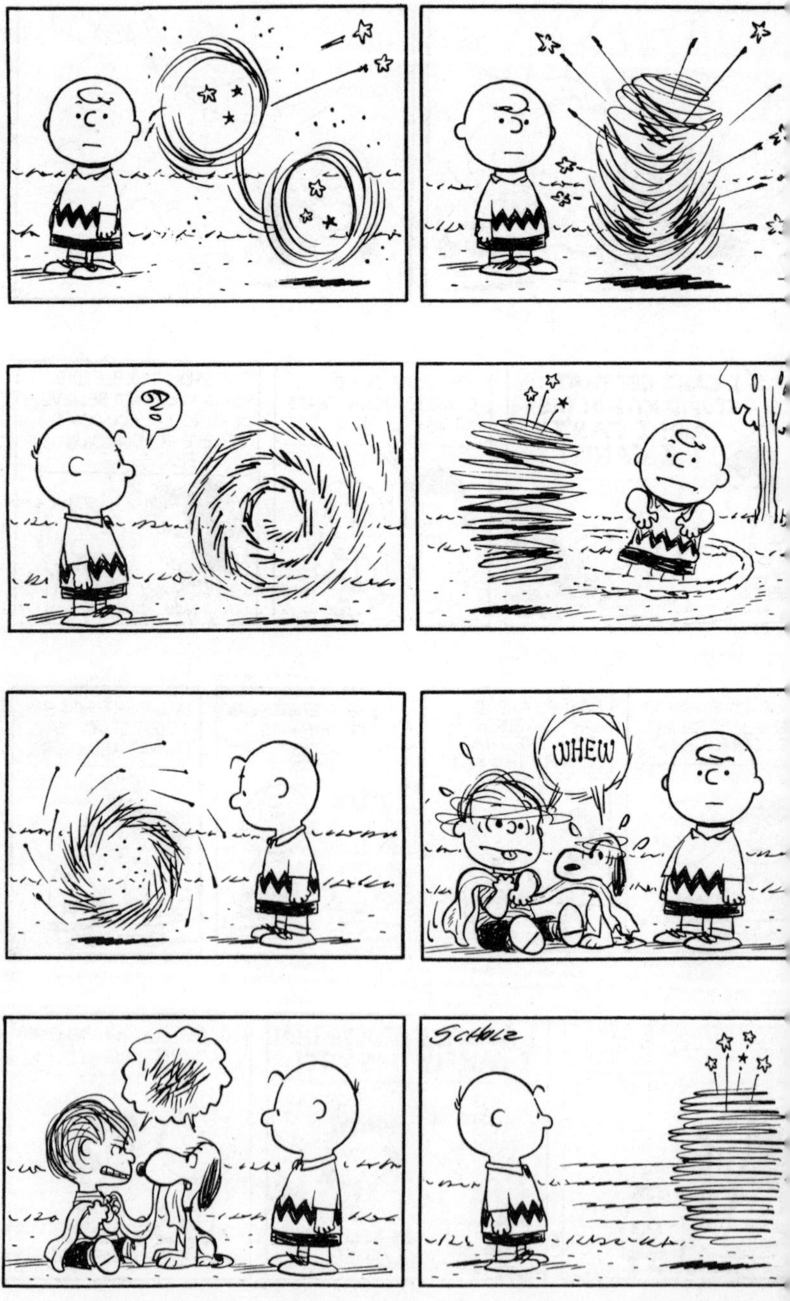
WHEW
SCHULZ

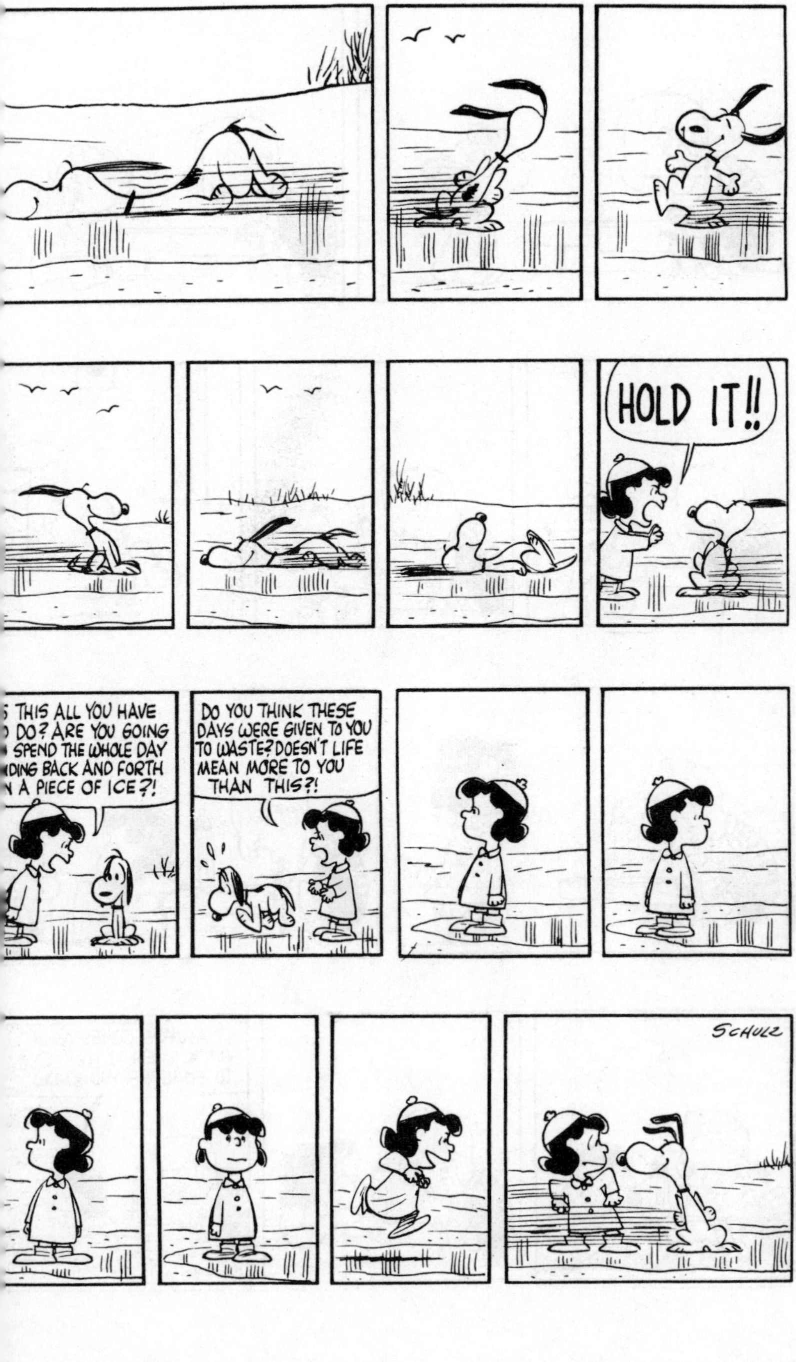
HOLD IT!!
THIS ALL YOU HAVE
DO? ARE YOU GOING
SPEND THE WHOLE DAY
DING BACK AND FORTH
A PIECE OF ICE?!
DO YOU THINK THESE
DAYS WERE GIVEN TO YOU
TO WASTE? DOESN'T LIFE
MEAN MORE TO YOU
THAN THIS?!
SCHULZ

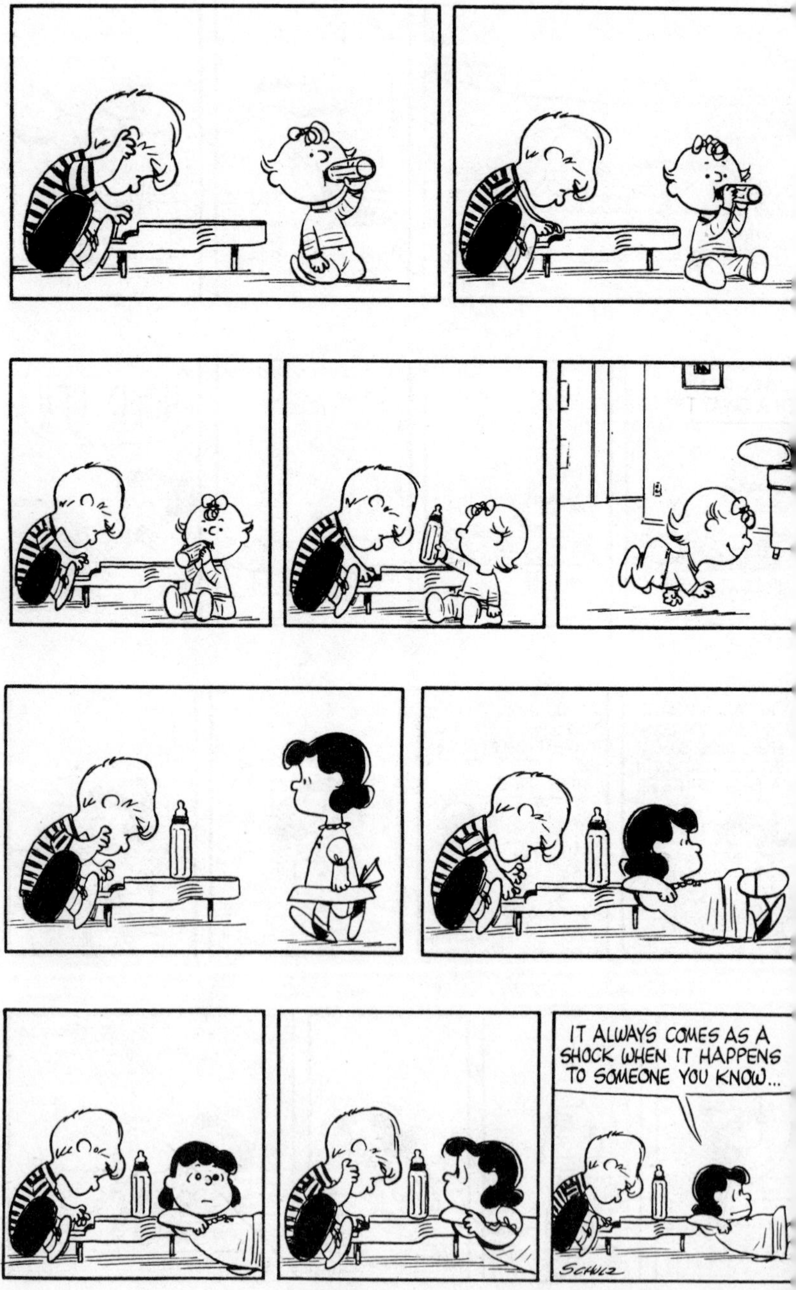
IT ALWAYS COMES AS A SHOCK WHEN IT HAPPENS TO SOMEONE YOU KNOW...
SCHULZ

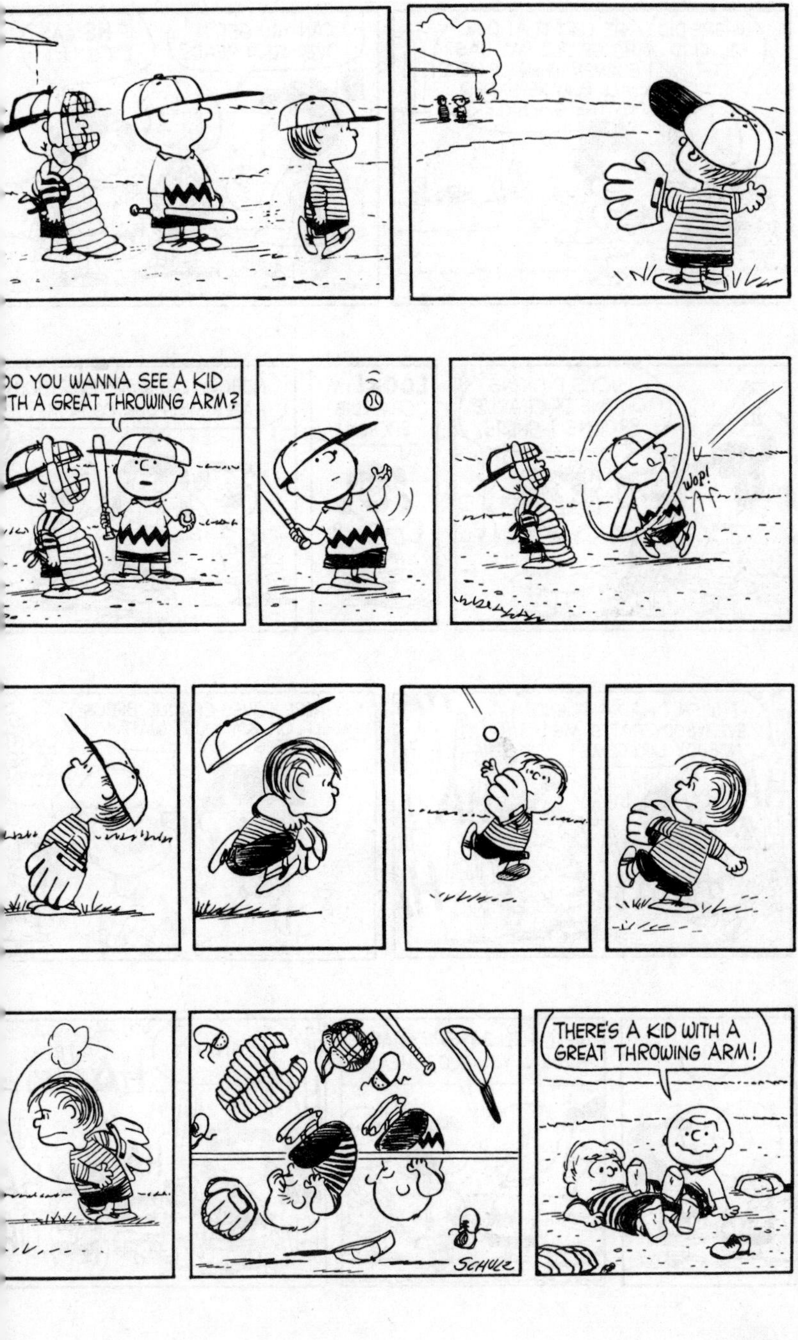

DO YOU WANNA SEE A KID
WITH A GREAT THROWING ARM?
WOP!
THERE'S A KID WITH A
GREAT THROWING ARM!
SCHULZ

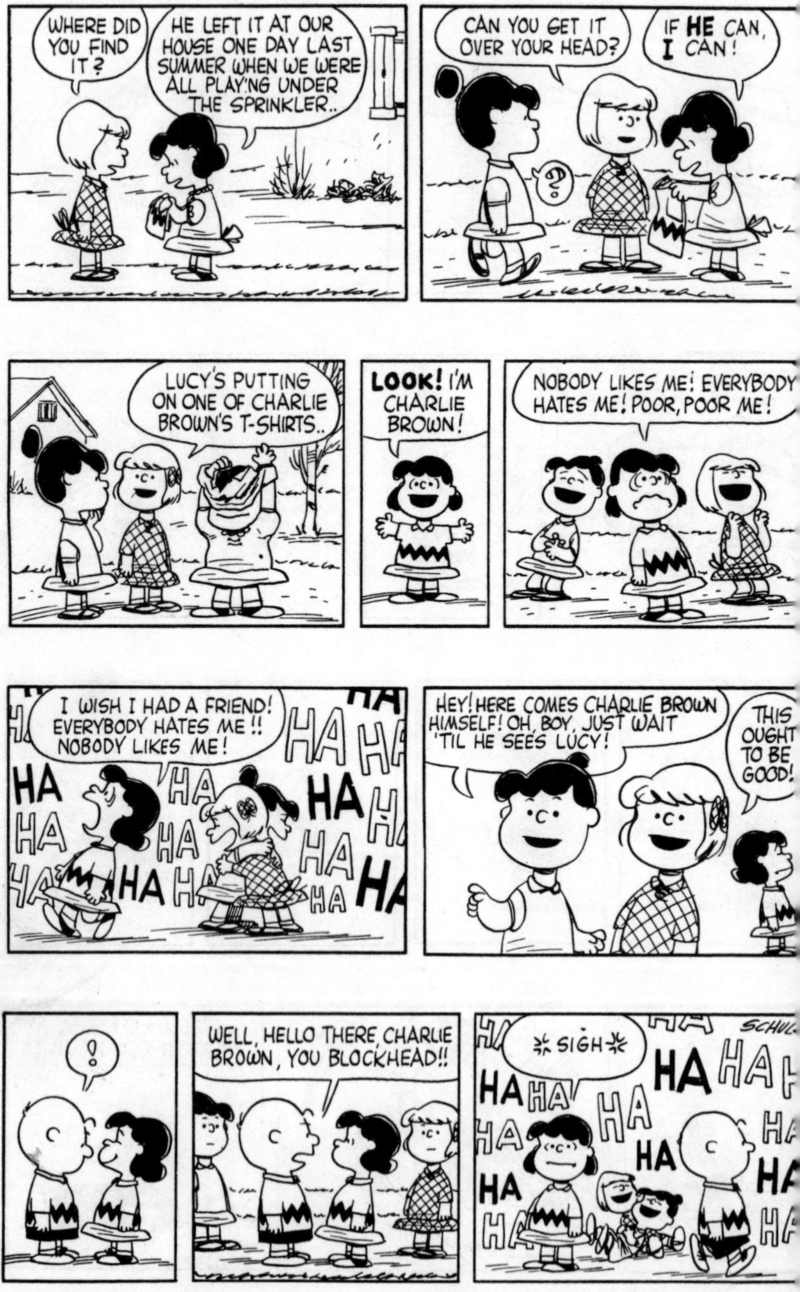
WHERE DID YOU FIND IT?
HE LEFT IT AT OUR HOUSE ONE DAY LAST SUMMER WHEN WE WERE ALL PLAY'NG UNDER THE SPRINKLER..
CAN YOU GET IT OVER YOUR HEAD?
IF HE CAN, I CAN!
?
LUCY'S PUTTING ON ONE OF CHARLIE BROWN'S T-SHIRTS..
LOOK! I'M CHARLIE BROWN!
NOBODY LIKES ME! EVERYBODY HATES ME! POOR, POOR ME!
I WISH I HAD A FRIEND! EVERYBODY HATES ME!! NOBODY LIKES ME!
HA HA HA HA HA HA HA HA HA HA
HEY! HERE COMES CHARLIE BROWN HIMSELF! OH, BOY, JUST WAIT 'TIL HE SEES LUCY!
THIS OUGHT TO BE GOOD!
!
WELL, HELLO THERE, CHARLIE BROWN, YOU BLOCKHEAD!!
SIGH
HA HA HA HA HA HA HA HA

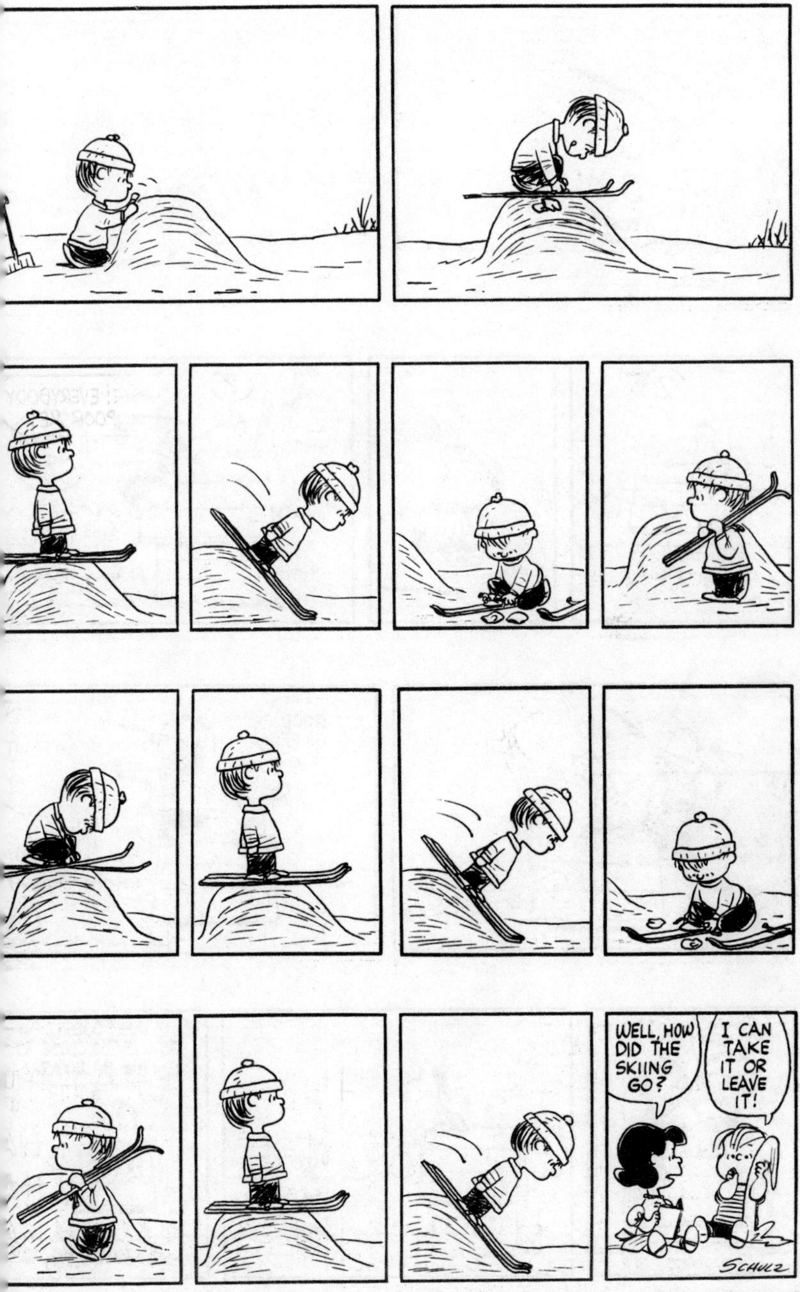
WELL, HOW DID THE SKIING GO?
I CAN TAKE IT OR LEAVE IT!
SCHULZ

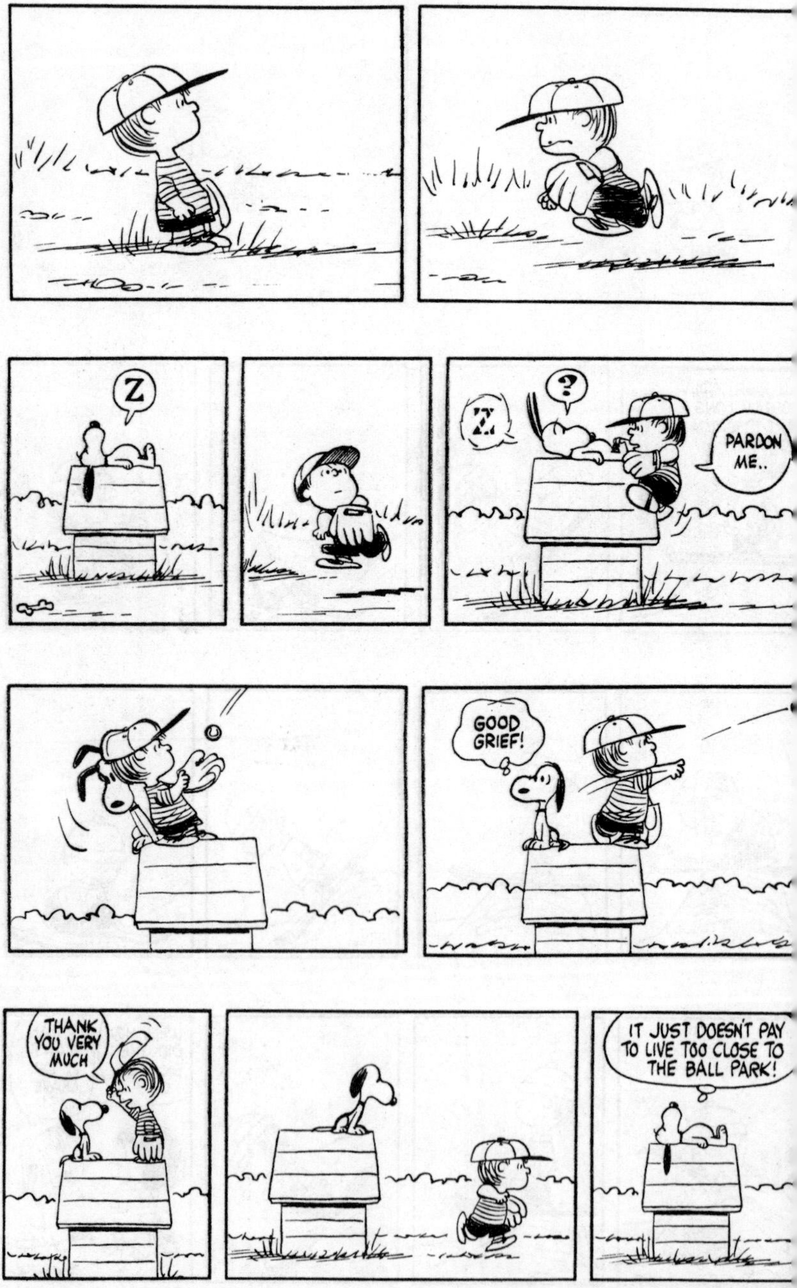
Z
Z
?
PARDON ME..
GOOD GRIEF!
THANK YOU VERY MUCH
IT JUST DOESN'T PAY TO LIVE TOO CLOSE TO THE BALL PARK!

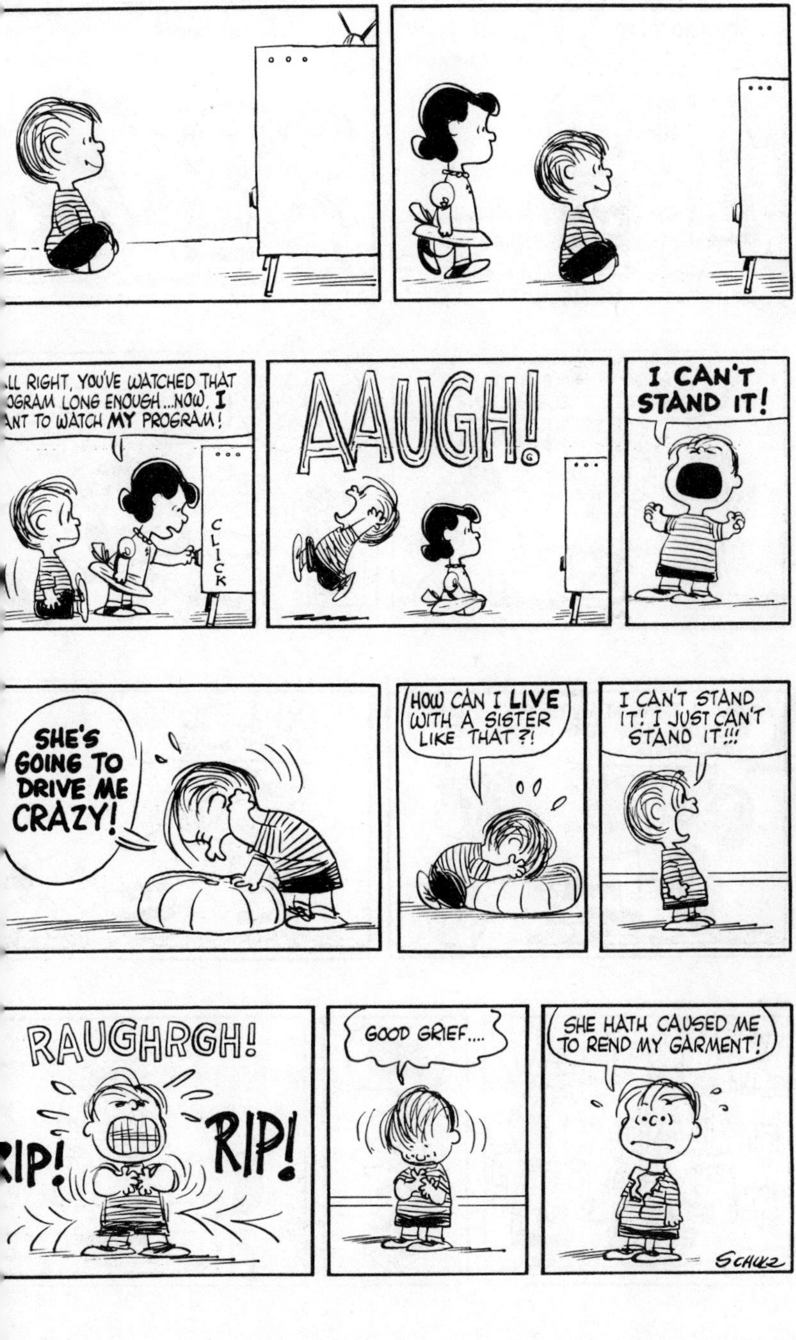
LL RIGHT, YOU'VE WATCHED THAT
OGRAM LONG ENOUGH...NOW, I
ANT TO WATCH MY PROGRAM!
CLICK
AAUGH!
I CAN'T STAND IT!
SHE'S GOING TO DRIVE ME CRAZY!
HOW CAN I LIVE WITH A SISTER LIKE THAT?!
I CAN'T STAND IT! I JUST CAN'T STAND IT!!!
RAUGHRGH!
IP!
RIP!
GOOD GRIEF....
SHE HATH CAUSED ME TO REND MY GARMENT!
SCHULZ

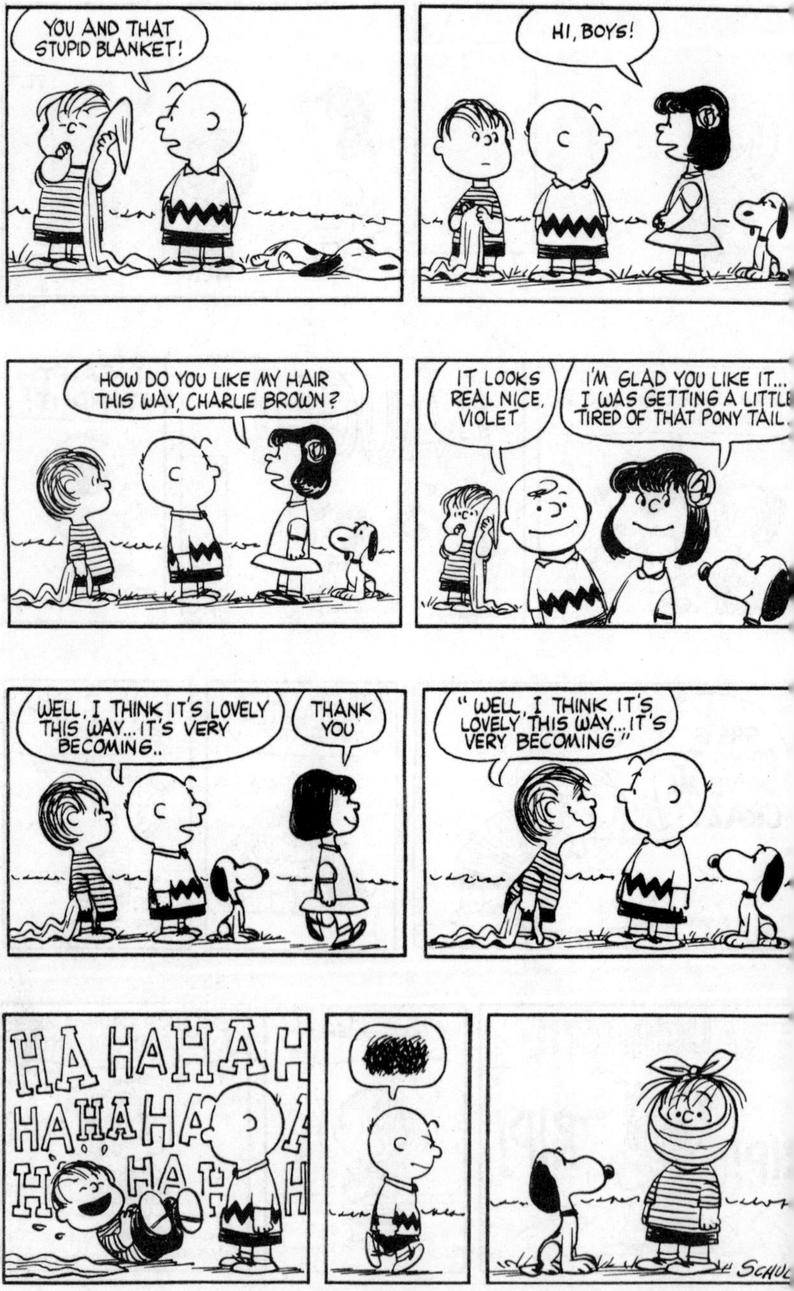
YOU AND THAT STUPID BLANKET!
HI, BOYS!
HOW DO YOU LIKE MY HAIR THIS WAY, CHARLIE BROWN?
IT LOOKS REAL NICE, VIOLET
I'M GLAD YOU LIKE IT... I WAS GETTING A LITTLE TIRED OF THAT PONY TAIL
WELL, I THINK IT'S LOVELY THIS WAY... IT'S VERY BECOMING..
THANK YOU
"WELL, I THINK IT'S LOVELY THIS WAY... IT'S VERY BECOMING"
HA HAHAH
HAHAHA
HA
SCHU

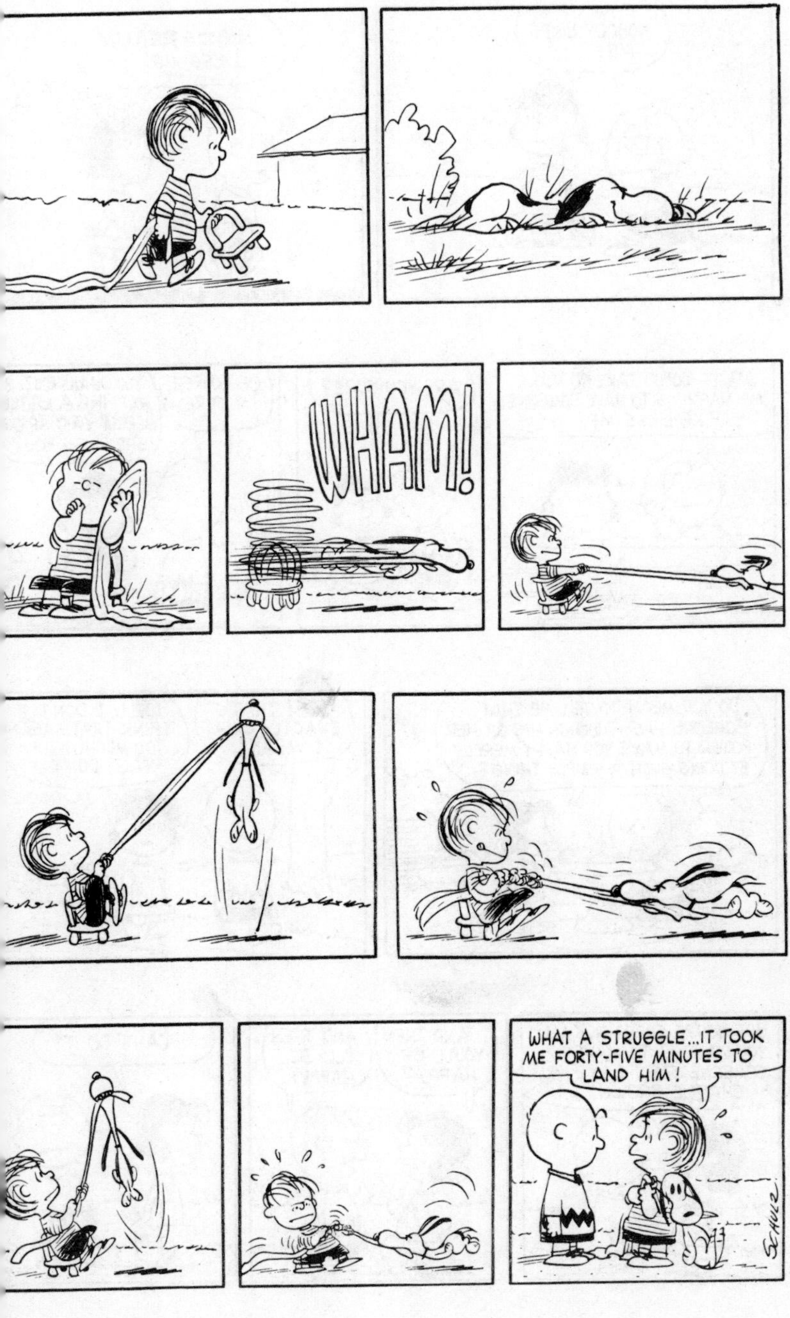
WHAM!
WHAT A STRUGGLE...IT TOOK ME FORTY-FIVE MINUTES TO LAND HIM!
SCHULZ

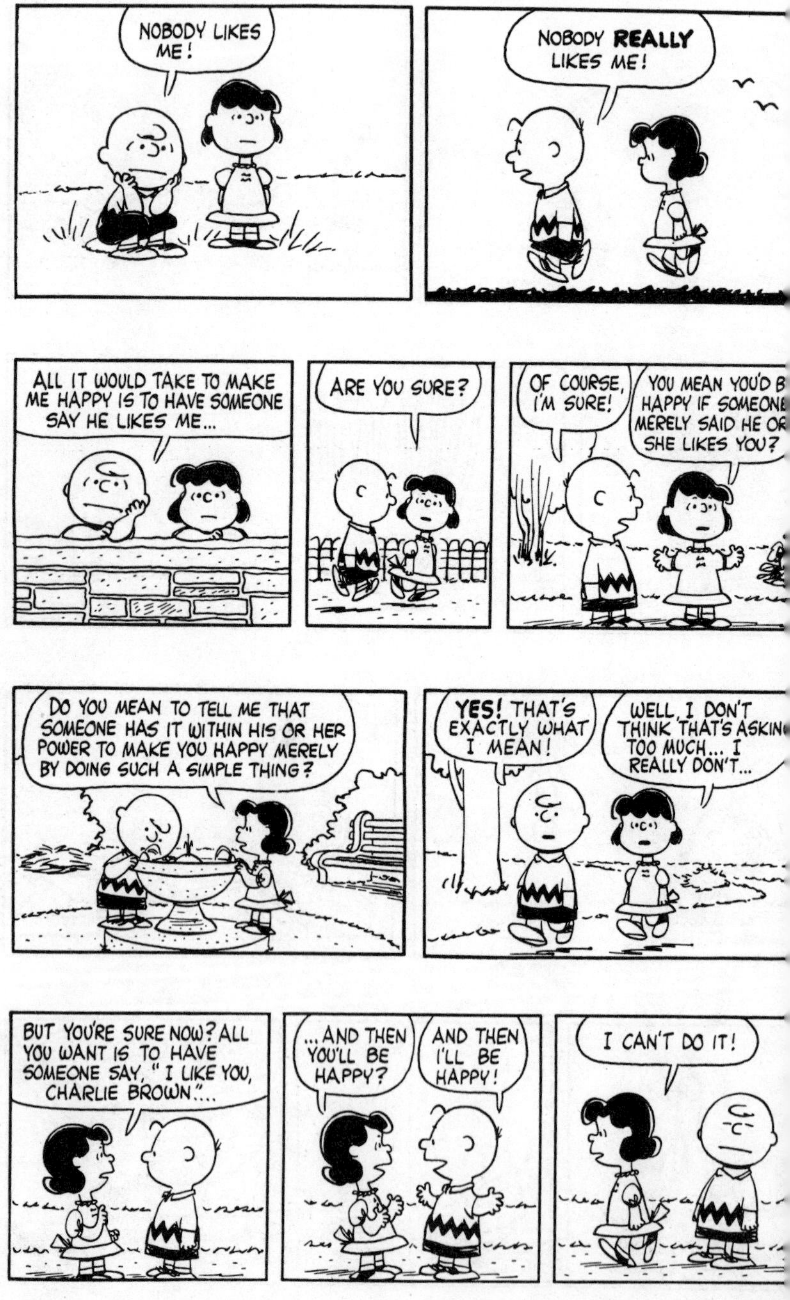
NOBODY LIKES ME!
NOBODY **REALLY** LIKES ME!
ALL IT WOULD TAKE TO MAKE ME HAPPY IS TO HAVE SOMEONE SAY HE LIKES ME...
ARE YOU SURE?
OF COURSE, I'M SURE!
YOU MEAN YOU'D B
HAPPY IF SOMEON
MERELY SAID HE OR
SHE LIKES YOU?
DO YOU MEAN TO TELL ME THAT SOMEONE HAS IT WITHIN HIS OR HER POWER TO MAKE YOU HAPPY MERELY BY DOING SUCH A SIMPLE THING?
YES! THAT'S EXACTLY WHAT I MEAN!
WELL, I DON'T
THINK THAT'S ASKIN
TOO MUCH... I
REALLY DON'T...
BUT YOU'RE SURE NOW? ALL YOU WANT IS TO HAVE SOMEONE SAY, "I LIKE YOU, CHARLIE BROWN."...
...AND THEN YOU'LL BE HAPPY?
AND THEN I'LL BE HAPPY!
I CAN'T DO IT!

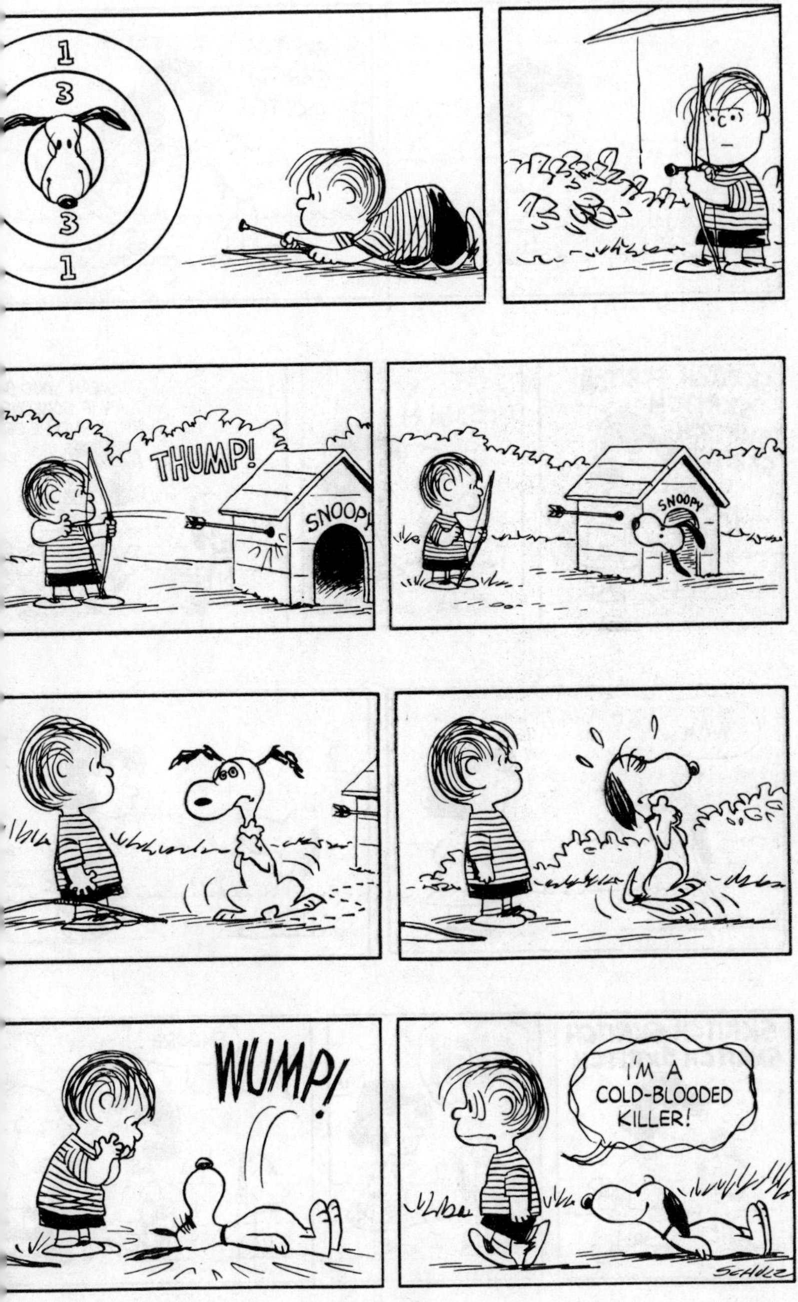
1
3
3
1
THUMP!
SNOOPY
SNOOPY
WUMP!
I'M A COLD-BLOODED KILLER!
SCHULZ

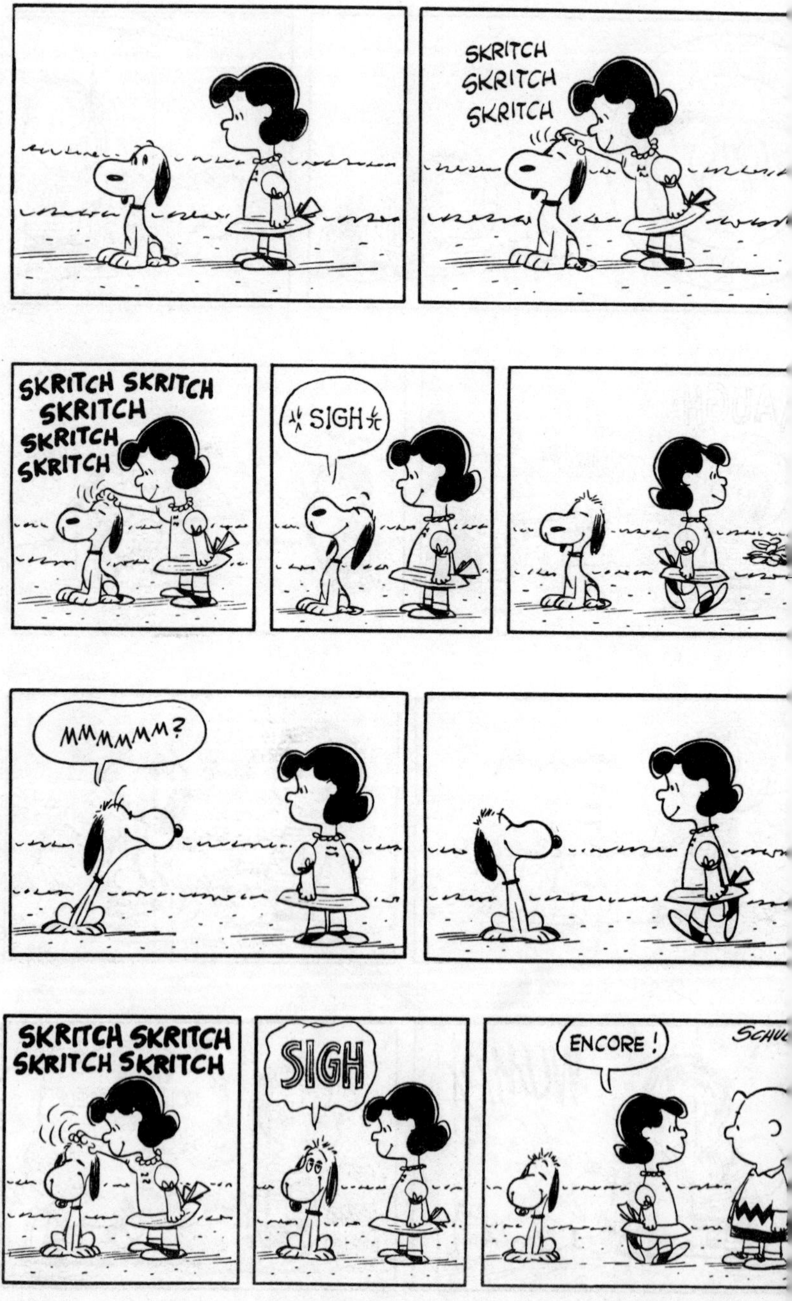
SKRITCH
SKRITCH
SKRITCH
SKRITCH SKRITCH
SKRITCH
SKRITCH
SKRITCH
SIGH
MMMMMM?
SKRITCH SKRITCH
SKRITCH SKRITCH
SIGH
ENCORE!

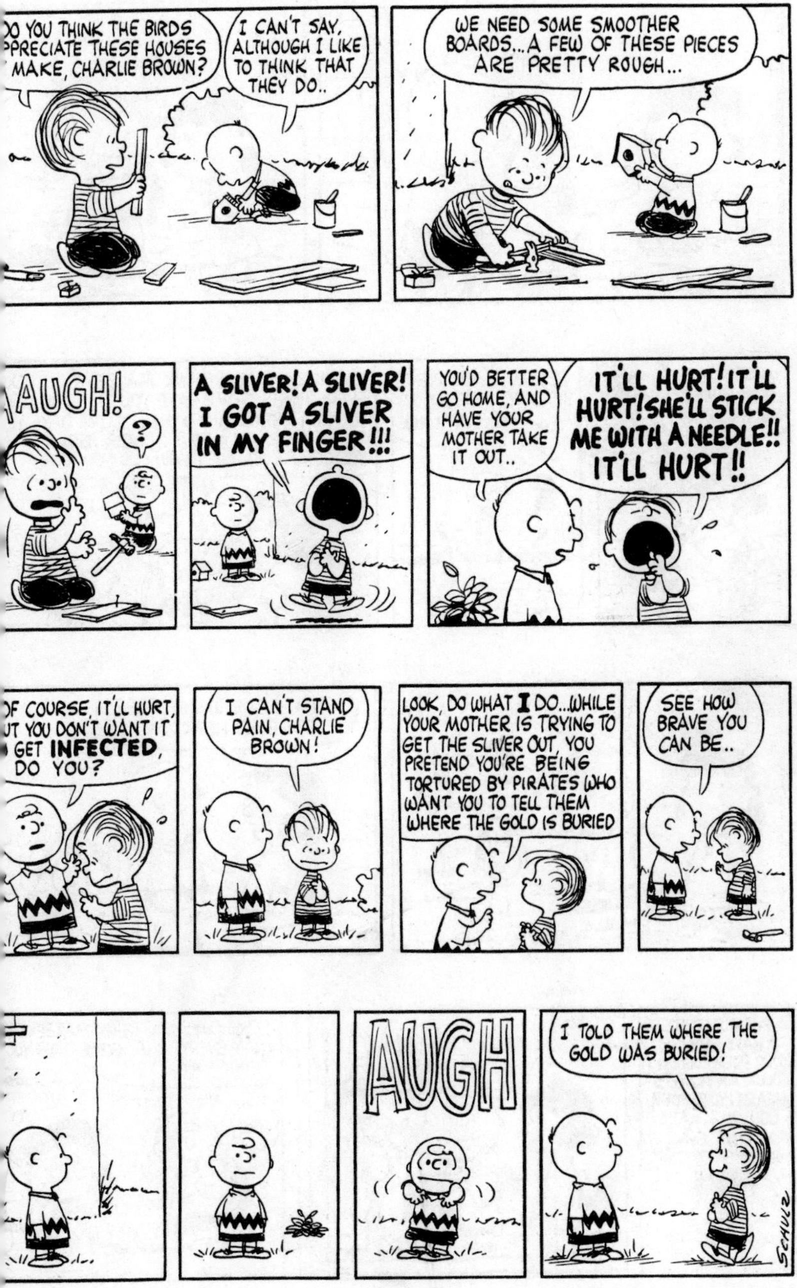
O YOU THINK THE BIRDS PPRECIATE THESE HOUSES MAKE, CHARLIE BROWN?
I CAN'T SAY, ALTHOUGH I LIKE TO THINK THAT THEY DO..
WE NEED SOME SMOOTHER BOARDS... A FEW OF THESE PIECES ARE PRETTY ROUGH...
AUGH!
?
A SLIVER! A SLIVER! I GOT A SLIVER IN MY FINGER!!!
YOU'D BETTER GO HOME, AND HAVE YOUR MOTHER TAKE IT OUT..
IT'LL HURT! IT'LL HURT! SHE'LL STICK ME WITH A NEEDLE!! IT'LL HURT!!
OF COURSE, IT'LL HURT, UT YOU DON'T WANT IT GET INFECTED, DO YOU?
I CAN'T STAND PAIN, CHARLIE BROWN!
LOOK, DO WHAT I DO...WHILE YOUR MOTHER IS TRYING TO GET THE SLIVER OUT, YOU PRETEND YOU'RE BEING TORTURED BY PIRATES WHO WANT YOU TO TELL THEM WHERE THE GOLD IS BURIED
SEE HOW BRAVE YOU CAN BE..
AUGH
I TOLD THEM WHERE THE GOLD WAS BURIED!
SCHULZ

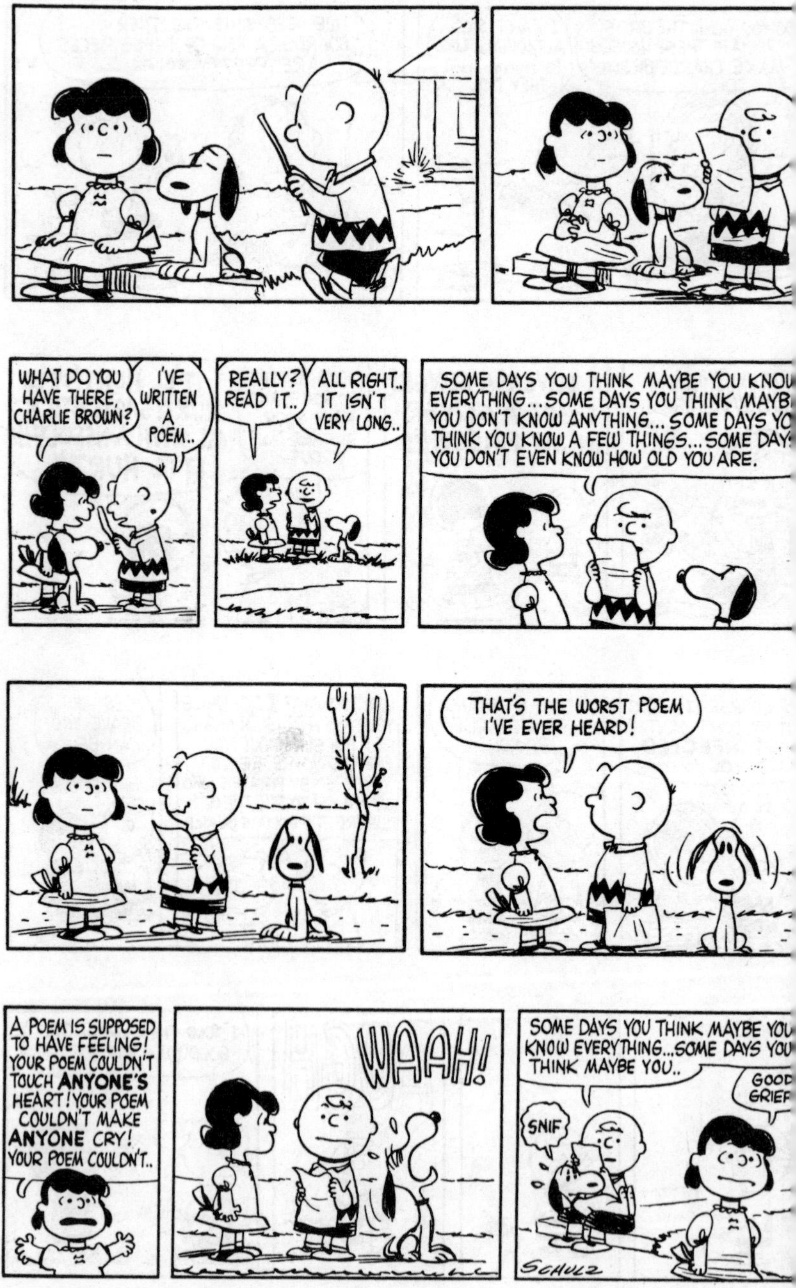
WHAT DO YOU HAVE THERE, CHARLIE BROWN?
I'VE WRITTEN A POEM..
REALLY? READ IT..
ALL RIGHT.. IT ISN'T VERY LONG..
SOME DAYS YOU THINK MAYBE YOU KNO
EVERYTHING...SOME DAYS YOU THINK MAYB
YOU DON'T KNOW ANYTHING... SOME DAYS YO
THINK YOU KNOW A FEW THINGS...SOME DAY
YOU DON'T EVEN KNOW HOW OLD YOU ARE.
THAT'S THE WORST POEM I'VE EVER HEARD!
A POEM IS SUPPOSED TO HAVE FEELING! YOUR POEM COULDN'T TOUCH ANYONE'S HEART! YOUR POEM COULDN'T MAKE ANYONE CRY! YOUR POEM COULDN'T..
WAAH!
SOME DAYS YOU THINK MAYBE YO
KNOW EVERYTHING...SOME DAYS YO
THINK MAYBE YOU..
SNIF
GOOD GRIEF
SCHULZ

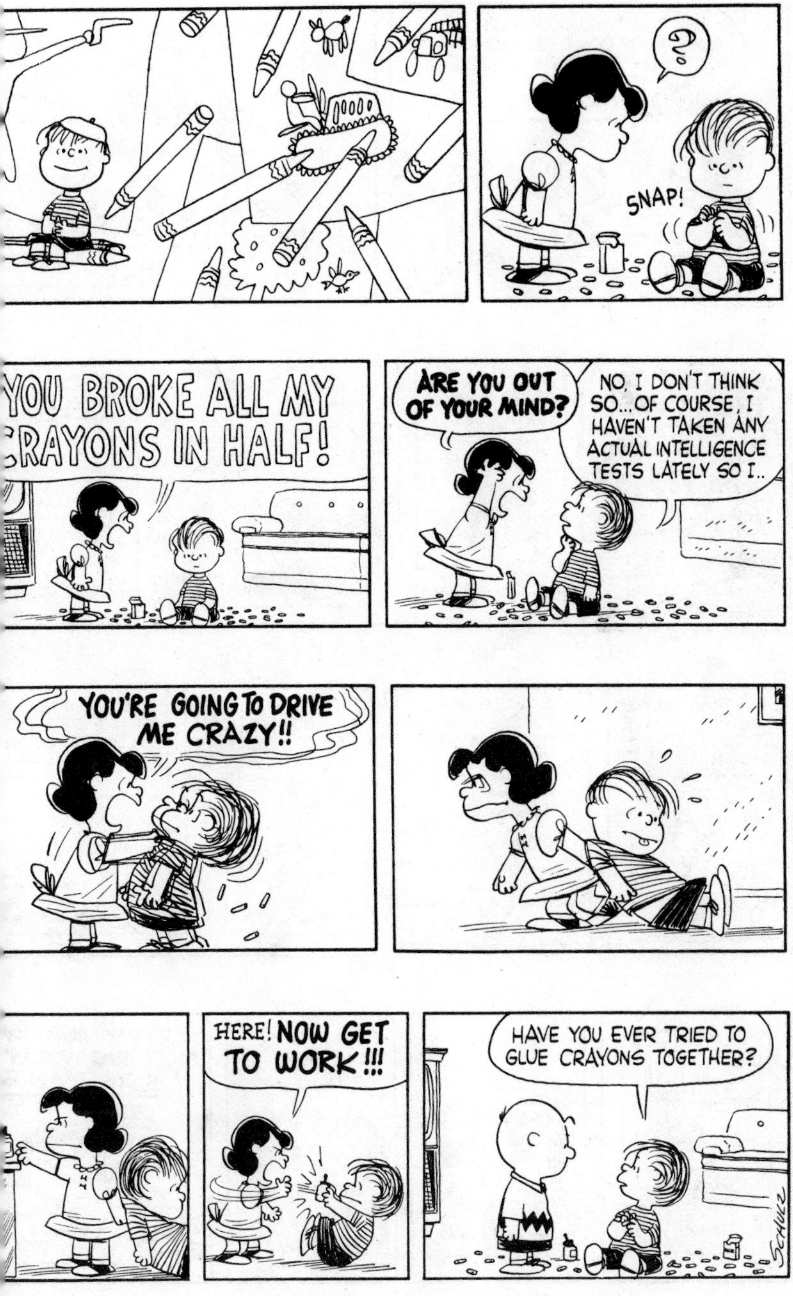
?
SNAP!
YOU BROKE ALL MY CRAYONS IN HALF!
ARE YOU OUT OF YOUR MIND?
NO, I DON'T THINK SO...OF COURSE, I HAVEN'T TAKEN ANY ACTUAL INTELLIGENCE TESTS LATELY SO I..
YOU'RE GOING TO DRIVE ME CRAZY!!
HERE! NOW GET TO WORK!!!
HAVE YOU EVER TRIED TO GLUE CRAYONS TOGETHER?
SCHULZ

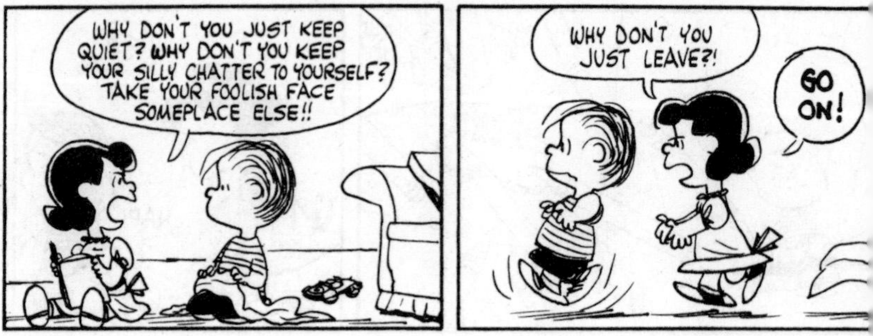

WHY DON'T YOU JUST KEEP QUIET? WHY DON'T YOU KEEP YOUR SILLY CHATTER TO YOURSELF? TAKE YOUR FOOLISH FACE SOMEPLACE ELSE!!
WHY DON'T YOU JUST LEAVE?!
GO ON!

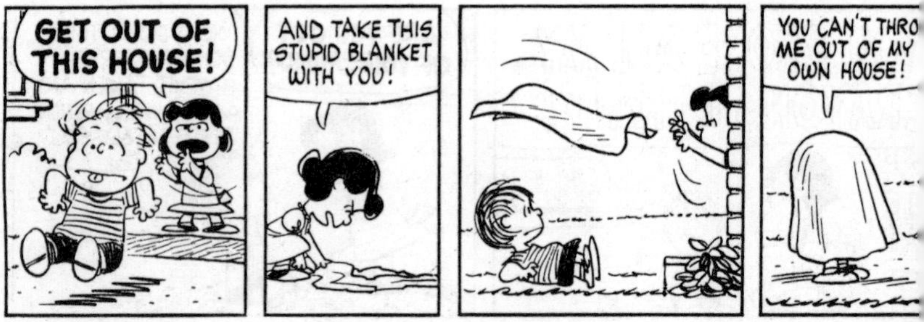

GET OUT OF THIS HOUSE!
AND TAKE THIS STUPID BLANKET WITH YOU!
YOU CAN'T THRO
ME OUT OF MY
OWN HOUSE!

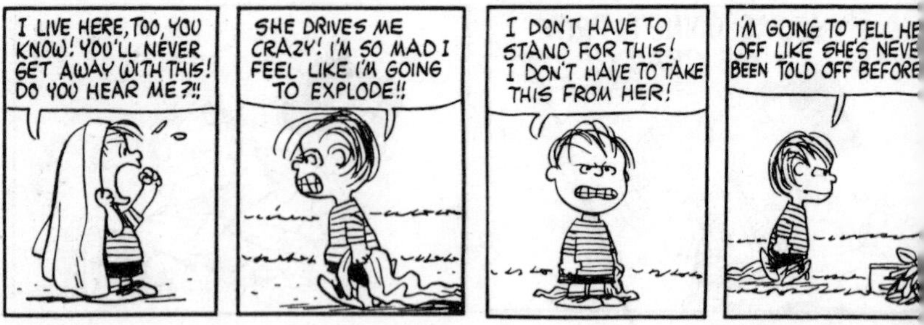

I LIVE HERE, TOO, YOU KNOW! YOU'LL NEVER GET AWAY WITH THIS! DO YOU HEAR ME?!!
SHE DRIVES ME CRAZY! I'M SO MAD I FEEL LIKE I'M GOING TO EXPLODE!!
I DON'T HAVE TO STAND FOR THIS! I DON'T HAVE TO TAKE THIS FROM HER!
I'M GOING TO TELL HE
OFF LIKE SHE'S NEVE
BEEN TOLD OFF BEFORE

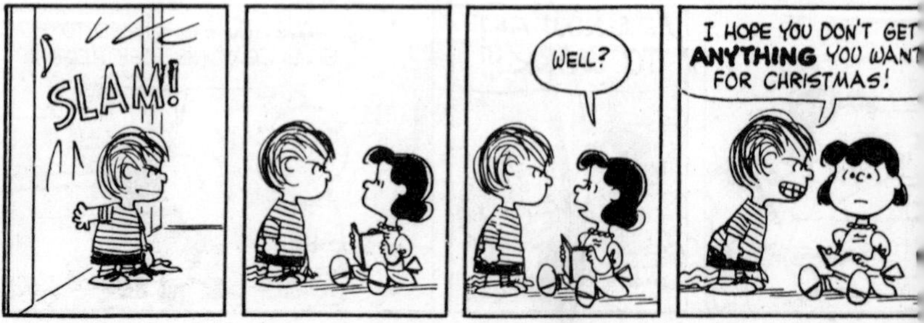

SLAM!
WELL?
I HOPE YOU DON'T GET
ANYTHING YOU WANT
FOR CHRISTMAS!

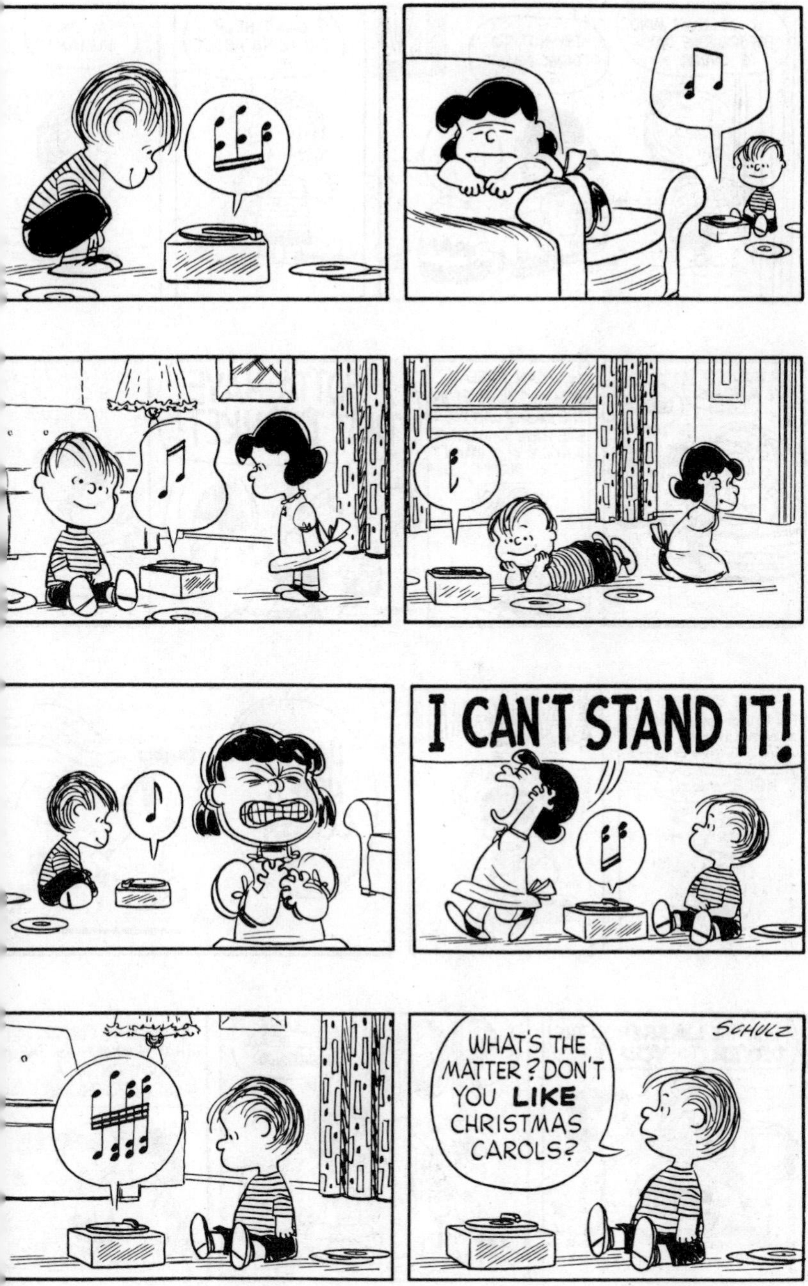
I CAN'T STAND IT!
SCHULZ
WHAT'S THE MATTER? DON'T YOU LIKE CHRISTMAS CAROLS?

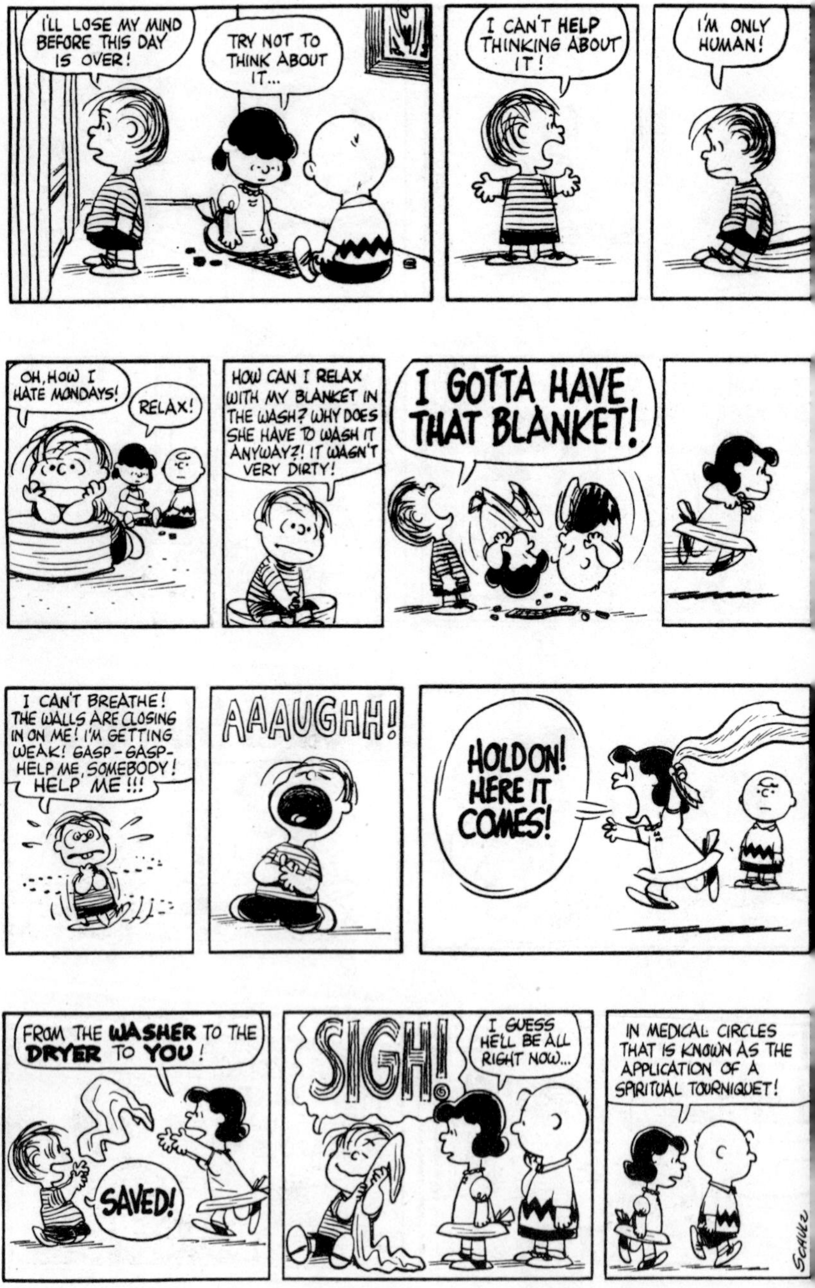

I'LL LOSE MY MIND BEFORE THIS DAY IS OVER!
TRY NOT TO THINK ABOUT IT...
I CAN'T HELP THINKING ABOUT IT!
I'M ONLY HUMAN!
OH, HOW I HATE MONDAYS!
RELAX!
HOW CAN I RELAX WITH MY BLANKET IN THE WASH? WHY DOES SHE HAVE TO WASH IT ANYWAY?! IT WASN'T VERY DIRTY!
I GOTTA HAVE THAT BLANKET!
I CAN'T BREATHE! THE WALLS ARE CLOSING IN ON ME! I'M GETTING WEAK! GASP-GASP- HELP ME, SOMEBODY! HELP ME!!!
AAAUGHH!
HOLD ON! HERE IT COMES!
FROM THE WASHER TO THE DRYER TO YOU!
SAVED!
SIGH!
I GUESS HE'LL BE ALL RIGHT NOW...
IN MEDICAL CIRCLES THAT IS KNOWN AS THE APPLICATION OF A SPIRITUAL TOURNIQUET!
SCHULZ

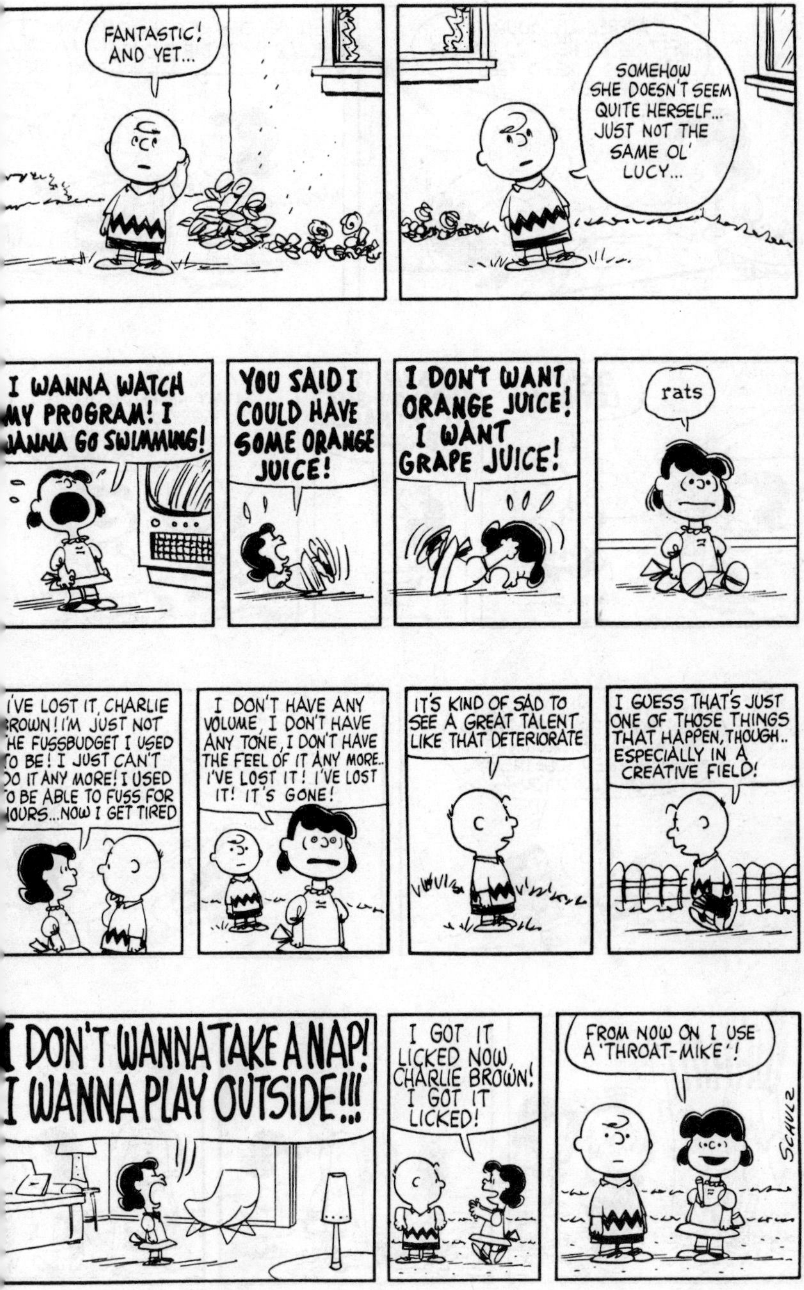
FANTASTIC! AND YET...
SOMEHOW SHE DOESN'T SEEM QUITE HERSELF... JUST NOT THE SAME OL' LUCY...
I WANNA WATCH MY PROGRAM! I WANNA GO SWIMMING!
YOU SAID I COULD HAVE SOME ORANGE JUICE!
I DON'T WANT ORANGE JUICE! I WANT GRAPE JUICE!
rats
I'VE LOST IT, CHARLIE BROWN! I'M JUST NOT THE FUSSBUDGET I USED TO BE! I JUST CAN'T DO IT ANY MORE! I USED TO BE ABLE TO FUSS FOR HOURS...NOW I GET TIRED
I DON'T HAVE ANY VOLUME, I DON'T HAVE ANY TONE, I DON'T HAVE THE FEEL OF IT ANY MORE.. I'VE LOST IT! I'VE LOST IT! IT'S GONE!
IT'S KIND OF SAD TO SEE A GREAT TALENT LIKE THAT DETERIORATE
I GUESS THAT'S JUST ONE OF THOSE THINGS THAT HAPPEN, THOUGH.. ESPECIALLY IN A CREATIVE FIELD!
I DON'T WANNA TAKE A NAP! I WANNA PLAY OUTSIDE!!!
I GOT IT LICKED NOW, CHARLIE BROWN! I GOT IT LICKED!
FROM NOW ON I USE A 'THROAT-MIKE'!
SCHULZ

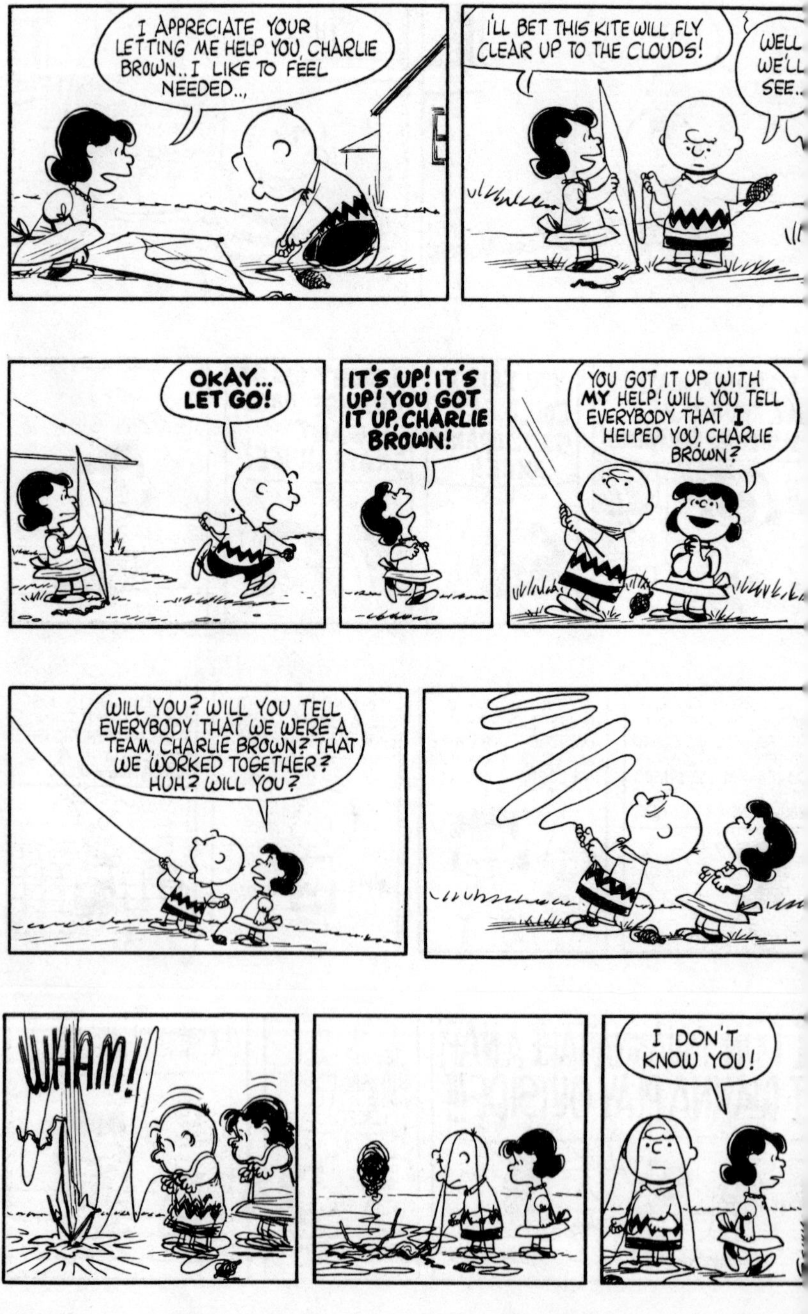
I APPRECIATE YOUR LETTING ME HELP YOU, CHARLIE BROWN.. I LIKE TO FEEL NEEDED..,
I'LL BET THIS KITE WILL FLY CLEAR UP TO THE CLOUDS!
WELL WE'LL SEE..
OKAY... LET GO!
IT'S UP! IT'S UP! YOU GOT IT UP, CHARLIE BROWN!
YOU GOT IT UP WITH MY HELP! WILL YOU TELL EVERYBODY THAT I HELPED YOU, CHARLIE BROWN?
WILL YOU? WILL YOU TELL EVERYBODY THAT WE WERE A TEAM, CHARLIE BROWN? THAT WE WORKED TOGETHER? HUH? WILL YOU?
WHAM!
I DON'T KNOW YOU!

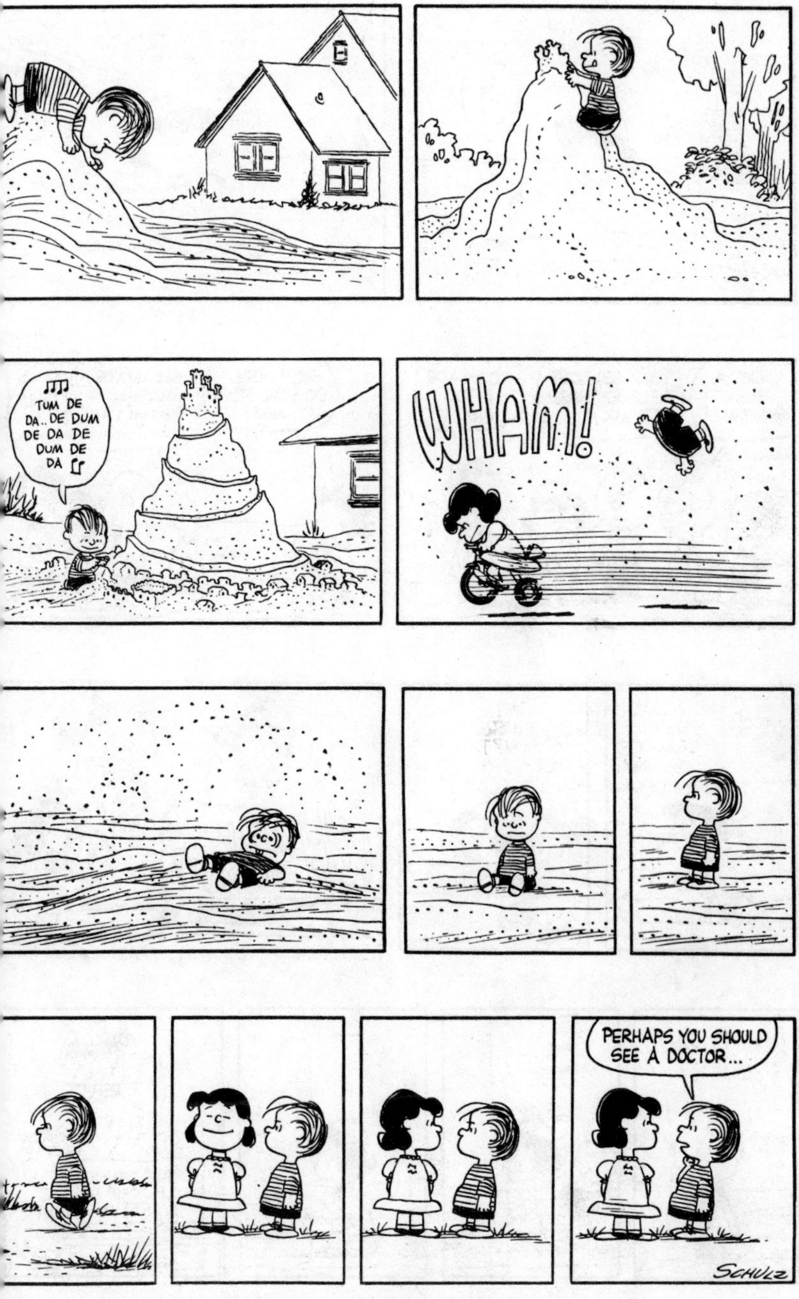
TUM DE DA.. DE DUM DE DA DE DUM DE DA
WHAM!
PERHAPS YOU SHOULD SEE A DOCTOR...
SCHULZ

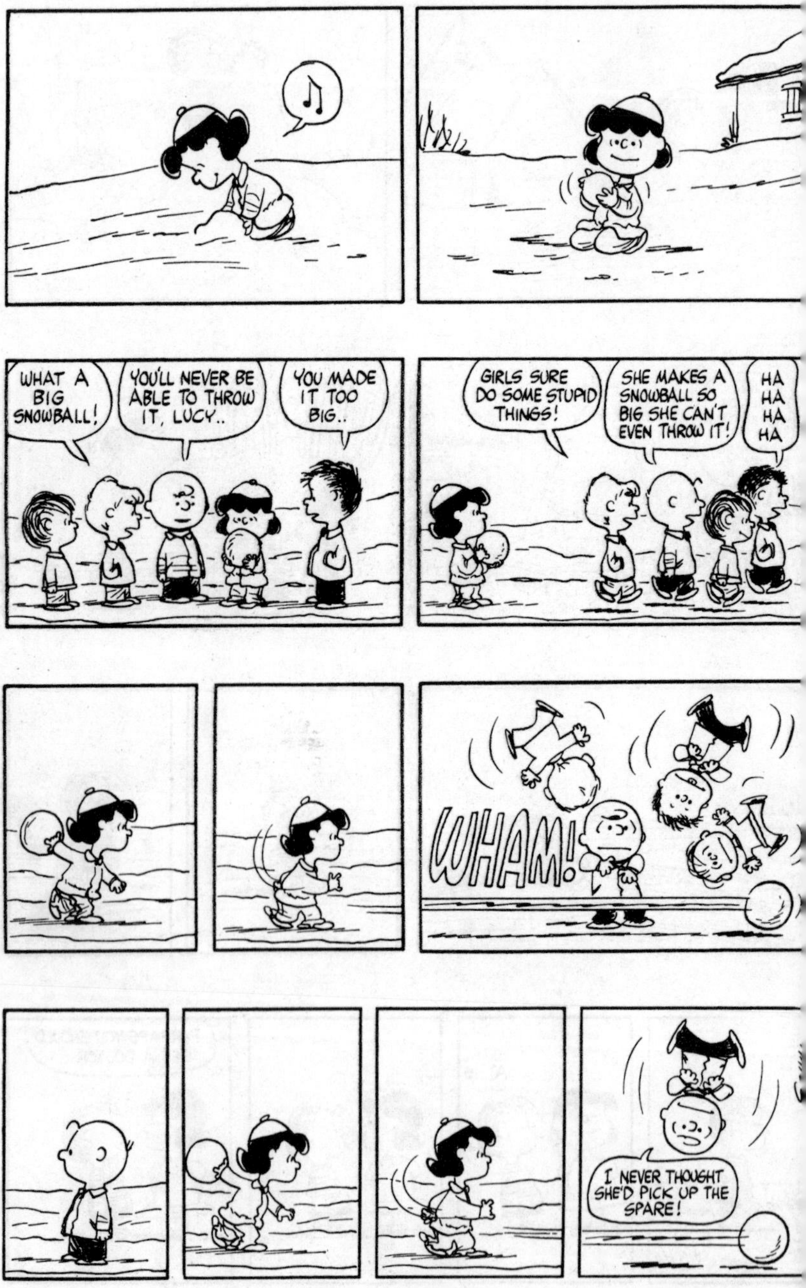
♫
WHAT A BIG SNOWBALL!
YOU'LL NEVER BE ABLE TO THROW IT, LUCY..
YOU MADE IT TOO BIG..
GIRLS SURE DO SOME STUPID THINGS!
SHE MAKES A SNOWBALL SO BIG SHE CAN'T EVEN THROW IT!
HA HA HA HA
WHAM!
I NEVER THOUGHT SHE'D PICK UP THE SPARE!

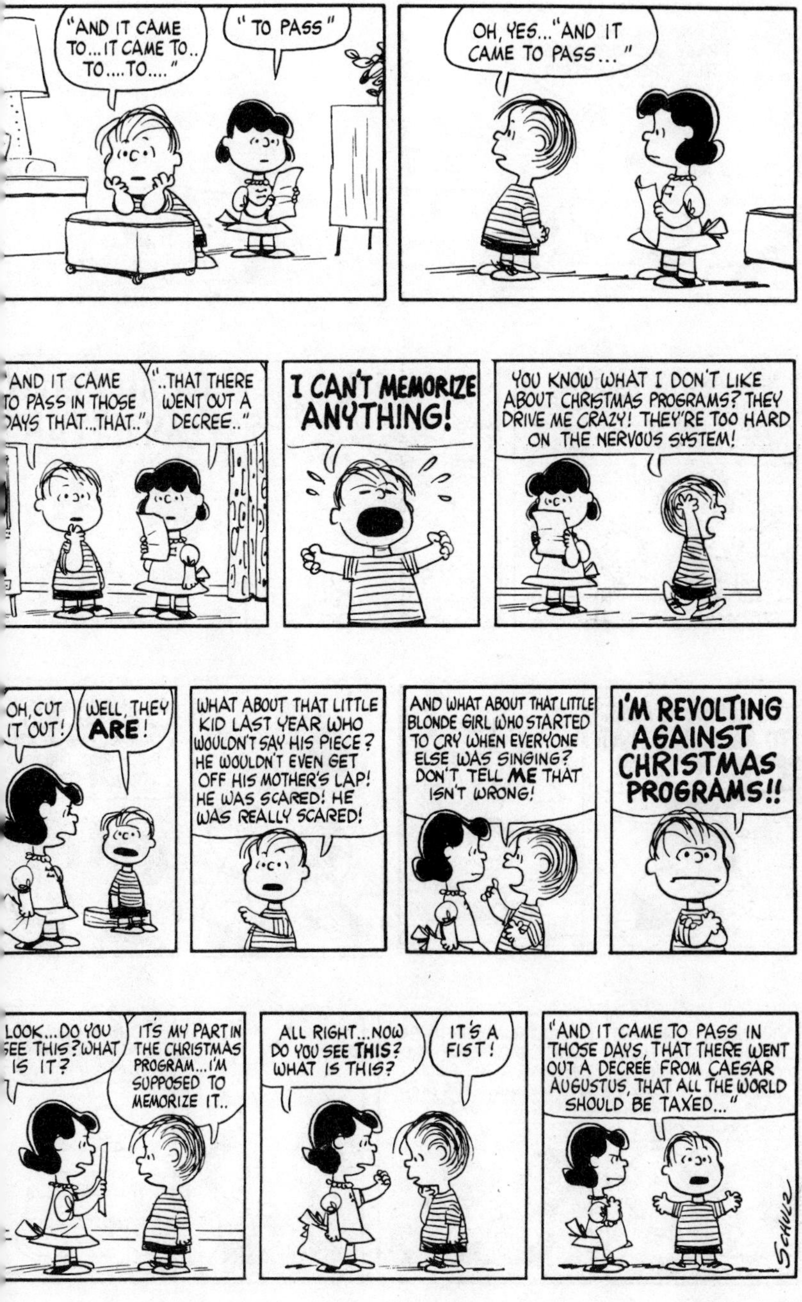

"AND IT CAME TO... IT CAME TO.. TO....TO...."
" TO PASS "
OH, YES..."AND IT CAME TO PASS... "
"AND IT CAME TO PASS IN THOSE AYS THAT...THAT.."
"..THAT THERE WENT OUT A DECREE.."
I CAN'T MEMORIZE ANYTHING!
YOU KNOW WHAT I DON'T LIKE ABOUT CHRISTMAS PROGRAMS? THEY DRIVE ME CRAZY! THEY'RE TOO HARD ON THE NERVOUS SYSTEM!
OH, CUT IT OUT!
WELL, THEY ARE!
WHAT ABOUT THAT LITTLE KID LAST YEAR WHO WOULDN'T SAY HIS PIECE? HE WOULDN'T EVEN GET OFF HIS MOTHER'S LAP! HE WAS SCARED! HE WAS REALLY SCARED!
AND WHAT ABOUT THAT LITTLE BLONDE GIRL WHO STARTED TO CRY WHEN EVERYONE ELSE WAS SINGING? DON'T TELL ME THAT ISN'T WRONG!
I'M REVOLTING AGAINST CHRISTMAS PROGRAMS!!
LOOK... DO YOU EE THIS? WHAT IS IT?
IT'S MY PART IN THE CHRISTMAS PROGRAM... I'M SUPPOSED TO MEMORIZE IT..
ALL RIGHT... NOW DO YOU SEE THIS? WHAT IS THIS?
IT'S A FIST!
"AND IT CAME TO PASS IN THOSE DAYS, THAT THERE WENT OUT A DECREE FROM CAESAR AUGUSTUS, THAT ALL THE WORLD SHOULD BE TAXED..."
SCHULZ

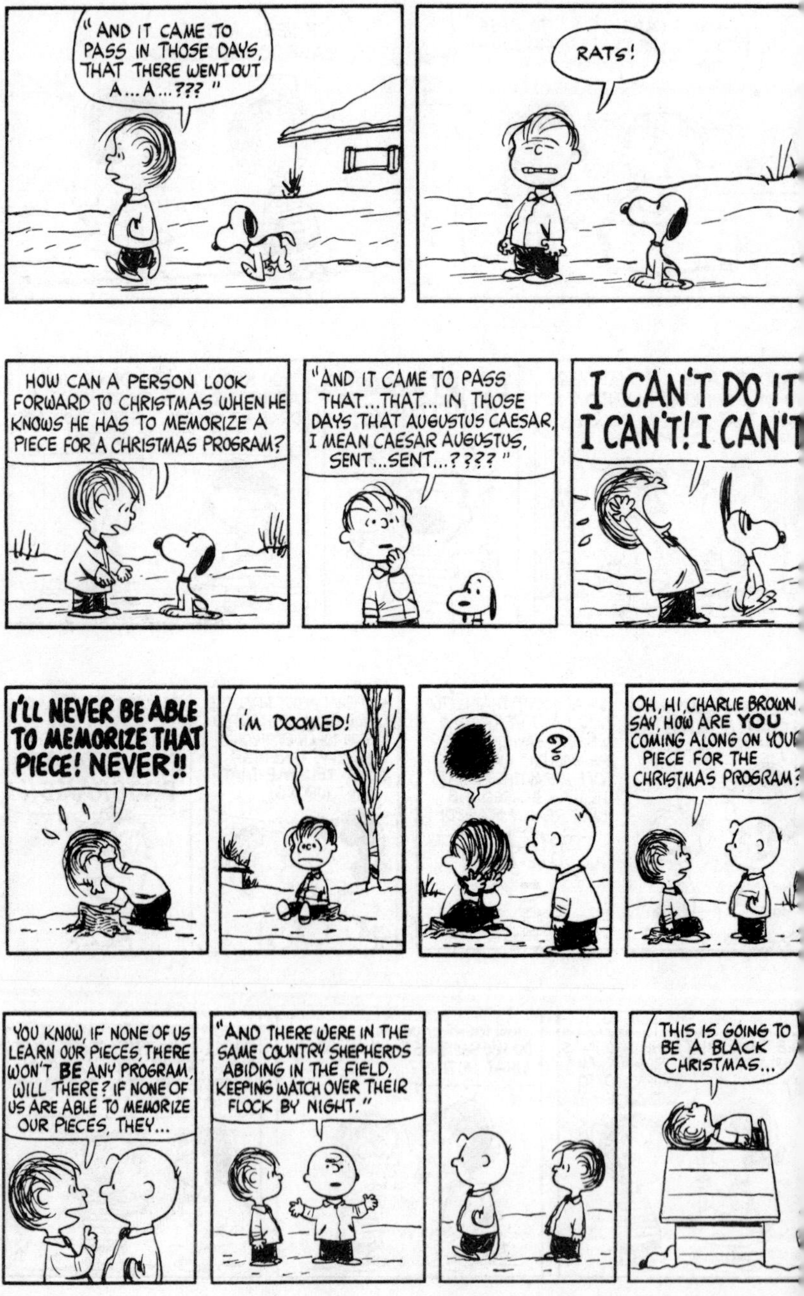

"AND IT CAME TO PASS IN THOSE DAYS, THAT THERE WENT OUT A...A...???"
RATS!
HOW CAN A PERSON LOOK FORWARD TO CHRISTMAS WHEN HE KNOWS HE HAS TO MEMORIZE A PIECE FOR A CHRISTMAS PROGRAM?
"AND IT CAME TO PASS THAT...THAT... IN THOSE DAYS THAT AUGUSTUS CAESAR, I MEAN CAESAR AUGUSTUS, SENT...SENT...????"
I CAN'T DO IT
I CAN'T! I CAN'T
I'LL NEVER BE ABLE TO MEMORIZE THAT PIECE! NEVER!!
I'M DOOMED!
?
OH, HI, CHARLIE BROWN. SAY, HOW ARE YOU COMING ALONG ON YOUR PIECE FOR THE CHRISTMAS PROGRAM?
YOU KNOW, IF NONE OF US LEARN OUR PIECES, THERE WON'T BE ANY PROGRAM, WILL THERE? IF NONE OF US ARE ABLE TO MEMORIZE OUR PIECES, THEY...
"AND THERE WERE IN THE SAME COUNTRY SHEPHERDS ABIDING IN THE FIELD, KEEPING WATCH OVER THEIR FLOCK BY NIGHT."
THIS IS GOING TO BE A BLACK CHRISTMAS...

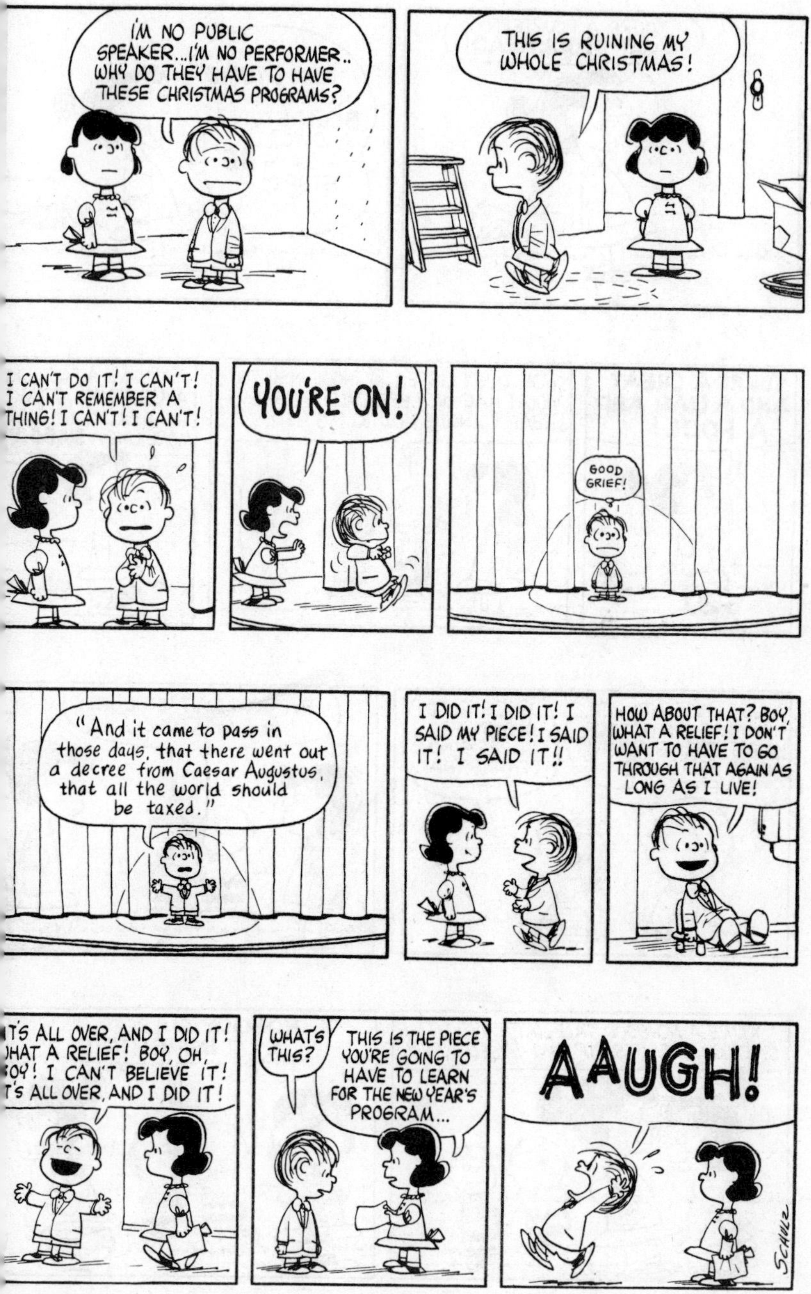

I'M NO PUBLIC SPEAKER...I'M NO PERFORMER.. WHY DO THEY HAVE TO HAVE THESE CHRISTMAS PROGRAMS?
THIS IS RUINING MY WHOLE CHRISTMAS!
I CAN'T DO IT! I CAN'T! I CAN'T REMEMBER A THING! I CAN'T! I CAN'T!
YOU'RE ON!
GOOD GRIEF!
"And it came to pass in those days, that there went out a decree from Caesar Augustus, that all the world should be taxed."
I DID IT! I DID IT! I SAID MY PIECE! I SAID IT! I SAID IT!!
HOW ABOUT THAT? BOY, WHAT A RELIEF! I DON'T WANT TO HAVE TO GO THROUGH THAT AGAIN AS LONG AS I LIVE!
IT'S ALL OVER, AND I DID IT! WHAT A RELIEF! BOY, OH, BOY! I CAN'T BELIEVE IT! IT'S ALL OVER, AND I DID IT!
WHAT'S THIS?
THIS IS THE PIECE YOU'RE GOING TO HAVE TO LEARN FOR THE NEW YEAR'S PROGRAM...
AAUGH!
SCHULZ

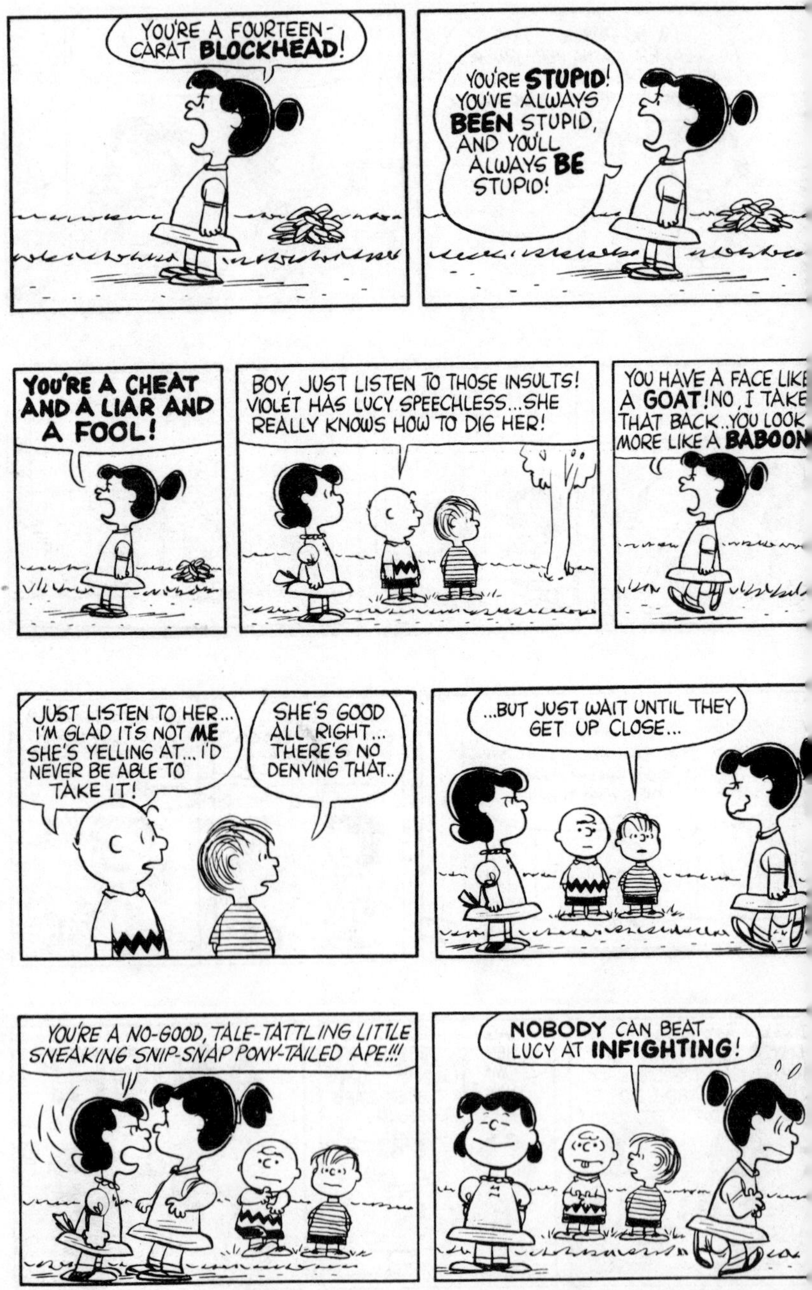

YOU'RE A FOURTEEN-CARAT BLOCKHEAD!
YOU'RE STUPID! YOU'VE ALWAYS BEEN STUPID, AND YOU'LL ALWAYS BE STUPID!
YOU'RE A CHEAT AND A LIAR AND A FOOL!
BOY, JUST LISTEN TO THOSE INSULTS! VIOLET HAS LUCY SPEECHLESS...SHE REALLY KNOWS HOW TO DIG HER!
YOU HAVE A FACE LIKE A GOAT! NO, I TAKE THAT BACK..YOU LOOK MORE LIKE A BABOON
JUST LISTEN TO HER... I'M GLAD IT'S NOT ME SHE'S YELLING AT... I'D NEVER BE ABLE TO TAKE IT!
SHE'S GOOD ALL RIGHT... THERE'S NO DENYING THAT..
...BUT JUST WAIT UNTIL THEY GET UP CLOSE...
YOU'RE A NO-GOOD, TALE-TATTLING LITTLE SNEAKING SNIP-SNAP PONY-TAILED APE!!!
NOBODY CAN BEAT LUCY AT INFIGHTING!

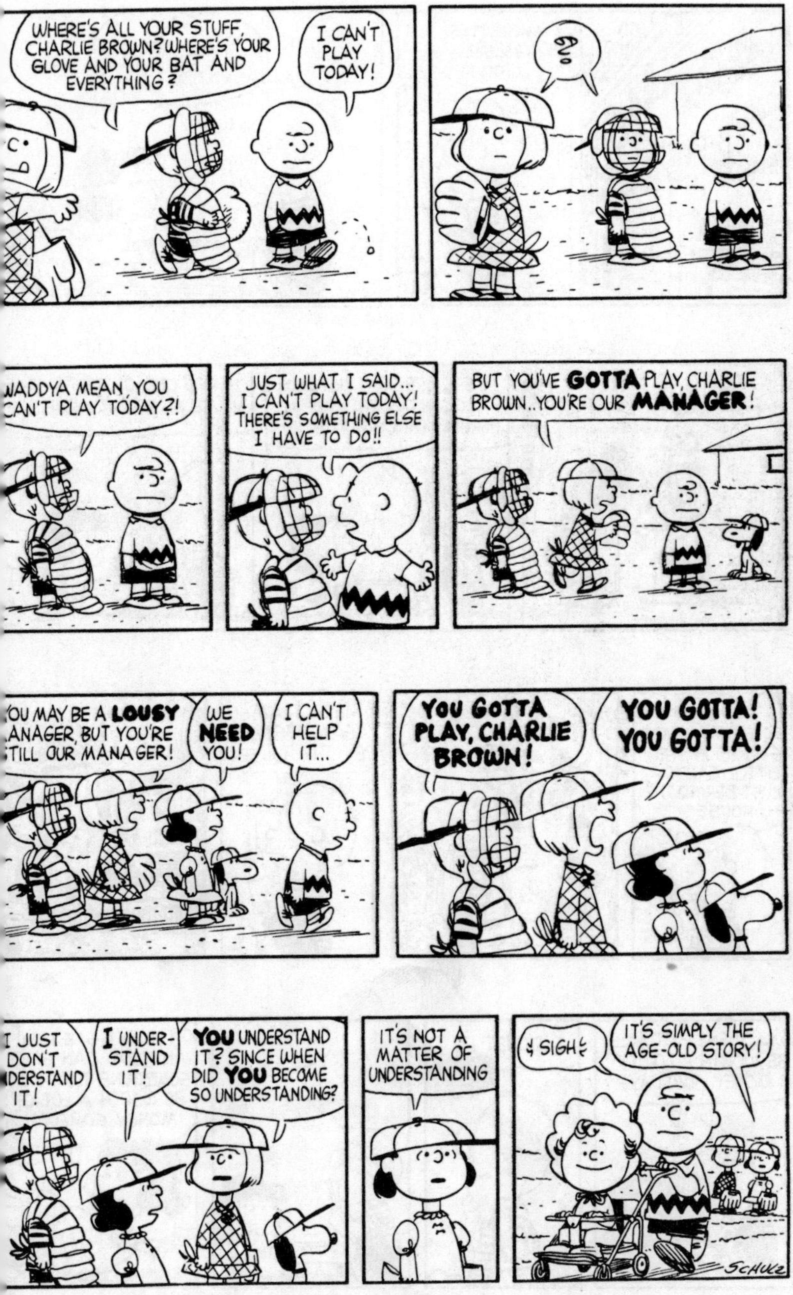
WHERE'S ALL YOUR STUFF, CHARLIE BROWN? WHERE'S YOUR GLOVE AND YOUR BAT AND EVERYTHING?
I CAN'T PLAY TODAY!
??
ADDYA MEAN, YOU AN'T PLAY TODAY?!
JUST WHAT I SAID... I CAN'T PLAY TODAY! THERE'S SOMETHING ELSE I HAVE TO DO!!
BUT YOU'VE **GOTTA** PLAY, CHARLIE BROWN.. YOU'RE OUR **MANAGER**!
OU MAY BE A **LOUSY** ANAGER, BUT YOU'RE TILL OUR MANAGER!
WE **NEED** YOU!
I CAN'T HELP IT...
YOU GOTTA PLAY, CHARLIE BROWN!
YOU GOTTA! YOU GOTTA!
I JUST DON'T DERSTAND IT!
I UNDERSTAND IT!
YOU UNDERSTAND IT? SINCE WHEN DID **YOU** BECOME SO UNDERSTANDING?
IT'S NOT A MATTER OF UNDERSTANDING
SIGH
IT'S SIMPLY THE AGE-OLD STORY!
SCHULZ

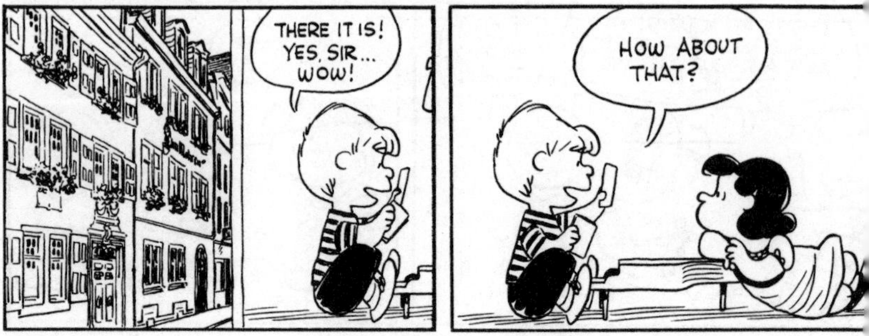

THERE IT IS! YES, SIR... WOW!
HOW ABOUT THAT?

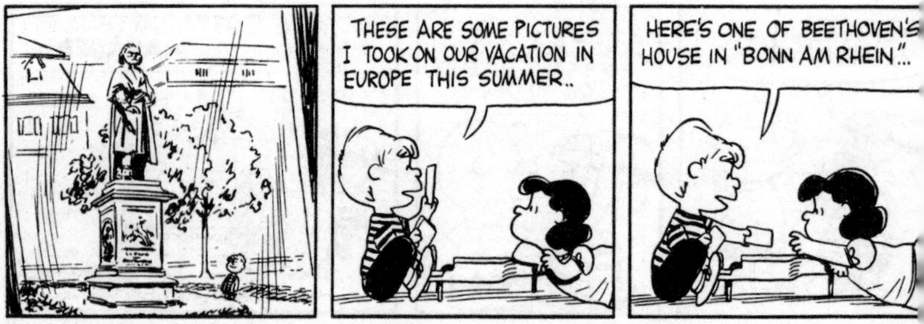

THESE ARE SOME PICTURES I TOOK ON OUR VACATION IN EUROPE THIS SUMMER..
HERE'S ONE OF BEETHOVEN'S HOUSE IN "BONN AM RHEIN"...

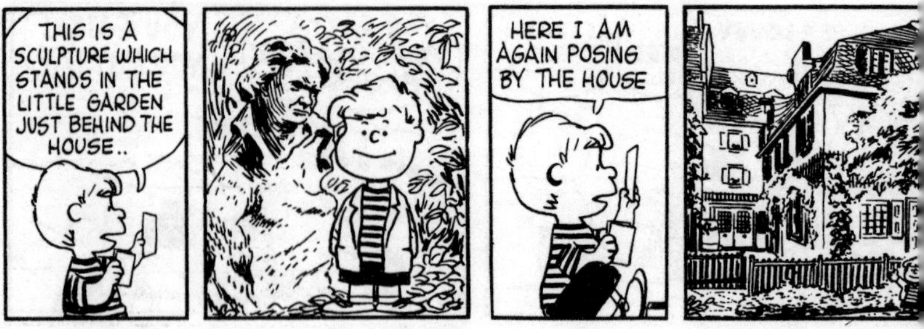

THIS IS A SCULPTURE WHICH STANDS IN THE LITTLE GARDEN JUST BEHIND THE HOUSE..
HERE I AM AGAIN POSING BY THE HOUSE

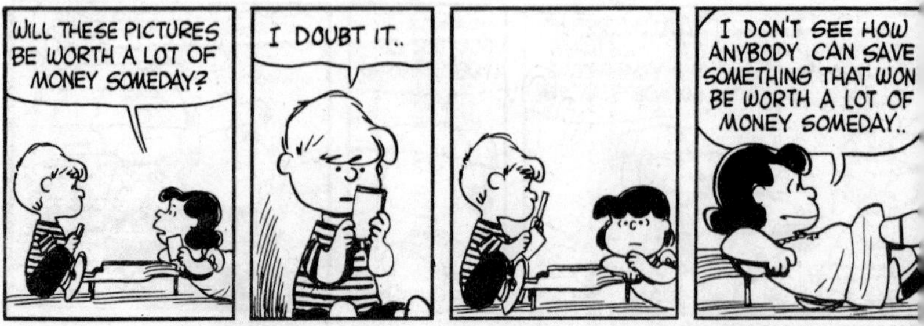

WILL THESE PICTURES BE WORTH A LOT OF MONEY SOMEDAY?
I DOUBT IT..
I DON'T SEE HOW ANYBODY CAN SAVE SOMETHING THAT WON BE WORTH A LOT OF MONEY SOMEDAY..

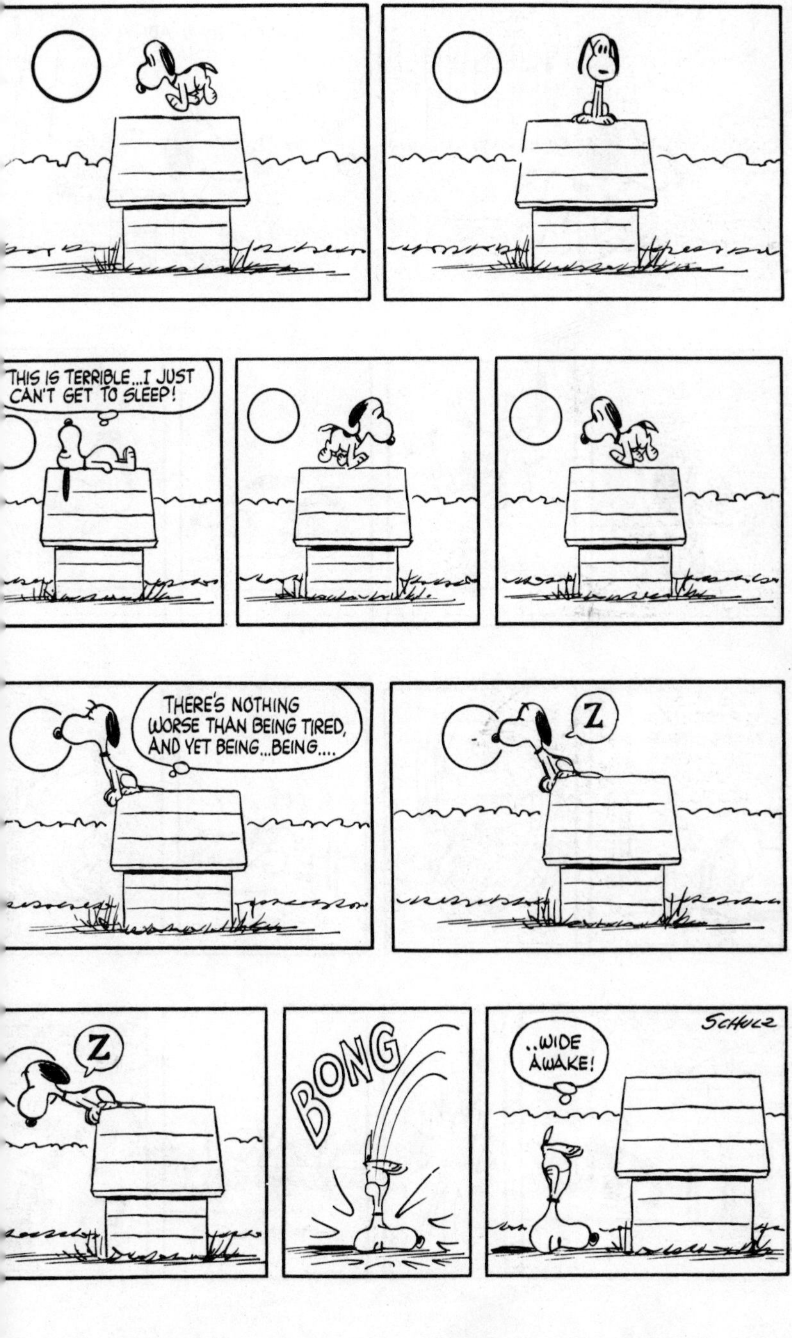
THIS IS TERRIBLE...I JUST CAN'T GET TO SLEEP!
THERE'S NOTHING WORSE THAN BEING TIRED, AND YET BEING...BEING....
Z
Z
BONG
SCHULZ
..WIDE AWAKE!

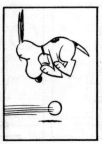

THUS ENDETH THE CROQUET GAME

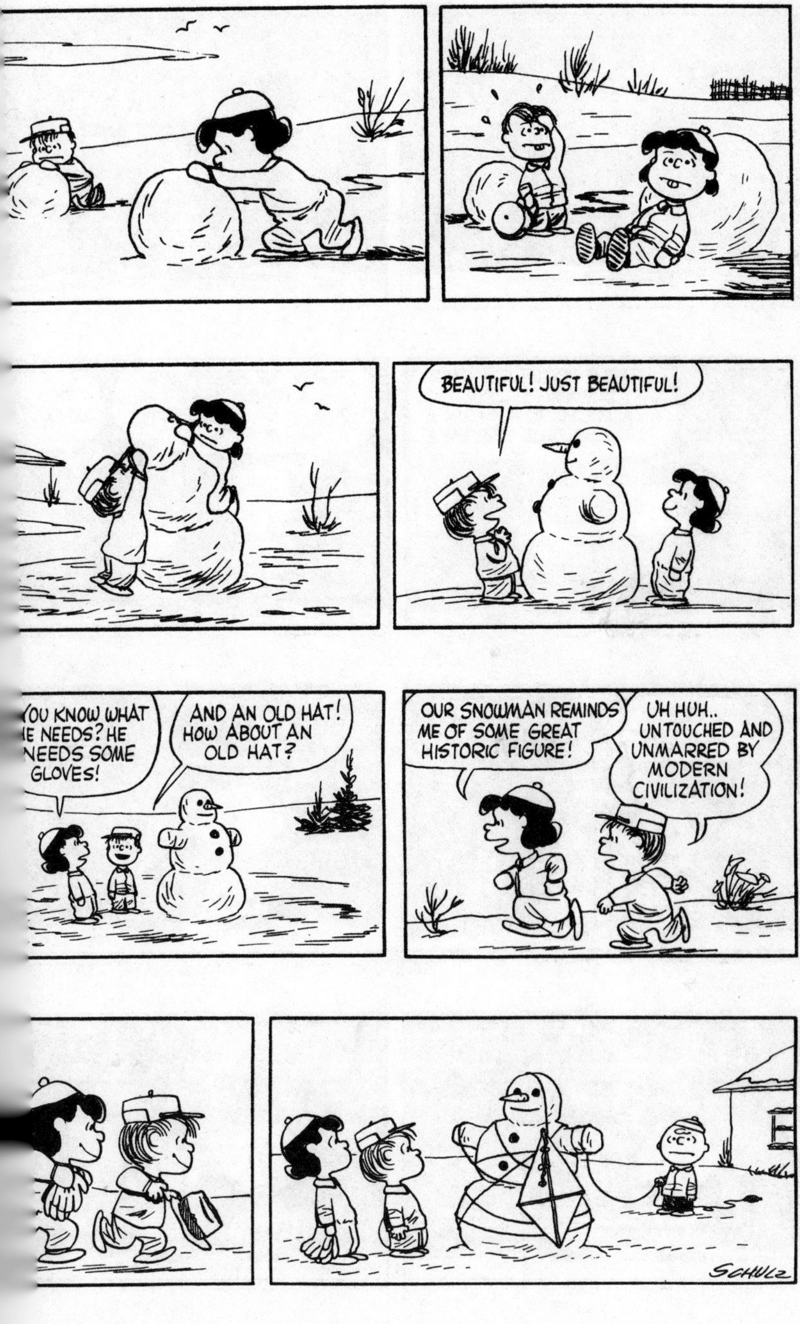
BEAUTIFUL! JUST BEAUTIFUL!
YOU KNOW WHAT HE NEEDS? HE NEEDS SOME GLOVES!
AND AN OLD HAT! HOW ABOUT AN OLD HAT?
OUR SNOWMAN REMINDS ME OF SOME GREAT HISTORIC FIGURE!
UH HUH.. UNTOUCHED AND UNMARRED BY MODERN CIVILIZATION!
SCHULZ

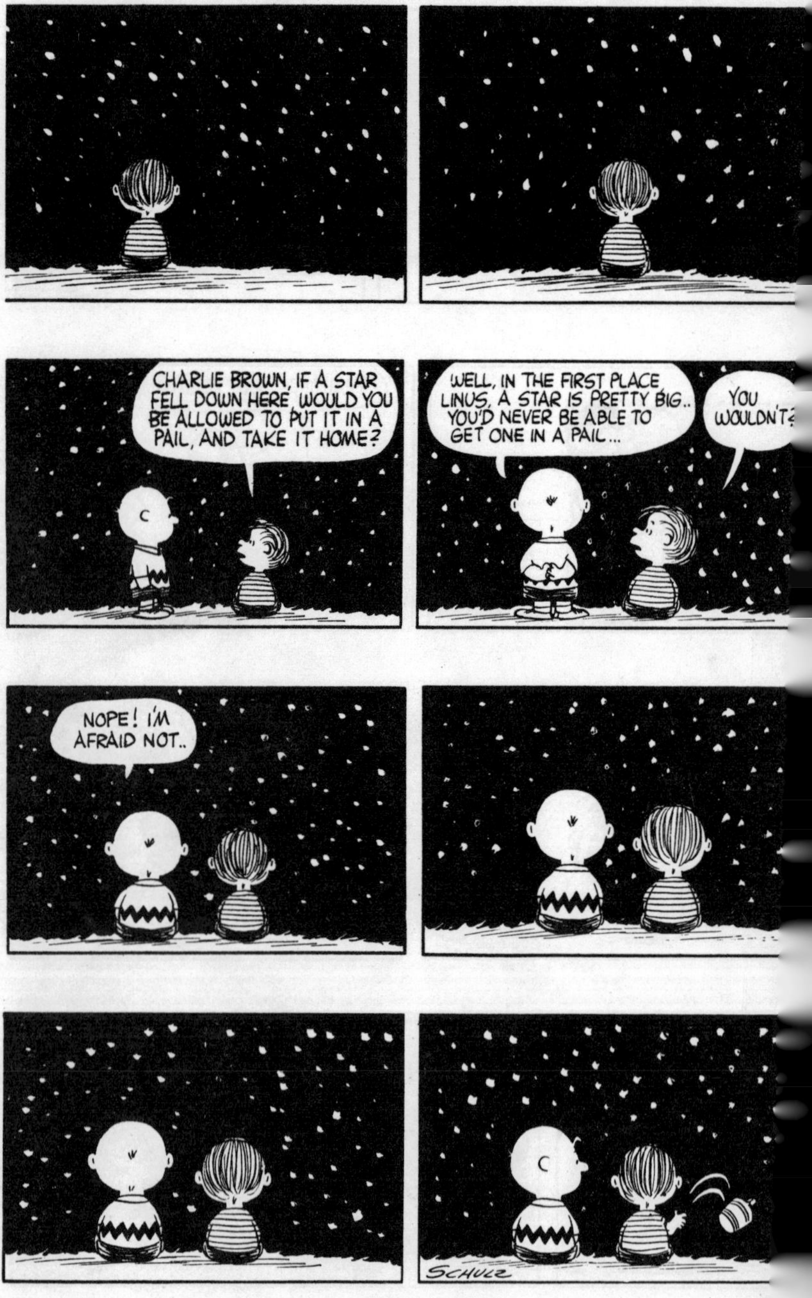
CHARLIE BROWN, IF A STAR FELL DOWN HERE, WOULD YOU BE ALLOWED TO PUT IT IN A PAIL, AND TAKE IT HOME?
WELL, IN THE FIRST PLACE LINUS, A STAR IS PRETTY BIG.. YOU'D NEVER BE ABLE TO GET ONE IN A PAIL...
YOU WOULDN'T?
NOPE! I'M AFRAID NOT..
SCHULZ